i'm not LIKE EVERYBODY ELSE

THE 1990s BRITISH MOD SCENE

Compiled and Designed by ENAMEL VERGUREN

SHA MAN publishing

MOD CHRONICLES Vol.2

First edition published in 2010 by
Shaman Publishing
21 Caedmon Road, London N7 6DH

Printed in Great Britain by Paul Hallam at Sterling Financial.
paul.hallam@sterlingfp.com

ISBN 978-0-9564882-0-6

MOD CHRONICLES Vol. 2

I'm not LIKE EVERYBODY ELSE

THE 1990s BRITISH MOD SCENE

Compiled and Designed by **ENAMEL VERGUREN**

PETER ROSTON & ENAMEL VERGUREN
Main Photographers

BRIAN KOTZ - CLAUDIA ELLIOTT - PAUL ANDERSON
Proof-Readers & Sub-Editors

in memory of **SEAN BODY**

SHA MAN
publishing

credits

with the precious help of

Paul 'Smiler' Anderson
Des Mannay
Mick Wheeler
Rob Messer and Mark Lusty

interviews with

Paul Anderson aka 'Smiler'
Gavin Gribbon
Rob Messer
Paul Hallam
Dave Edwards
Des Mannay
Eddie Piller
Dean Rudland
Richard Searle
Mark Lusty
Mick Ferrante
Simon Clowes
Kevin Walker
Milton Astley
Al Richmond
Phil Otto
Matthew Braim
Dom & Claire Strickland

photos by

Enamel Verguren
Peter Roston
Steve Brown
Darren Russell
Phil-Hip Beauvais
Dom & Claire Strickland
Paul Anderson
Milton Astley
Nickie Divine
Tina Vaughan
Steve Hall
Rachel Harmond
Mary Perazzoni-Nimmo
Toski, Mark Lusty
Rob Messer
Matthew Braim
Mark Raison, Janine Snow
Yann & Kim Vatiste
Andrew Catlin and Frank Noon

with comments from

Paul Lobb
Paul Sawtell
Caspar De La Mare
Stephen Twigg
Jayne Pountain
Mark Raison
Ken Sweeney

We have done our best to insure that every information that appears in this book is accurate. If you have any queries or questions, please contact us: *modchronicles@hotmail.com*

Entirely edited & designed, and partly written & illustrated by: **Enamel Verguren.**

NB: When the author talks directly to the reader, the font of the text changes from **VAG Rounded** (Guest's interview) to Eurostile - **Condensed** or **Extended**- (Author's comments).

By the mid-'80s, the mod scene, still surviving from its 'Revival', slowly started to fall apart. Had it become too elitist to admit new members? Was it bored of its frantic nights? Was it fed up with the regularity of its clubs and the difficulty to find new music?

We wish to apologise to **CARON MALCOLM**, who should have been credited for photos on P.159 (Dennis Greaves), P.184/185 (Makin'Time) & P.189 (The Untouchables) on Mod Chronicles - volume 1: "This Is A Modern Life". Also, **MATT WOODHAM** was the owner of some of the photos attributed to Rob Messer...

articles & press cuttings
from
The Sun
Daily Mail
Daily Mirror
Daily Star
New Society
Hastings Observer
I-O-W Weekly Post
Sounds
Smash Hits
Scootering
Time Out
Just 17
I-D
The Face
Melody Maker
Mojo
Mirror
Evening Standard
South Wales Argus.

The Author in 1999 Photo: Berit Boettcher

Then came The Untouchables, a group of purist Mods who enjoyed partying...

and suddenly everything started up again...

Paul Hallam: "Once a Mod,

If you were into it that much

always a Mod.

your heart will always be into it"

Suddenly, the scooters were in fashion again; I don't know if it was due to the *Scooterboys*' influence, but by the late '80s and mainly throughout the '90s, we all started to put a bit of effort into the design of our machines. I could even say that at some point, my *Vespa* - or my *Lambretta* was the most important asset in my life. In a way you would need to buy more music and clothes to 'renew' your identity, or you'd get bored after a while; you'd need money... but once your scooter was up and ready, only a gallon of petrol and you could happily hang out all week long, to be seen everywhere...

And you'd get noticed straight away! More of a visual impact than say, a smart suit or a Steve Marriott haircut.

The sensation is unique. As soon as you kick-start your scooter (even more when it is nicely covered with chrome and accessories), straight away, you join the ranks of a WW1 pilot (on a *Vespa*) or of the knights of the modern times (on a *Lambretta*).

You instantly feel knighted when you drive a scooter covered with chrome

London Ride Out - 2000 - Photo by the author

MODS WERE THE PUNKS OF THE 1960s!

To be a Mod in the 1960s, in terms of fashion, meant to be MODERN; to live in harmony with the new technologies at the time, and to accept all the new concepts in design, fashion, music... but coming from the point of view of a working class upbringing only - quite political after all, even if the movement has always pretended to be apolitical. Basically, you'd be eventually driving the newest sports car in '64, which in our eyes today wouldn't look that bad at all; or, because you couldn't afford it, what would be more modern than this 'portable moving chair' called a motorscooter (brand new invention which had invaded and revolutionised the whole world since the early 1950s)? The scooter has this advantage on the motorbike that, one: it's got a spare wheel, and two: it's much more comfortable for your passenger.

In terms of attitude, the Mods obviously had to answer to the sarcasms of *Rockers* who would find these machines (as well as this fashion) ridiculous, even if some of the - earlier - *Coffee Bar Cowboys* & *Ton Up Boys* were spotted on *Lambrettas* a few years before. Clashes happened, both camps suffered from it, for years, until the early 1980s in some places. It appeared to be very unfair sometimes, leading to fights at the scale of five against one...

The other thing that was crucial in the gap between these two cults (though those movements had so much in common: riding bikes, a working class background...) was the music and the attitude towards it: Mods listened to *Blues*, *R'n'B* from America and were interested in new sounds as well, mainly in what England had to offer at the time as an answer to this new wave (brand new bands such as *Who*, *Kinks*, *Yardbirds*... the list is endless). Their influence was strictly black American music. The *Rockers* - even if they were drawn to the same music in the beginning - had white idols, which very quickly related them to the 'rednecks' of the southern USA, and their political views.

On top of that the mod gear - then & now - looked much more conventional than the black leather flying jacket covered with grease. Does that make the Rockers seem cooler, or more rebellious? We proved that wrong, in the first volume of this series... Mods were the *Punks* of the 1960s !!!

To be a Mod in the 1990s, or even for the previous 20 years, means something completely different; you are living out of your time. There is no more Modernism as such, you are constantly influenced by the 1960s. Real modernism, or whatever you see of it around you, disgusts you.

You've been through the terrible 1980s, the 'dark years', when nobody understood the reasons to be a Mod, or even to listen to '60s music. You've been preaching the good taste of '60s design and fashion, even if nobody wanted to listen to you, and you start seeing it coming back into the field. That's what the '90s were; an acceptance from society that we were right, that this 'line' would come back one day. For the first time, we didn't have to go to second-hand shops; we could buy off the peg.

The attitude is slightly different though. The working-class hatred of middle-class values has been enhanced by the *Punk* explosion of the 1970s; the new Mod has to be much more than its predecessors, in every way. More arrogant, better looking and a better dancer.

Phil-Hip **& girlfriend back in 1993**
Photo: Phil-Hip Beauvais

Rob Messer: Even though I love that book, the "Mods" book by *Richard Barnes* - it's the Bible for any Mod - but in a very few cases you'll see one of them on the photos being really smart; everyone of them has got a thing that is just not quite right. What we did in the 1980s is: we took the best bit of each individual one, put it together and created our own style. And we looked better! We did better than them, and same with the music.

In a way, we were ahead of our time
Gavin Gribbon

SMILER: The scene, just after **'Sneakers'** at the *Bush* had closed, completely changed. Prior to that there'd had been a lot of fights on Shepherd Bush Green... with *Casuals*, there had been a big row outside the 'Donut Dinner'. A lot of people stopped coming because of that. Shortly afterwards, on *February 22nd of 1986*, a band that still was quite respected, **The Scene**, played their last gig (on the Saturday). The next day **'Sneakers'** closed its doors. A lot of Mods stopped attending mod nights from then on. 'Sneakers' had moved to the **Clarendon** in Hammersmith, but you never saw some of the old regulars again. They knew that an era was gone, that it would never be the same.

THE RHYTHM AND SOUL SET
— Presents —
★ Rhythm, Soul, Jazz & Boogaloo ★
AT THE MAYFAIR SUITE, THE GRAND HOTEL
Undercliff Road West, Felixtowe
SATURDAY, 23rd JULY, 1988
7.30 p.m. — 2.00 a.m.

★ D.J's : ROB, MACE, JON, PID, RALSTON ★

ADMISSION £3·00   Dress to impress !

London Ride-Out and London Run - 2000 -

Photos by the author

Because it was impossible to cover the entire British scene in Volume 1, we have added some information relating to the different scenes in towns and countries throughout the UK and the Commonwealth (taken from fanzines gathered by *Des Mannay*), in the next ten pages, as well as a few press cuttings from early to the mid-'80s (confirming, once again, the good reputation of Mod at the time) although most of the photos (gathering several accounts of rallies during the early 1990s) have no connection with the texts.

RALLY PASS
MUST BE HANDED IN AT ENTRANCE TO GAIN RE-ADMISSION.
I.O.W. SCOOTER CLUB RALLY, 1984
NOT TRANSFERABLE

POLICE BEAT OFF INVASION BY THE MODS AND ROCKERS

ON YOUR BIKE!

TWO policemen grab a rowdy Rocker in clashes on Brighton seafront   Picture by DAVID HILL

Britain in battle of the beaches

- THESE were the flashpoints in the round - Britain battleground that faced police from Scarborough to Brighton. Thousands of Mods and Rockers yesterday set out to re-enact their Easter holiday seaside punch-ups of the Sixties.

- But police chiefs were ready for the invasion. They were under orders to "keep 'em apart, and keep 'em on the move."

Big seaside clampdown halts holiday punch-ups

By PETER BOND and ALASTAIR TAYLOR

NO-NONSENSE police yesterday slammed the brakes on thousands of warring Mods and Rockers.

They routed the invasion by thugs at a dozen seaside towns during the Easter Monday Madness.

Their short and sharp message to troublemakers was: "On your bike, son!"

And hundreds of them headed for home before the day was out.

Police halted many gang fights at the first sign of trouble.

Arrests

SOUTHEND suffered one of the biggest invasions of Mods and Rockers.

More than 1,000 roamed the Golden Mile. There were several fights and 72 arrests. And last night a 60-strong mob of Millwall soccer fans went on the rampage and smashed up a seafront pub.

But Superintendent Charles Harper said last night: "Considering the large number of tearaways in the town, there has not been too much trouble.

"Not one policeman has been hurt and there has been virtually no damage to property.

"We are sick and tired of this behaviour, and we set out to stop it."

Several hundred Mods on scooters were greeted

A Punk is arrested at Clacton

by heavy police patrols at MARGATE.

There was sporadic fighting—and 38 arrests.

And police moved in quickly at CLACTON to halt trouble.

SCARBOROUGH was worst hit by the invasion.

Angry hotel owners and shopkeepers cleared up the debris of a three-day siege and said: "It must never happen again."

Police arrested 217.

Seven of them were yesterday fined a total of £1,715 on public order offences.

Hundreds of Hell's Angels tried to roar into the town for a showdown with the rival Mods.

Police patrols sent them packing.

BRIGHTON was hit by fights between 3,000 Mods and gangs of Rockers shouting "aggro." There were 40 arrests.

Patrols

Police said they were worried by the number of teenagers carrying offensive weapons.

There were 68 arrests at WESTON - SUPER - MARE, Avon. More than 600 youths and girls roamed the streets, fighting and hurling abuse. Police kept them apart.

There were several arrests at RHYL, North Wales. Police said the mobs were "under control."

Sun man attacked

- BEDRAGGLED Sun photographer Terry Richards dries out . . . after being kicked and punched by Mods at Southend yesterday and thrown into the sea. A gang of 20 had turned on him and another photographer.

- One of his cameras was stolen and another thrown into the water. Terry said: "One of them grabbed me and they all piled in."

FIREBUG FANS GO WILD

FIREBUGS brought a mad new horror to soccer yesterday.

They started a fire under a stand holding Sheffield United fans at Blackburn. Several fans were arrested. No one was injured.

And a Molotov cocktail exploded in the crowd at White Hart Lane, Tottenham, in London.

The petrol bomb was thrown from the Arsenal section into a crowd of

Spurs supporters. It set alight a wooden section of the terrace. No one was hurt.

Spurs manager Keith Burkinshaw hit out: "Society is too soft with these people."

In another orgy of violence, Millwall fans set fire to a toilet and wrecked three coaches of a soccer special train bringing them back from Southend.

BRITAIN'S YOUNG TRIBES

MODS, Rockers and Skinheads are in the news again after the battles that shattered the holiday peace in seaside towns.

But youth lost its innocence back in the Fifties when teenage idol Marlon Brando was asked what exactly he was rebelling against. "Whaddya got?" he mumbled—and the generation gap was born.

That was twenty-five years ago. Now there are more youth cults than ever before, each speaking with the voices of a generation divided against itself. And it is music, the powerful force that first bound them together in simple rockin' and rollin' that is now tearing them apart.

Here the Mirror talks to the young tribes of Britain.

MODS MARCH BACK INTO BIG TROUBLE

THE revival of the 'Swinging Sixties' super-slick look has made Mods an easily-identifiable target for violence.

Traditional enemies such as the Rockers are still around but not in great numbers. The gap has been filled by the Skinheads, many of whom have only recently shed their Mod mohair suits and put their scooters up for sale.

Before you can say "bovver boots" they're in there kicking hell out of the Mods. And the Mods are not slow to respond.

"They think we're just a load of tarts. Well we're out to prove ourselves to them," says ace-face Roger Willey, a 17-year-old gas board fitter from Birmingham.

Best

An ace-face is a Mod who's got everything going for him. A classy Lambretta scooter, an expensive mohair suit, a neat haircut and a cool manner.

"Being a Mod is about being the best," announces Nigel Bolton, an 18-year-old engineering worker from Coventry.

The Mods love their "hairdryers," and the have survived for . . .

SMART SET: Mods on parade in Coventry.

But the nicknames are not one way—outsiders refer to the Mods' scooters sneeringly as "hairdryers."

The Mods love their "hairdryers," and the have survived for . . . . rival And so far so . . .

tend to be very good fighters.

Sheridan Truelove, an 18-year-old student, was kicked in the chest a few weeks ago by a rocker and narrowly avoided serious injury.

"This Smelly just started coming at us

Praise for visiting Mods

BOTH the police and management of Ryde's Solent Court Hotel, have praised the behaviour of the 450 Mods who visited the Island over the bank holiday weekend.

Police Chief Supt. Dennis Challis said the rally had gone "very well" while Mr. Stuart Griffin, manager of the Solent Court, where entertainment for the Mods was laid on, described their conduct as exemplary.

"They were fantastic, in fact better behaved than some of the local people who use the hotel," he added.

Police were involved in only one major incident, when late on Sunday night, young Mods were involved in skirmishes with people filing out of a blues concert held at Ryde Pavilion opposite.

Six Mods were arrested and five later charged with public order offences. The other was released with a caution.

Rally organiser Mr. Tony Class apologised to police over the incident and later pledged to root out and expel troublemakers from the group which prides itself on the smart appearance and good reputation of members.

Thugs who brought terror to a seaside Bank Holiday

Held : Police grab a youth in Clacton

Held : Detective helps to handcuff a boy in Clacto

Continued from Page One

the promenade railings cheered as scuffles broke out between the youths and the police.

A massive police operation prevented a confrontation between the mods and rockers who arrived on motorbikes.

Hooligans used bottles, stones and chains in one beach clash.

Some sea front bars put up their shutters and vetted customers as several cafe windows were smashed and a bus shelter was wrecked.

Last night rival gangs clashed in Brighton's town centre and scores of extra police had to be drafted in. The number of arrests topped 60.

At Southend, families took refuge in amusement arcades and cafes as 1,000 skinheads paraded along the Golden Mile.

The trouble was made worse as some of the youths confronted a swathe of disgruntled Millwall fans leaving the local football ground.

During the day police made

72 arrests in the town and shepherded many of the youngsters onto soccer specials back to London.

Supt. Charles Harper of Southend police said : 'Thank God no one has been seriously hurt. But these lads were terrorising a lot of respectable people out for a pleasant weekend.'

At Clacton fighting broke out among rival groups of punks, teddy boys and mods. A policeman injured in the fights was taken to hospital. Twenty people were arrested.

At Margate police made 20 arrests among the hundreds of mods in the town.

At Weston-super-Mare about 50 arrests were made.

In London last night police and British Rail staff were on the alert at stations to cope with the gangs returning by train from the resorts.

Police said a number of people were arrested.

● A petrol bomb was thrown by hooligans during the Tottenham - Arsenal match at Tottenham's White Hart Lane ground yesterday.

Held : A police dog in action at Brighton

MARCH OF THE MODS

HUNDREDS of rampaging Mods, Rockers and Skinheads were marched out of town at sun-up yesterday.

Posses of police had rounded them up at two resorts after a night of violence and petrol bombing.

Police from all over the South coast had been drafted in to clear the streets of Brighton and Southend. Then early, yesterday, the rioters were finally coralled.

Said one battle-weary copper at Brighton : "They expressed a willingness to leave town . . . and we were willing to escort them"

The March of the Mods moved off as the sun came up.

About 200 were taken to the station and penned in before being railroaded out of town.

And on the trains there were transport police to make sure there was no further trouble.

At Southend, hundreds of skinheads were caged

By DON MACKAY

in one part of the beach before they, too, were ordered out of town.

But for some of the bovver boys it was just a short walk . . . to the court house.

The rampaging gangs were branded "animals" by Brighton magistrates' chairman Mr Ray Long.

And he handed out fines totalling £1,200

against five of them at a special court.

Skinhead Michael Donnelly, 18, of Field Road, Hammersmith, London, was fined £500.

He was caught trying to ambush Mods, wielding a three-foot post with two six-inch nails in it.

Mr. Long said : "If you had hit anyone with

that you could easily have killed them."

And he told a Mod who objected to being escorted along the sea front by police : "If you behave like animals you must be expected to be herded like animals."

The Mod, 18-year-old Wayne Kavanagh, of Bearsted Terrace, Beckenham, Kent, was fined

£250 for threatening behaviour.

Police Sergeant John Ainsley told the court : "There was a serious outbreak of violence, almost amounting to a riot.

"Nearly 300 youths had come to Brighton with the express idea of causing trouble in the town."

Picture: TIM CORNALL

Confrontation . . . Skinheads fighting at Southend.

TREND SETTING

WHY ON earth are you continuing with this pathetic babble about casuals, trendies or whatever they like to call themselves. Surely a magazine (?) called *Sounds* should be about just that, not bunches of little kids just prattling on about the clothes they should wear.

Keep that kind of nonsense for the *Face* which is already full of it.

The majority of these so called casuals are just little twelve, 13 and 14 year old kids who just copy what they see older people doing. A few years ago they would have called themselves mods, the majority of whom didn't know what the hell they were doing and just latched on, exactly the same as today.

HASTINGS AND ST. LEONARDS
Observer

No 8383   *Telephone 428231 (6 lines)*   **SATURDAY, APRIL 17, 1982**   PRICE 12p

● **FLASHBACK**
to last Easter and
the now inevitable
scenes of violence

Angry traders threaten: Tougher measures or we become rates rebels

STOP THE JACKALS

HASTINGS business people are rising in revolt against holiday hooligans who come to wreck and destroy.

by Francis Cornwall

Nearly 100 people many of them with businesses in the Old Town have signed a petition demanding tougher action, and a ban on suspected trouble makers. Otherwise they are threatening to withhold rates.

Within a few hours of the petition being launched — later presented to police headquarters at Bohemia Road — there was a rush to sign it.

Organised by Mr Andreas Christoforou of the Charcoal Grill, East Parade, it says: "The people of Hastings are greatly concerned about the hooligans invading our town.

"The majority of the businesses in the town are seasonal, depending on the three or four summer months in order to make their trade, particularly at Bank Holidays.

"But when tourists are driven away by the hooligans, then the trade of the individual is also driven away.

"Therefore, we the undersigned, demand a much tougher approach to the situation, namely, to stop them from coming into the town from the main roads leading into Hastings."

Sixteen shop windows were smashed in Hastings and 72 arrests made during the weekend.

FEAR

Old Town traders fear a repetition next Bank Holiday—only weeks away — and are threatening to withhold rates and taxes unless action is taken.

Mr Christoforou said. "Although we were lucky enough to escape damage there was no trade and practically all the cafes were closed by 7 pm on Sunday night."

Deputy Borough Tourism officer Roger Dennett said that stories published in some papers about damage at the White Rock Pavilion were completely inaccurate.

"There was absolutely no damage, merely mess."

Although there was some damage to glasses, optics and furniture at the Palace Bars where a fight started, there were no injuries.

Chief Inspector Keith Beard said: "We are never satisfied with any situation like this, but the plans we had made coped with the majority of problems. The support we received from outside the sub division was adequate."

See pages 6 and 7

COPS HURT IN GANG BATTLE AT DISCO

THREE policemen were injured when a new wave of gang warfare erupted outside a disco.

Trouble broke out for the second weekend in succession as 50 to 100 members of the Casuals gang confronted 150 Mods at Chesham, Bucks.

Bottles

Pcs Stan Carruthers and Christopher Howell and acting Inspector Paul McKeown were hurt.

Four youths were later charged with police assault, possessing weapons and other offences.

Disco organiser Alan Jenkins claimed last night that the Casuals had taken to attacking the scooter-riding Mods.

"They've been throwing stones, bottles and glasses at the scooters, causing damage," he said.

"I have offered to put on discos for them, but they don't seem to want to be bothered.

"It's a great shame because the scooter boys come from as far away as Windsor, Reading and even Yorkshire to attend the discos."

The previous weekend three other policemen were injured in running battles near the disco.

Sixties

LONDON police officer James Porker, (left), aged 19, likes to let the Sixties scene rule when he returns to his home in Patterdale Close, Cyncoed, Cardiff at weekends.

"I like this look — paisley shirts, striped jacket, etc — and it's a lot better than being dressed in scruffy jeans," he explains.

But he is prepared to spend quite a lot of money on getting the necessary garb.

FEET FIRST ... this skinhead came off worst when he tangled with the strong arm of the law at Southend

MIKE'S BIKES
By Mike Nicks

YOUNG mods have never had it so good.

They no longer have to wait until they are 17 before hopping on a scooter and cruising down to the coast.

For Vespa are offering a unique scooter, for the "sixteener" market, which is limited to 50cc machines with a top speed of up to 45 miles per hour.

Called the Vespa 50 special, it really needs a downhill run to hit that figure. But despite the meagre performance I enjoyed my test ride.

Pete Townsend, of the Mod's favourite band, The Who, would probably have loved to play tunes on the special's four-speed gearbox when he was a kid.

Apart from its tiny two-stroke engine the 50 Special is a full-sized scooter in most other respects.

Glitter

It has sophisticated front and rear springing, powerful drum brakes, and traditional scooter bodywork to hide the engine and keep the rider's clothing clean.

Mods like their machines to glitter. So here's a huge range of chrome-plated accessories, including carriers, back rests, mirrors and wheel trims, to fit all Vespas.

Fuel consumption is better than 100 mpg, so owners won't have to dig too deeply into their parkas for petrol money.

But the 50 Special has drawbacks. Oil has to be mixed with the petrol, yet few garages serve this old-fashioned "petroil" blend.

The gear-change is sloppy, as on most scooters, and it's easy to hit a false neutral.

Indicators, essential on today's busy roads, cost £48 on top of the Special's £448 basic price.

And the restricted power, a hazard common to all "sixteener" machines thanks to misguided legislation, means that car drivers are often breathing down the rider's neck on the getaway from traffic lights.

MY VERDICT: Expensive, but the only machine for 16-year-olds who hate conventional mopeds.

Scoot into the big time with lots of style

Mod magic . . . Mike and the 50 Special

Terror as the Mods hit resorts

Daily Mail Reporter

MODS, rockers, skinheads and punks went on the rampage at resorts up and down Britain yesterday.

They brought Bank Holiday terror to thousands.

The chaos that started at Scarborough during the Easter weekend was spread by invading gangs of youths to Southend, Brighton, Margate, Clacton, Weymouth, Weston-super-Mare and Great Yarmouth.

At Scarborough, which was worst hit, a special court fined a 19-year-old Doncaster miner £650 for assaulting a policeman and threatening behaviour.

Smashed

An 18-year-old chef from Leicester was fined £500 on similar charges. And five others, including three girls, were ordered to pay a total of £565.

During a weekend of

---

park anger

Rubbish hurled in shops

AT Rock-a-Nore, on Sunday night youths continued their orgy of destruction.

Not a window survived their onslaught at Rock-a-Nore garage. Wall panelling was kicked in, the computerised section of a petrol pump was smashed and "Mods rule" was spray painted on a van in the forecourt.

A battery was missing and a phone was ripped out.

Vandals emptied rubbish bins through shop-fronts and hurled a stolen radio through the window of the Wood Shop, where a bemused Reginald Pye was offering bits of broken glass free to his customers on Tuesday.

His windows were barred, but youths took about £250 worth of stock, which they made bonfires of on the cliffs and beach.

Mr Pye said: "I came down to the end of the road but the police had cordoned it off and they wouldn't let anyone down."

Fish salesman George Rich arrived for work at 4 am on Monday to find rubbish thrown through his window. He said: "It's really terrible, I don't know why they did it."

Eye injury

THE holiday clashes led to one youngster receiving an emergency eye operation on Saturday. Fortunately the boy, Andrew Wilder, aged 16, of St Helens Park Road, is not in danger of losing his sight. His condition is satisfactory.

● Vandalised wood shop Rock-a-Nore. Sign reads: "Free piece of glass to every customer."

Mob target 2

● Boarded up Rock-a-Nore garage.

Mob target 3

● Smashed: Wisdens, Claremont.

● Mods gather at the seafront.

---

400 MODS IN SEAFRONT RAMPAGE

By IAN BOYNE

MORE than 400 mods went on a seafront rampage in Paignton, South Devon, last night at the end of a three-day scooter rally. Hotel windows and bottles were smashed.

The main group was scattered by police, who used a helicopter to track down smaller groups.

Seven people were arrested, taking the weekend total to 32.

But elsewhere, the bank holiday weather seemed to have dampened "bovver".

Seaside police reported fewer arrests, especially in the north, where it was mainly cold and windy.

At Southend, Essex, there were 20 arrests. Trouble began when three skinheads were taken to hospital after running battles along the seafront with punks and mods.

One skinhead had serious head and leg injuries after being dragged nearly 100 yards along a road by a car. Later there was more seafront fighting, and youths were arrested.

Special train

In mid-afternoon, police escorted about 250 skinheads to a special train for East London.

Similar trains have been laid on by British Rail for about two years to get rid of Bank Holiday youths.

Southend police said: "It was old rolling stock and there were plenty of British Transport Police on board.

"Overall there have been a few disorders, but no major incidents. It's been a comparatively quiet day."

At Brighton, Sussex, there were isolated clashes between mods and skinheads, and seven arrests.

Police searched skinheads as they arrived by train from London, and confiscated bootlaces.

Police at Margate, Kent, made ten arrests, "just like a typical summer weekend."

The Look: Neat mohair suits, Hush Puppies, parkas, Fred Perry shirts and a scooter.

The Music: Tamla Motown, The Who, early Beatles, The Jam and Secret Affair.

■ **MANDY McCABE, 13, from Birmingham, schoolgirl:** "I was a punk when I was ten, a rockabilly last year, but now I'll be a mod forever.

"Most of the music was made before I was born but I'm not living in the past. There are millions of mods. If there were only a few I'd feel horrible.

"My Mum doesn't worry about me because she was a mod herself.

"I would only go out with a mod—though you've got to watch them. Sometimes they slip pills in your drink and then you're up all night."

■ **WILLIAM McMULLEN, 18, from Birmingham, butcher:** "Mods have a violent reputation, but we never go looking for trouble. Rockers and skinheads start more fights than we do.

"Mind you, the police aren't exactly a mod's best friend. I've got a Lambretta and I'm always being stopped.

"The police are always looking for drugs, too. You've got to take something to keep you awake if you're driving all night."

'We're sick to death' — says magistrate

HASTINGS is "sick to death" of youngsters who come and spoil the fun of other holidaymakers, said a magistrate this week.

Mr Victor Bray's attack came at Hastings Court on Tuesday when eight youths were found guilty of public order offences connected with bank holiday violence.

The eight, who pleaded guilty, were ordered to pay fines totalling £555. Twelve other defendants were released on bail.

Mr Bray told some defendants: "Most of you seem to think this is highly amusing. Well I can assure you it is not, so you had better think a bit more seriously about it."

During the hearing he said: "Towns such as Hastings are sick to death of young people such as you coming here at holiday time and spoiling the holidays of other people.

"You are a public nuisance. My advice is that you stay away in the future."

Five youths admitted threatening behaviour, for which they were each fined £75 and bound over for 12 months in the sum of £50.

They were: Paul Phillips, aged 18, unemployed, of Priory Road; Richard Hill, aged 17, unemployed, of Gordon Road; Martin Davies, aged 17, unemployed, of Ealing; John Shaw, aged 17, a post office worker, of High Halden, Kent; and Andrew O'Connor, aged 18, unemployed, of Church Road, Hastings.

Nathan Jones, aged 18, unemployed, of Linley Drive, who admitted obstruction, was fined £20.

Anthony Goodwin, aged 20, a student, of Otford, near Sevenoaks, was fined £10 for being drunk and disorderly.

Twelve people charged with threatening behaviour pleaded not guilty and were released on bail. They were: Warren Welby, aged 18, of Woodland Vale Road; Charles Smith, aged 18, of Brighton; Patrick Cunningham, aged 17, of Cotswold Close.

Derek Stepanek, aged 18, of Middle Street; Paul Clarke, aged 19, of Oakwood Close; Sally Terrell, aged 17, of Bembrook Road; Kevin Hildon, aged 17, of Ashford; Neil Pennington, aged 20, of Lower Park Road; Karen Burton, aged 18, of St Peter's Road; John Wilkins, aged 18, of London Road, St Leonards; Nicholas Downs, aged 18, and Dennis Spice, aged 21, both of Malvern Way.

Nine youths had already appeared in court on Monday to face charges of breach of the peace and receiving stolen goods. Five were fined and bound over.

BAGGED!

Mods, boneheads and normals on the front

Ian Walker joins the mods at Brighton; **Chris Moyse** took the pictures.

Could *this* be the start of something big? A flurry of parkas, up the steps leading from Brighton beach to the promenade, turns all those heads getting hot in the queue for the Palace Pier. At the rear of this charge of the mods, a stockbroker's clerk, Andy, clomps the last few steps in his brown suede Cuban heels. Storm in a teacup, he says, watching about 30 fellow members of the Essex Thunderbirds running nowhere in particular.

It is Sunday dinner time. Mods are still arriving, by scooter and car, coach and train. Andy left Hornchurch on his Lambretta GP200 at six o'clock last night, got into Brighton at eleven and made camp near a golf club. Sitting outside a cafe on the front, he squints into the sun and says, languid, that they were stopped and searched twice en route.

Andy is 17. Though he has been a mod for three years, it's only since he started working that he's been able to go "completely mod." Before then he sometimes had to wear straight clothes.

He's wearing a suede-fronted cardigan above permanent crease trousers. His Cuban heel boots are killing him, he says, walking towards the fairground. Being a mod is an expensive hobby. "We used to go to this club in Southend, Scamps, on a Saturday night. It's 25 miles, which is two quid in petrol. Then it's two quid to get in. It stays open till two, so you're going to do a tenner. Which when you're on £14 a week supplementary, you done it. And people do. Live for the weekend."

Another member of the Thunderbirds starts walking alongside, plying Andy with stories of last night's fights. Andy listens stoically. "The whole thing sickens me actually," he says, after his friend has disappeared. "Some people can't enjoy themselves without having a row. I mean, I will defend myself. I will defend my scooter. I think it's ridiculous if the police are going to nick you for that. Mine's left down there now. Cost me £300 and it could be kicked to pieces. Get no insurance for that."

Tonight the Thunderbirds will conceal their scooters in a copse near the Lambretta. "To be on the safe side," he says, walking past the Penny Wonderland amusement arcade, nodding to all the familiar faces. There's been rumours of hordes of East End skinheads—mods call them "boneheads"—coming down here, but so far Andy's only seen ten.

About 80 scooters are parked opposite the Volks miniature railway station, and a few hundred mods are sunning themselves on the grassy slope above the tarmac. Andy sits down next to another Hornchurch mod, Eric, who is a trainee chef for Hambro's Bank. "I hate going to work," he says. "But you got to work. Otherwise I wouldn't be able to do this." Eric's scooter, which he's buying on HP, will cost him £1,000 all told. He takes home £45 a week.

Eric is wearing a West Ham scarf, but he says that it's just to keep him warm on his scooter. Like Andy, he isn't interested in football. "Better things to do on a Saturday. Saturday mornings we go looking for clothes in the orig-inal shops in the East End that are all closing down, in the West End too, and in markets like Roman Road," he says, raising a hand to a short boy called Kev whose tape recorder is playing soul at full volume.

Kev is a DJ. He does rhythm and soul nights every Tuesday and Wednesday at the Sebright Arms in Hackney. He's got 500 soul singles, he says, and hundreds of LPS. Daytimes, he too works as a stockbroker's clerk. If he can find a hotel room he's going to organise a party for tonight, he says.

Although he owns a scooter, Kev says he is banned from driving for a year. He was breathalysed? "Nah. Forged number plates, no L-plates, no tax, no insurance, bird on the back."

He nods his head to the first few chords of the next soul single on the tape. A lot of Kev's record collection, which he's built up in just two years, comes from a shop called Final Solution, just off Oxford Street. Strange name for a record shop? Mods, Andy says, don't much go for politics, but there are a few fascists here and there: a scooter club called the Viceroys which is all British Movement, a mod fanzine called *Patriot*, that kind of thing. Mod colours always have been red, white and blue.

At about 6.30 pm the Thunderbirds start picking themselves off up the grass. Some go and get changed before walking into town, to the Royal Oak, one of the few pubs that doesn't have men standing outside denying entrance to mods and skins this bank holiday.

By 9pm the Royal Oak was shut, lights off and doors closed. Skinheads had been in one bar, mods in another. Three thunderflashes were let off. Police cleared out all the mods, who retaliated with stones and bottles as they were moved on down towards the promenade, and finally penned in on the open ground before the Volks railway station, which was petrol bombed.

The phone started ringing in the booth by the station, just as it was being smashed up. Someone picked up the phone, explained what was happening, and carried on wrecking the booth.

At 2.30 am, police were still rounding up all the mods. One group of 60 or so, who'd been fighting on the front with a small contingent of the crumpled green tonic jacket, down the promenade. "We didn't co trouble," explains Steve, who was on train. "Just to have a good time, th

Gas board workmen are cleanin wreckage round the Volks station, just three scooters parked opposite them is owned by Mart, who says halfway to London and back last eyes are black through lack of sleep left school this summer, but he has a to next week, as an electrician.

"Last night," he says, "they [the po all our cardigans and parkas, nicked chucked all the crash helmets in the r was watching us all night. At four o' started letting people put their shoe their toes were falling off."

Early morning on the grass (the girls are not those referred to in the article)

Boy on scooter knifed to death

Sunday Mirror Reporter

A TALL, vicious killer who stabbed a teenage motorscooter rider to death was being hunted last night.

Police also mounted a round-the-clock guard on the dead youth's friend, who watched helplessly as the killer struck.

William Kirby, 18, was the victim of a frenzied knife attack while on his scooter near his home in Corby, Northants, on Friday evening.

He was stabbed repeatedly — for no apparent reason — as he and his 17-year-old friend stopped their scooters at a road junction.

Nearly 100 officers are involved in the hunt.

They include 20 members of Northamptonshire county's elite uniformed support group, set up recently to deal with major incidents such as terrorism and murder. "This was an unprovoked and apparently motiveless attack on a innocent young man," said Detective Super intendent Peter Sharp deputy head of North ants CID.

Police, who are no naming William's frien say the killer was accom panied by a youth, age about 18. After the stab bing they both ran off without saving a word.

The man police war to question is aged abou 23, 6ft, 3ins, tall with broad shoulders. He wa wearing a shiny black leather bomber jacke and faded blue jeans.

His companion ha long straight hair and was wearing a tan suede jacket.

DAILY MIRROR

New Society 3 September 1981

Early morning on the grass (the girls are not those referred to in the article)

rockers, were the last to be taken down to the pen by the beach. "It's called police harassment," whispered a boy whose tonic suit wasn't warm enough now the night had turned cold. I walked down towards the Palace Pier behind a mod couple, a sleeping bag draped round the boy, a blanket round the girl. There had been 15 arrests. At 6 am all the scooters were escorted out of town.

Darrin, walking down from the station next morning at 11 o'clock, wants to know what happened. He's down from Romford for the day. He wears the inverted y peace symbol on his American flying jacket. He got interested in CND, after looking round a bookshop in Exeter while on holiday. Darrin, 16, has been looking for a job since he left school in July.

On the train Darrin met Mark, another 16 year old claimant. Mark has been a mod three years now. "Great life," he says, this fat boy in

Darrin hands out some cheese sandwiches his mother made for him that morning. Six skinheads stand talking to police by the railings beyond the station. "Hello," shouts a mod girl called Maria. "I'm a skinhead. Can I crawl up your arse?"

Maria, a 19 year old dental nurse, sits with her younger sister Rosemarie. "I never wanted this to happen," says Maria, pointing at the burned-out station. "I thought that was disgusting." Her sister, and their two friends, Angie, who works at Chelsea Girl boutique and Caroline, who's studying at catering college, all agree. These four girls, all members of the Essex Thunderbirds, managed to find a B&B late last night.

"My mum knows I'm down here," says Caroline, who's wearing a green tweed two-piece she got from a charity shop. "She was one of the original mods. Used to tell me what to do. Tactics."

Rosemarie works in a jewellers in Oxford Street. She says that mods were quite respectable back in 1979, before you got all hangers-on and posers. A poser, she continues, is anyone who is a part-time mod. These four have different club memberships for every night of the week. "Good clubs they are. You don't get no trouble there," says Rosemarie.

"I'm just despondent about the whole life," groans Maria, the other mods agreeing. It's a grey day, looks like rain. Police across the pond are supping tea from plastic cups. "It's not a holiday home. You're supposed to be working," yells Maria.

Rosemarie says she is a communist, while her sister is 'Frank NF.' Angie's brother is a rocker. Home life can get complicated.

Because most of the boys in the Thunderbirds had their scooters away, they avoided getting run out of Brighton. They arrive in ones and twos, sit down by the girls. Post mortems are going on all over the grassy slope, on which some 200 mods are sitting, by one o'clock. Eric, the trainee chef, sniffs in disgust at a headline in the *Star*: PETROL BOMB TERROR. "It was only a little vodka bottle," he says.

Someone else has heard that the police get £10 an hour for working bank holidays. He advances his theory that they have a vested interest in bank holiday bundles.

At just gone 2 pm the police start moving everyone off the grass, up the steps onto the promenade. "You just want everyone up there, on the main street, chanting 'We are the mods,' so you can nick us all," says Maria to one of the policemen.

"It's not us, honestly," he replies. "It's those geezers in the flat hats. They tell us what to do. Everyone'll be off rioting now, and it's us who have to put up with the bottles and bricks. Everything was nice and cool. Everyone sitting down." He walks away, exasperated.

The four girls get up. Maria pulls on her purple raincoat. All four pick up their cream overnight cases, start walking alongside the railway track, past the Astro Liner ("Take a trip to the future, 50p") at the edge of the fair, and up the steps towards the promenade.

They are joined by Tom, a 14 year old mod who has been in trouble with his headmaster for wearing eye-liner. Tom intends going into the army as an engineer. "Eight normals want a fight, down by the slide," Tom whispers to the girls. "But they just want the big ones. Keep it quiet." He rushes off. Rosemarie laughs.

A hundred yards further on two skinheads stand flexing their muscles before a group of 20 mods. The girls, led by Marie, break up the fight by dragging away skinheads. A police Transit screeches to a halt. Men burst out the back door, start chasing a dozen mods up Bedford Street. Of those who are caught, some get taken away in the Transit. Others just have to surrender the laces from their Hush Puppies.

"If there'd been a bunch of skinheads we'd of joined in fighting," explains Rosemarie, matter-of-fact. "But when there's just two boneheads you've got to break it up."

The four girls turn off the main streets into the bus station. They're going home early. It hasn't been much of weekend.

At Brighton station police have segregated the passengers for the 4.05 to Victoria. Normals at the front of the train. Mods in the back. At least it never rained.

10,000 MODS ON THE WAY

ORGANISERS of this year's Island scooter rally have still not officially told the County Council that they plan to use a site near Newport.

With the rally only just over a month away the council says it is still waiting for confirmation that scooterists plan to use 30 acres of farmland near Vittlefields Cross off the Forest Road.

Deputy County Secretary and Solicitor Mr. Felix Hetherington said: "While we have seen unofficial reports that they want to use Vittlefields we have not received in writing confirmation of the site and the name of the landowner.

"The ball is firmly back in the organisers court. Until we have received that information it canno considered by a spe called meeting of County Public Prote Committee."

The council has also to receive an official w ing from organisers they expect their overn gathering to exceed 5, people although under terms of the IW Act authority only has the power to act after the gathering has taken place.

Organiser of the rally — planned for August Bank Holiday — Mr. Chris Burton has already forecast at least 10,000 people will attend despite the fact that Mods have their own separate mainland rally on the same weekend.

Police well-prepared for any clashes between gangs of skinheads and mods on the seafront at Brighton yesterday. There were a dozen arrests.

A bundle on the promenade . . .

LIVERPOOL

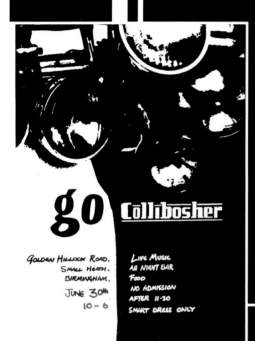

go Collibosher

GOLDEN HILLOCK ROAD.
SMALL HEATH.
BIRMINGHAM.
JUNE 30th
10 - 6

LIVE MUSIC
ALL NIGHT BAR
FOOD
NO ADMISSION
AFTER 11·30
SMART DRESS ONLY

In Liverpool we are 100% Mod - PURISTS!
I know you're going to slag me off for being narrow-minded, living in the past etc.. but, quite frankly, I can find nothing which compares with both:
1) the proper mod way of life which I consider is totally TIMELESS - why should it apply to only 4/5 years in the late '50s/early '60s???
2) *Black music* in general, but particularly the period 1958-1968. To be honest, we don't like the new mod bands, and we don't consider *Rickenbackers* and a scissor kick in the air to be Mod. *The Who/The Jam* etc... Mod??? NO WAY!!! Maybe we're just a bunch of self-opinionated boring turds, you tell me.

Liverpool clubs:
THE DOLPHIN CLUB, Paradise St, Liverpool. Every Friday, 8pm-12pm, 20p.
MAXWELLS, Hanover St, Liverpool. Every Thursday, 8pm-1am, entry free.
Both clubs are smart dress only. DJs: *John Gall* and *Allan Griffiths*.
The **Weekend Dancer** newsletter is handed out free on the door at the clubs. It is produced by Liverpool Mods for Liverpool Mods.

John Gall
NATIONAL MOD SCENE
From GoGo n°3 (1985)
Editors: *Jackie & Bernie*

BIRMINGHAM

There are around 30/40 Mods in Sutton itself (including a few girls), although these tend to keep to themselves in groups of about 6/8. In the whole of Birmingham including the Black Country, I'd guess at about 3000 Mods in total. Probably the largest contingent of Mods and *Scooter Boys* is in Aldridge. Other groups of Mods include the *Sutton*, the *Four Oaks*, the *Streetly*, the *New Oscott*, the *Kingstanding* and the *Boldmere*.

Clothes are easy to come by as Brum City Centre is not that far away by bus or train. This means that a lot of the Mods have a good clothes selection. There are a few scooters, however, a lot of Mods (including myself) are getting cars or already have them.

The only mod disco in Sutton is held every 3/4 months at the *Four Oaks TC* when *Tony Reynolds* (the Midlands N° 1 Mod and *Northern Soul* DJ) plays a lot of '60s music which annoys the majority trendy audience. For the more adventurous there is the *Manor Disco* in Aldridge, *the Whit* in Walsall or the *Streetly Disco* in Streetly, however, I haven't been there for years.

In Brum centre the main mod shops are *Gear Oasis*, *Nelson Houses* (there's about 7 of them), *Style* (near Bingley Hall) and various other shops like *Jeansville, Harry Parkes, Clogs* that sell good *Lonsdales*, shoes, *Levis*, boxing boots etc. *HMV, Virgin, Smiths* and *Subway* have a good selection of records, however, for the enthusiasts there's *Reddingtons Rare Records* and a good record shop close to *Ryans cafe* where a lot of Mods hang out, including some of my mates, but if you decide to go there beware of the *Black Rudies* 'cos they take great pleasure of massing into large armies of niggers and kicking in small groups of Mods and Modettes.

SUTTON MOD SCENE From '**In The Crowd**' no. 8 (1983)

I.O.W - 1994 - Photos by the author

SHEFFIELD

Those of us who live in or around London are lucky enough to have a choice of clubs and gigs to go to every night. Not everyone is that fortunate.

There're lots of *Scooterboys* here, not many Mods; lots of *Soulies* too, dating back to the early and mid-'70s. Weird. Lots of northern Mods dig "Ski-ing In The Snow" and "Footsie", AWFUL!! Such records bring back horrible visions of flared trousers. You can get *Carnaby Cavern* clothes in Sheffield, from *Pulse* in Cambridge Street, and also shit like *Jam* shoes and *Melanddi* gear from *X Clothes*.

FANZINES -Impossible to get unless by mail direct, hence my distribution idea which will offer an efficient outlet (regular mail-out lists, stalls, mail-order ads etc.). It will be called *U.N.C.L.E. Distribution*. There are three local fanzines: mine, which is the best known (big headed bastard!); **First Impressions**, from Sheffield, run by *City Limits Modernist Society* - poor but will improve. **The Target**, the worst fanzine I've ever seen - any out - sider reading it would have thought that there was no mod scene at all (or it finished with *Small Faces/Who*).

BANDS - **The Gents** you already know. **Beat Street** are a '60s band with maybe too many *Beatles* influences for their own good, but had a promising single out last year called "Egg On My Face". **The Way** are a four-piece who have only done 3-4 gigs so far. They do a lot of *Jam* covers, but they're being ousted in favour of some promising self-penned stuff, such as the very excellent "Sock It!". A demo is on its way, on the *U.N.C.L.E.* label (of course). **Revolver** I know nothing about except that they're a three-piece Rotherham mod band.

Lots of *Northern Soul* nights to go to. It's extremely common here and is not really a mod thing. Sixties night at The **Leadmill Beat Club** every Wednesday in Sheffield - all the **City Limits** lot go. down.

RECORDS - **Amazing Records** in Cambridge Street, Sheffield is crammed with the occasional gem, '60s stuff, *Soul*, etc. Expect to browse for hours.

A brief run down! Things are picking up now with more Mods getting in touch with each other and arranging things etc. *James Blonde* (**Generation X** fanzine).

NATIONAL MOD SCENE
From **GoGo** nº3 (1985)
Editors: *Jackie & Bernie*

Des Mannay: The *psychedelic* scene happened just in time - in 1982, because the bloody mod club in Cardiff had been closed up. It had been packed or bombed in a modern car-park by a bunch of... there was nowhere to go, literally. Nothing happened until those clubs opened up again. As *psychedelic* ones. Then you had a really weird mix, all sorts of people went along there; Mods growing a more *psychedelic* look and all sorts of other people as well. The person who set up the *psychedelic* night in Cardiff was an *ex-Punk* of the first lot - he was a mate of one of *The Clash*. A nightmare; he was a good lad but he was just clueless. He hired the club because he liked the wallpapers, he thought it would look nice with the music. The fact that it was fucking impossible to get a taxi from there at night didn't matter.

I got into the *psychedelic Revival* for a bit and I just got fed up with it in the end. Somewhen in the middle of the '80s, the club had closed down as well; that's when I started getting back into *Soul*. All of Cardiff's *psychedelic* bands were playing on rent anyway. We had one *psychedelic* band in Cardiff: **The Neverminds**, who had an excellent drummer, *Chris Ales*. Then they turned the *psychedelic* night back into a mod night, when you had **Street 66** playing in there, their second-ever gig.

Nowadays, *Northern Soul* drowns everything out; it tends to drown everything once it catches on. It's a shame because there're so many different types of music and so many different kinds of creative things that you could listen to.

SCOTLAND

The most obvious centre for the largest group of Mods is **Aberdeen**. Of the several hundreds in the city that call themselves Mods, only about half of them are dedicated or reliable when it comes to the mod way of life. That is, 99% of the time they're wearing their parkas, suits, etc. It's unusual to see the Mods in Aberdeen in really big groups, except for the occasional Sunday, when they assemble in Golden Square for a scooter Run. However, Mayday seems to bring out every single person who has, or used to have a parka. This year, we'd estimate that 80/100 Mods stood in groups along Union Street, while another 150 occupied Union Terrace Gardens.

A rough guess at the number of scooters would be about 80/100. The largest percentage of which seem to be owned by *Scooter Boys*. The only shops which cater for Mods, in records and clothes are **1-UP**.

Buckie appears to be doing pretty well for itself on the mod scene and has a fairly surprising amount of Mods for the size of the area. Despite living on the wrong side of 40 miles from Aberdeen, they're well up-to-date with the national scene and news, and aren't slow to organise coaches to gigs.

The scene in Dundee is pretty small if you go by the size of the place. Most of the scoots are owned by *Scooter Boys*. As for shops, the main place to get clothes is **Breeks** and records from **Grouchos**, both of which are outlets for *"007" fanzine*.

Stonehaven probably experiences the greatest changes in mod numbers. A couple of years ago there were only half a dozen, and the number of scooters was just less. More recently, the numbers vary between 15 and 20.

The only scene in the Montrose area is at St. Cyrus or Arbroath. The first has 5 Mods and 2 scooters, while the latter has a fairly big scene for the size of the town.

Scooter clubs in the North-East used to include: **The Faces, Woodside, Garthdee, Rampant Lions**, and **Scooters Inc.** (easily the largest). The latter eventually broke up and new smaller groups were created, such as **The Stylists**. The main group in Dundee is the **Stars & Stripes**, the majority of which are, again, *Scooter Boys*.

As for fanzines, there are only three that we know about. These are "Shout", by *Bruce Innes* and friends in Buckie, and "Third Degree", by *Pete Mathieson* from Aberdeen. And "Just Once", that you're reading at the moment. Together, the three of them have a direct selling area from about Buckie down to Dundee. All three are also available from *1-UP* (where else!).

N.E. SCOTLAND SCENE

From **Just Once** n°2 (1986)
Editor: *Robert Lee*
(Laurencekirk, Scotland)

EDINBURGH

In Edinburgh, there are about three or four hundred Mods. However, most of them are younger so there are only about one hundred proper Mods.

We have two mod bands, **THE PRIDE** and **THE MIRRORS**. *The Pride* were formed originally in May 1983. They have a distinct *Pop-Art* sound and some excellent songs like "Push 'N' Shove" or "Pity Or Pride", when playing live they do all their own numbers. The band are all heavily influenced by Mod, e.g. they range from *Squire, The Jam ,The Church, The Action* and *The Creation*. They play gigs quite frequently and usually attract a fair sized crowd.

The Mirrors are also a four-piece and are heavily into Mod. They've been going for about two or three years. When playing live however it is mostly cover versions that they play.

We also follow the *R'n'B* band **Blues'n'Trouble**. They play very hard *R'n'B* and have a scruffy image, but they are still worth going to see. Some of us also go to the "Kaleidoscope" *psychedelic* club to see local *psychedelic* bands like **The Green Telescope** and also other bands like **The Playn Jayn** who come up from London.

The main mod society is **The Avengers Mod Club** who organise mod nights quite frequently, often with bands playing, e.g. *The Mods May-Day* gig at the *Maybury Roadhouse* in Edinburgh where *The Pride* and *The Mirrors* pulled a crowd of around 400 Mods. Other mod clubs are **The Cliche** (which play mainly *Soul*) and **The Maximum Speed Mod Club**, which have recently been formed and concentrate mainly on mod *Revival*. There are also *Northern Soul* allnighters in Edinburgh every two or three weeks and we sometimes go to the **Hoochie Coochie** club which is *Soul and Reggae* (but a problem is that it's popular with queers). There is also a mod pub called **Close Encounters**, plus a mod cafe called **Cross-Winds** and there are three or four youth clubs which are popular with the Mods...

EDINBURGH MODS
From **Happening Right Now** n°1 (1985)
Editor: *Johnny Hamilton* - Antrim (Ireland)

In Stirlingshire the mod scene is slowly breaking up, but it was great in its prime (83/'84). Scotland isn't the best place in the world for a Mod, but it has quite a few dedicated followers of the fashion. I live in a small town called *Denny*, after moving from my home town of Glasgow when I was young. I grew up in Denny and I became a Mod in the beginning of '82 after hearing about the good *Revival* bands such as *The Chords, Purple Hearts, Squire*...

There was a club for Mods in a small town called Grangemouth that held discos but was stopped after being raided by the pigs, and resulted in a few under age drinkers getting done. Then another club in Falkirk had mod nights, but everybody only danced to *Soul* and only the Denny Mods danced to *Revival* music; saying we danced like *Punks*; but we eventually got them to appreciate good music and they danced to it as well. Hearing of the *Ilford Alldayer* in London, five of us decided to go down and see it after being invited down by *Jeff Shadbolt*. Here we got introduced to the *Purple Hearts* and got autographs & records & Parkas signed. It was the first time we'd heard of *The Scene* and *Makin' Time*, but we thought they were all brilliant. So after sleeping in the train station (never again) we went back to Scotland where most of the Mods had turned poser or *Skin*.

The *Nightspot* discos were getting worse, nobody was turning up and so us Denny Mods arranged *The Gents* and *The Pride* to do a concert which was a let down; and resulted in the Falkirk Mods fighting the Edinburgh Mods (God knows how) and when *Makin' Time* played in Edinburgh none of the Mods from Stirlingshire were allowed in!!! Because of the trouble the previous weeks. Anyway the scene will either get better or worse but our fanzine "Millions Like Us" sells like wild fire.

From **Fabulous**
Editor: *Des Mannay*

I.O.W - 1988 - Photo: SMILER

IRELAND

Although a handful of mainly British Mods were in Dublin in 1979 it didn't boom until 1980 when **The Blades** were beginning to emerge. A large turnout of about a thousand Mods occurred in the holiday resort of Bray in 1980 and with nobody to fight they chased the local police until they were rounded up and sent back to Dublin. That year *Gaeity Green*, a large outdoor market was the scene for many fights between Mods/Skins and dirty *Greasers*, sadly the Mods, outnumbered, rarely won! In 1981 the market was closed and the Dublin Mods started to hang about at a monument in O'Connell Street, it was suitably re-decorated and is still 'the place'. In 1981 there were around 2000 Mods in Dublin, now in 1983, with between 300-400 *Scooter Boys* there is a population of around 500 Mods, mostly with *Vespas* but a handful with the new *Lambrettas*. Some of the biggest scooter Runs in recent years have been at Tramore in 1982 and '83 and at Bray this year. The one at Tramore last year was widely covered by the press and had the biggest turnout of Irish Mods so far. The largest following of Mods in Eire now are at Drogheda, Dublin, Wexford and Waterford on the East coast and also at Cork, Limerick and Galway. There are two clubs in Dublin, one at "Bubbles" in Fleet Street which is held on Wednesdays, Fridays & Sundays, while the Dublin *R&B Scooter Club* is held monthly.

Beat Boys fanzine was founded in 1981 by *Dev* and *Gribbo*, two Southside Mods from Dublin. The first *Beat Boys* was a crude photo-copied job though it still sold well with an interview with *Secret Affair*, Mari Wilson, drummer *Paul Bultitude*. *Beat Boys* was started in the wake of an explosion of Irish Modzines, "Distant Echoes", "Steppin' Out", "Reflections", "Biff Bang Pow" and "The Changing Face". *Beat Boys* number 2 was printed as a forty page booklet with a wide distribution of 10,000 copies. Its popularity was due to the fact of it coming out more like a popular music mag and an interview with Dublin's favourite sons *The Blades*. More issues followed, though in 1983 the *Beat Boys* editors split. In the summer of this year me and *Dev* went over to London and got interviews with *Tony Meynell* and *Beggars* old guitarist *Jeff John. Dev* is bringing out a new mag, though the title is as yet undecided. There are now only a couple of Modzines left in Eire: THE CHANGING FACE, BEAT BOYS, DISTANT ECHOES.

THE BLADES
The band with the biggest following in Southern Ireland is easily *The Blades* - though they're not strictly a mod band - they don't want to classify themselves with any movement. I can assure you that the band have some ace dance tunes up their sleeves, proof enough is in the latest single, "Downmarket"/"You Never Ask" (*Reekus Records RKS 010*) a brilliant slice of *Soul/Beat-Pop* with some great brass sections. Formed in 1979 the band have released four singles previous to the latest. The debut single was "Hot For You" (*Energy*) released in '79 and followed by "Ghost Of A Chance"/"Real Emotion" (*Energy*), the release of which coincided with a UK tour and some very favourable press over here. Surprisingly recent press coverage has been none existent since then although the band have had three more singles released in the meantime, "The Bride Wore White"/"Revelation Of Heartbreak" and of course the current "Downmarket" gem.

The band have moved on from their inception as a jangly/Jammy three piece '60s *Beat-Pop* group to a more *Soul* orientated direction now. Interesting news too is that the band have just signed a five album deal with the *US.Elektra* mega-label. The band's current line-up is: *Paul Cleary* on vocals and guitar, *Brian Foley* on bass, *Jake O'Reilly* on drums, *'Fitzer'* on organ and also the horn section, 'The Blue Brass', two members of which used to be in the popular, but unrecorded Irish mod band, **The Mod-L's**.

ZEN ALLIGATORS
The Zen Alligators have now split up into another, non-Mod band called **The Hosts**, but they did share a single with another mod group, **Side One**, which was released on *Hotwax* earlier this year. The *ZA's* side was, "I Never Forget A Face" - a song dedicated to *Pete Coffney*, an Irish Mod who died after falling off his scooter last year.

SIDE ONE
Side One are awful, they play about twenty *Jam* covers and some *Small Faces* numbers. At a gig last month at the *Ivy Rooms*, Dublin, I had to endure their entire set which includes a desperate version of *Squire's* "It's A Mod Mod World", with some dodgy lyrics added. I've been asked not to quote them because they are extremely embarrassing, but here goes anyway, instead of "And It's Ready Steady Go On My PX 200", *Side one* sing: "Heavy Heavy Heavy, *Paul Weller* I love you". At one point in the gig they said, "Now we're going to play some of our own material", at which half of the Mods walked out. It was later revealed that the rest of the audience were relatives of the band. I'm told that they dress in cardigans and wide lapelled suits, more *Mafia* than Mod. Anyway, I think that *Side One* deserve a mention for being so silly. Incidently their side of the *Zen Alligators* single was called, "Diary Of A Forgotten War".

MOD IN EIRE
From **Time For Action** nº 2 (1983)
Editor: *James Blonde*

Southend
- 1999 -
Photo:
Steve
Brown

Canadian Mod Scene 1986

Canada's thriving West Coast Scene!

"Is there a mod scene in Canada?" you ask. Are you in for a shock! We here on the West Coast have an active and thriving scene.

Now if you're thinking of the Southern California scene, you are wonderfully mistaken (A few of our Mods went down to L.A. and suffered severe culture shock!). Unlike the U.S. scene, we are styled after the original British Mods.

Clothes are available but we really have to dig around. The guys wear three-button suits, *Fred Perry* tennis shirts, desert boots, Chelsea boots. Girls wear skirt suits, sleeveless turtle necks, ski pants, and loafers. Most girls have bobbed hair. Fishtail parkas abound everywhere. Since we can't just walk down to *the Cavern*, we have to search thrift stores and alter our own clothing, sometimes using old '60s patterns to make our own.

We've got two mod bands at the moment, **On The Go** and **Times 4**. We have no regular hangout (except maybe *the Pig and Whistle* on weekends), not even a cafe (but we're working on one), so the bands play at regular venues where we have to fight *Punks* and *Trendies* for a spot on the dance floor.

So with few clothes shops or entertainment spots to spend in, most of our money goes on scooters. There are three main scooter clubs; **The Saints**, **The Royal Westminster S.C.** and **The Upstreet Racers** (that's me!). Including the independent scooterists, there are easily fifty scooters buzzing around. Most of them are *Vespas* (as there used to be a dealer in town) but there are quite a few *Lambrettas*, a couple *NSUs*, and a *Manhurin*. (No Fap Crap allowed!) Older, classic bikes are preferred.

We don't go in for racing - our love lies in runs. Nearly every long weekend in the summer is booked. We usually go in search of other scenes which we've found in Victoria (B.C.) + Bellingham, Seattle, and Portland, USA. Scooters are "furnished" in the traditional ways; lamps, mirrors, and lots of chrome. (No murals - they are scooters, not vans!)

Keeping a solid bond, Susan.

Torquay
- 1991 -
Photos:
Phil-Hip
Beauvais

I.O.W - 1990 -
Photos: Phil-Hip
Beauvais

COUNTDOWNUNDER
PARTY AT HANGING ROCK

The UPBEAT ▲ The SAINTS ▲ The REASONS WHY ▲ UPS And DOWNS
The DYNAMIC HEPNOTICS ▲ STUPIDITY ▲ SONS OF GUNS ▲ HAPPY HATE ME NOTS
GROOVEYARD ▲ The MUSTARD CLUB ▲ PAINTERS And DOCKERS ▲ The HUXTON CREEPERS

ently I came
...ss a couple of
...cles in daily
...ers and one in a
...ic paper, in
...tralia, which pro-
...ms the existence
...Mod in this far-off
...ntry...

Ray Patriotic (1983)

THE KING LUD. WELL MATURED WINES & SPIRIT

RANT
CAFE—VARE PROFIT

L MATURED WINES & SPIRITS

**.O.W - 1994 - the *King Lud* in Ryde,
entre point of the lunchtime session**

Photos by the author

SYDNEY & DIVISION 4

There is quite a strong scene "down under," the stronger ones being in the capital cities of each state. The main fanzine in Australia is "Get Smart", which organised Australia's first mod Alldayer in Sydney. It is edited by *Anita Janelsins*. There are now a few clubs where the Australian Mods can go and listen to live bands or dance to records. The bands they listen to include:

The Introverts who play an aggressive set in a style of music that only could be compared to that of *The Chords*.

The Reasons Why are another band they listen to. They used to be **The Clones** but they split up, and when reformed, they changed their set.

Division 4 have recently split up, but here is an article on them sent in by *Anita Janelsins. DIVISION 4*, one of Sydney's premier mod bands, seemed to have it rough from beginning to end. They made their debut in 1981 at the legendary *Sussex Hotel* - home of the Sydney Mods. Back in those early days they were rough, really rough. At first Mods paid no attention to the consistent banging of their drums, which almost drowned out the jukebox in the upper bar of the pub. But soon *Div.4* got a medium sized following of Mods. Their early set included lots of '60s *Punk & Pop* stuff, but it was good to have a slam to. They supported **The Sets** on the "Sydney Mods Easter Weekend Melbourne Invasion" but after travelling all that way, they only got dragged through the dirt by the music papers.

Soon, their bass player *Antony* left (booted out), and they recruited a new one (who happened to be a Mod) named *Ian*. The other members of *Div.4* have always dressed Mod, but they didn't really want a mod label put on the band as, understandably, it would be bad for their progress.

By the time *Ian* had arrived, their set had changed considerably, but still mainly consisted of covers including: "Dirty Water", "Watcha Gonna Do About It", "Run, Run, Run", "Show Me The Way" (off a *Pebbles* album), "Legal Matter" and many more. They were a great dance band and their gigs were always packed with sweating, exhausted, speeding Mods. But at the same time, they were being continually slagged off by the press, other bands and a majority of older ex-Mods.

Again they were to lose their bass player. *Ian* found he could not be in a band and lead a full mod way of life at the same time. So he left.

After a long break they were back on the road with a new bass player called *Mark*, who was never a Mod to start with, but was made to get his hair cut and wear acceptable clothes on stage.

Div.4 once more returned to an enthusiastic mod audience, as good as ever and with a few new covers, "Action Women" from *Pebbles* Vol.1 and "I Can't Pretend" by *The Barracudas*, also a few new originals which appeared to be on their feet at last.

Their EP "On the Beat" was released in 1982 and included two originals "I Can't Give You Everything" and "Stop Dreaming" plus one cover "She's Just Not Anybody". The band were not really satisfied with the EP. It did moderately well.

The band's third bass player left, (yes, what did they have against bass players??). After a VERY long break they were back with yet another bass player *John Salway*, formerly of another great Sydney band **The Clones**. *John* not only played bass, but he sang and wrote his own songs. So, this time when *Div.4* returned they were completely different. They had dropped all their former set and were now playing mainly originals which *John* wrote. This sudden change shocked the Mods and because the band didn't do any of their old favourites, but instead, songs which were alien to their audience, they weren't very popular for a while. Myself, and a few others thought they were still great, the originals were different to what we were used to, but were ultra '60s and very good. Soon Mods were back seeing and dancing to them again, but not for long. After a couple of months, the fact that the band weren't getting many gigs, plus a few personal problems between them, proved to be the last straw, and they decided to call it a day.

They played their last gig on *28th January 1984*.

To me, they were a band who deserved much more credit than they got from critics. They were one of my favourite Australian bands and it was more than a shame to see their demise. In the future two new bands will be forming from the members. One will be quite similar to *Div.4*.

From **What's Happening Today** nº 4 *(1984)*
Editor: *Gaz Poundall*

By late '79 New Zealand's main largest city, Auckland, had given birth to a new group of teenagers, the Mods. They started out as a collection of like-minded individuals who had not as yet come together to form a definite group. Local pubs and clubs played a major part in uniting the Mods as well as local, up and coming *Pop* bands. The most popular group was **Pop-Mechanix** who played pure *Pop* music at that time. But there were also various *punk* bands that appealed to early Mods too because of their '60s sounding music and style (not so much of the style though). These included **The Swingers**, **The Terrorways**, **Toy Love & The Primmers** to name only a few.

A lot of early Mods were university students who already rode scooters, and were the first to come together because of their working relationships. Scooters were a common sight in New Zealand and unlike Australia they were treated as an ordinary form of transport by the public in general. This meant that the Mods could fit into society without causing a sensation with their strange, two wheeled vehicles. The scooters were all *Vespas* except for one *Lambretta LI 150* and one *Punch* (and one *Triumph Tigress* which spent its life in pieces on a garage floor). *Vespas* numbered about 40 and consisted mostly of *GS 160s*, *150 Supers* and *180 Super Sports*, and were distributed by a shop similar to "Tony's" in Annandale, run by a bloke with dollar signs for eyes. Two Mods were given probation for breaking into the '*Vespa* Shop' on a mission of revenge for all the 'shithouse' scooters he had sold.

More bands were starting to form, purely for the mod following. Such bands as **Blam Blam Blam**, **The Screaming Meemees** and **Penknife Glides** were all started by university students, and all appealed to Mods (these three bands have all recorded material for record companies). There were also bands that came from the Mods such as **Vivid Militia**, an amateur *Pop* band, and **Active Eye**, a just as amateur *ska* band, both of whom died 'before they got old'. By mid-1980 cult groups consisted of Mods, *Punks*, *Rude Boys* and *Rastafarians*. There were also a fair number of *Bootboys* but they never did constitute a cult group. These groups, with the exception of *Rastas*, all drank at the same pubs and went to the same nightclubs and generally got on well together. The only trouble came from the *Yobs* and *Rastas*, but they were no great threat.

The Mod's week would start on either Monday, Tuesday, or Wednesday, depending on whether there was a good band on. If there was a band on early in the week it would usually be at the university for a couple of dollars. On Thursday night everybody would head up to *The Parrot Bar*, a gay bar that doubled as a meeting place for Mods. From the *Parrot Bar* the Mods would go on to one of the many night spots to see a band. Most venues were small and dark and nearly always upstairs. Favourite venues were "The Rumba Bar", "The Reverb Room" and the "Cellar" (similar to *The Sydney University 'Cellar'*). After the band everybody would meet up at "Al and Pete's", a takeaway fish shop that was in the vicinity of a lot of Mod's households. From there it was either a party or an all-night coffee shop. Much the same thing would happen on Friday night although the raging would go on into the early hours, ending in a mad scramble to find a comfortable place to crash. In the morning those who were awake or still coming down would visit *Cook Street Market*, similar to *Paddington Market* but held in a warehouse near the city centre. At about two in the afternoon there was usually a gig at *The Rumba Bar* featuring **The Androids** or some other amateur *Pop-Rock* band. Then it would be off to a chicken shop or takeaway for dinner. At about 7.00pm everybody would start to turn up at the "Vic", a sleazy pub and notorious hangout for the *Bootboys*. It was here that the Mods bought and sold drugs before heading off to a gig.

On Saturday night a great place to go would be *Mainstreet*, a converted ballroom that featured up to four bands for as little as four dollars. From there you would either end up at a party, on a *scooter Run* or just crash out 'round one of the university mod squats. Sunday was the anti-climax with either a soccer match at the *Auckland Domain* or a booze-up to bring your weekend to a close. Coming home was like stepping into another world where you would be cut off from everything except school, university or work.

MOD IN NEW ZEALAND
From **Pow** - Australia Editor: *Dave Turner* - no date, probably 1982 or '83

NEW-ZEALAND

Torquay - 1991 - Photo: Phil-Hip Beauvais

The Hip Cats and Smiler - **1990** - Photo: SMILER

'Oxford' Martir
Clive Bushnell
Stuart Everett

Tony Schokman, Dom Bassett
and Matty who became a famous DJ in
the *Techno/House* industry, aka **Jim Masters**
Photos: SMILER - **1989** -
Clive Bushnell, Tina Vaughan, Phil Reeves

Paul Davy
Photo: Mark Lusty

SCOOTERING

Number 5. £1.20.
January/February 1986.

By Mart.

INSIDE: Win a PK 125S!
FREE COMPETITION FREE COMPETITION

Everything you need to know about the
scootering world: Customs, vintage, the new
T5 Vespa, Redcar run, Milan show —
plus special features on the faces
in the Mod scene '64-'86.

THE 60's MODS

THE 80's MODS

and certainly weren't at war with them
(too concerned with the creases in our
suits for that), and besides they'd simply
turn out to be old mates from school
(exactly like in Quadrophenia) — all the
stuff we saw in the papers was unreal,
press hype — and we knew it. We didn't
mind strutting about though ... didn't do us
any harm, you know? The enemies
weren't rockers at all, but bills — dry
cleaning bills and scooter repair bills. We
kept a lot of folk in work, we did. Crash
damage wasn't worn with pride, like a
badge; I wouldn't turn out if even a single
mirror was broken (those alone cost me a
fortune).

Fashions changed; all the chromey bits
were slung into the back of the coal shed,
and "The Thing" suddenly became the
stripped down look — everything off
that'd unbolt, and you'd get stopped by
the police for dangerous parts about twice
a week. And it's a funny thing, but I really
can't remember what became of that
maroon, cream, and lime green TV/SX; I
must have sold it, but in the way that I
remember buying it like it was yesterday,
I've got no memory at all of selling it. Lost
interest. Moved on. By '68 there was
more going on — different things — hair
got longer, and the hippie generation
picked me up and swilled me along. Tell
you another thing though, you don't
forget. Oh no. What I do have left is the
stack of singles: worth fortunes nowadays
I'd imagine ... and I'll tell you summat else,
you're not having them, not for anything.
Okay?

still got the cutting from The
Manchester Evening News. It's gone all
brown now, but is still in the back of me
Dad's old, red A-Z, on the page covering
Moston in North Manchester. It's the
Motorcycles, Scooters, and Three
Wheelers column, and ringed in biro is a
1975 — asking price £45; good clean
example. Actually, it wasn't all it seemed
— it had an SX150 engine, truth be
known ... a stolen SX150 engine; but then
those days as much stuff seemed to be
nicked as was straight. Dunno what things
are like these days ...

Me dad ran me up there in his Ford
Anglia (the 1200 cc Deluxe model, as it
happens) and I paid the asking price and
rode the thing away. It had a few bits and
pieces on it — front and rear crash bars,
and a vertical spare in a tartan cover —
and an SX front mudguard. Fair enough, I
was well happy.

There was a very strict line of status,
when it came to the sort of scooter you
rode. No-one in our crowd rode Vespa —
none at all; LIs were run-of-the-mill, LDs
were the bottom of the pile along with
125s, and SXs were the business. When
the GP range was introduced they caused
a real stir and were instantly "The Thing
to Have". Top of the heap before that was
my mate Dave — a crazed police cadet
with a big bore conversion on an SX200
who certainly should never have made it
to the force, looking back ...) So my
TV/SX was okay. Respectable.

The thing was maroon and cream —
and I added a lime green fluorescent flash
to the side panels (and repainted the
bastards every time they fell off and went
clattering down the road). The little
screen came next — with leopard skin
surround (and the oval clamps kept
dropping down over the hand controls!);
then — gradually — a dozen mirrors, a
smart set of Fiamm dual air horns, a red
and black shaped mat that never fitted too
well, a radio in the tool box, a red and
cream striped seat in real leather, a long
black mudflap that dragged on the ground,
a whip aerial with a tiny Union Jack on the
top, a back-rest trimmed in matching fur
(also, a pair and a set of "Florida bars"
that ran from just behind your feet,
diagonally up the panels, and bolted to the
rear crash bars ... these made the panels
virtually inaccessible, and if/when you
were lucky enough to get a bird on the
back she inevitably snagged her tights on
them. My lasting impression is of
outstanding tackiness; the front crash
bars tore huge holes where they were
bolted through the leg shields, the back
rest snapped through on the Chester
road late one night and left a smart kid

called Ronnie bouncing along the outside
lane, and the twin megas — which
sounded a treat and were very long and
very chromey — snapped off from the
main box about once a fortnight.

The bike itself was never of any
interest. The add-on bits were everything.
I would only get my hands grubby — and
then with great reluctance — on the not-
infrequent occasions when cables
snapped (through lack of routine
maintenance like lubrication). Long as it
looked right — and that usually meant
looking all right at night — nothing else
mattered. No murals. No silly names. All
done to an accepted formula. All very
tribal. We thought ourselves individualists
— but we didn't half conform to our own
cult.

We tended to be out and about most
nights of the week; certainly Thursday,
Friday, Saturday and Sunday were all
solid virtual all-nighters — each week,
every week. Dunno how I kept it up.
Dunno how I afforded it — drinking lager
and lime, buying cherry brandies for girls
you had little real chance of getting off
with.

Saturday night was "The Night",
unsurprisingly. You'd start mid-afternoon,
zooming around, meeting up by ESP
rather than any specific arrangement, and
then into town to tour the clothes shops
and the record stores (and you didn't have
mega record stores in those days — just
snotty places staffed by old blokes whose
main income came from Stravinsky and
The Seekers, and you had to really get the
old buggers to work if you wanted to get
your hands on obscure Tamla singles). By
five o'clock all the scooters would be lined
up, parallel, on a 45 degree angle, by the
side of the Co-op, facing the bus station
(all these places long since demolished
and replaced by a huge shopping
precinct). That was the understood haunt;
the place you sorted plans for the
evening, and caught up with the girls
who'd be catching buses home between
5.30 and 6 o'clock.

There was a funny gap then; home for
tea and watch Juke Box Jury. That was
really crappy (except for the one time the
entire panel was made up of The Rolling
Stones, and they really took the piss, and
David Jacobs didn't know what to do with
himself) and nothing like Ready Steady
Go; that was un-missable on Fridays —
they played the music and the audience
set the fashions (the guys mostly, who
really worked at it; the girls — even Kathy
McGowan herself — were never quite
that into it in some way). Even Thank Your
Lucky Stars and Top Of The Pops (still on
a Thursday night, even then) were better

than Juke Box Jury.

By eight o'clock you'd be out of your
casual gear (if you'll pardon the modern
aspect of that expression) and into the
night gear; the suit, the roll-neck nylon
pullover, the shiney best shoes — topped
off with the great-coat to keep the road
muck off (replacing the "surfer" jacket of
the daytime — rarely a parka, in point of
fact). Then down to a pub; meet up, get
into the mood, zoot up a bit, and off down
the venue — inevitably a club, any one of
a number. It was the greatest feeling in
the world; a couple of dozen of you,
dressed up to the nines, zapping through
the suburbs under the yellow neon light,
riding like nutters (who cared?), out on the
town. You knew who you were. You had
your mates. You knew you looked good.
Knew you were right.

The club would be very hot and very
sweaty: The dancing took a bit of practise
— I was okay — not the best — but okay.
From time to time there'd be a bit of "A
Problem"; not too often though — there
were a couple of brothers in our mob (who
had a beautiful and much desired sister,
name of Theresa, who was known as a
certainty) who always seemed to be
flashing blades at people outside the club
at closing time. There wasn't that much
though — and while a few of us did get
hurt in scooter crashes (I lost a knee,
nothing; a mate smashed his legs and
pelvis and was really badly off) I don't
recall anyone getting seriously hurt in the
odd scuffles. Our lot kept away from the
seasides in the main; never saw rockers

Scootering

Foreigners and even British folk
unaccustomed to London's much famed
Carnaby Street might be forgiven for
thinking themselves in some kind of a
time-warp — for the look of the Eighties,
Frankie Says T-shirts and rah-rah skirts
and the like is now finished. The style of
the Sixties is once again with us. The
Mods are back. There are those of you
who might say they've never been away,
but no, the current revival is undoubtedly
the biggest we've seen since Mod first got
on its way, over twenty-one years ago.

1985's Mod is actually a far different
creature from his Sixties predecessor,
according to Paul Field, editor of 007
Modzine, the bestselling Modzine
currently available. "Today's Mod is into
getting somewhere in the world, back in
the Sixties, Mods had things easy. There
wasn't such a thing as unemployment,
there was always plenty of cash to go
round; nowadays, things are harder, and
Mods seem to have a lead on other young
people, they're always well dressed and
looking smart — that counts for a lot
when it comes to jobs."

Mods, according to those I met and
spoke to in Carnaby Street on Saturday
the 6th July '85 — in case you were
there! — have four main interests in life
and they pursue each vigorously. Music,
clothes, scooters and girls, and if there is
a fifth then it's "style". But then style is a
vital part of each of their other four
attractions.

"Mods do everything with style —
whether it's making out with a girl or just
making a boring old cup of tea!" says
Nick Allen, a bearded ex-Mod, now 18, with
more than a little bit of sarcasm. But no,
Mods do do everything with just a little bit
extra verve. Take their music for instance,
although you might never see their

favourite groups of Top Of The Pops or
The Tube, they're incredibly loyal to the
bands they follow. Of the Mod bands
currently around, probably the most
popular is The Gents, followed by The
Scene, The Moment and Beat Direction
— a group of Mods that come all the way
from Canada. A Miss Eleanor Rigby is
their favourite pin-up, she's a singer and
her single, provocatively named Can I
Sleep With You? is one of 1985's
bestselling Mod records. Eleanor's even
got her own fan-club and fanzine. The
Mod records are not easy to get hold of,
very few record shops bother to hold
them, so Mods get them in the main
through mail order companies, such as
St. John Sixties Supplies, based in
Carnaby Street. Their Andrew St. John
showed me letters from all across the
globe; Mod music may be based in
London, but Mods from as far afield as
Sydney, Australia, to Brantford, Canada,
write to Sixties Supplies for their favourite
sounds.

Scooters are as popular as ever with
the Mods. Carnaby Street was full of talk
about shock absorbers and engine
chroming. Managing Director of The
Cavern, a Mod clothes shop, is Martin
Benjamin, a bearded ex-Mod, now 27, he
grinned ear to ear when I asked him if the
Mod movement was continuing to grow.
"Yes, it is, we're busier than ever and the
scene is looking really healthy at the
moment." I asked him to be more
specific. "Take the Modzines for instance.
There's over sixty of them in regular
production. That's three times the number
that were around in '82/'83. Mods have
been getting write-ups in the national
press and not for causing aggro on the
runs, but for being well dressed and cool."
The Cavern was incredibly busy while I

was there and the Mods were looking
pretty sharp.

But what of Mod girls. What are they
into? With a deep breath I approached a
hoard (is three enough to be a hoard?) of
them, who were posing by the public
at the top of the Street! They were Debbie
Brady, 16, Michele Ely, 15, and Pauline
Taylor, 17. Denise and Pauline were
decked out in those tight-fitting ski pants
while Michele preferred the original
Sixties look; her clothes came mainly from
jumble sales, Camden market and her
mother's sewing machine.

The one thing missing from Carnaby
Street was in fact trouble. A few years
ago, there were almost permanent battles
with skinheads, but in '85 trouble was
nowhere to be seen. I asked Pauline,
who's been coming up to Carnaby Street
regularly for four years now what has
happened. "The skins don't bother us
much now. We've developed a live and
live relationship with them and once you
get to know them they're not that bad.
One of me best mates, Shaun, is a skin,
and he's been coming up here for longer
than I have."

So, by the look of things, there are a
multitude of reasons for Mods current
boom. The energy of the Modzine editors,
the business sense of shops like The
Cavern, and mail order companies like
Sixties Supplies who deal in old and new
Mod records. I spent six hours in all in
Carnaby Street and came away more
impressed. The Mod scene is strong at
the moment, if the organisation behind it
keeps up its side I can only see it growing
even stronger.

you need wheels...

Steve Marriot, original mod from 1966.

''Don't call me a modette. I'm a mod girl,'' says Donna (17) from Beckenham. She works for a Chartered Accountant ''but they don't mind the way I look because my boss used to be a mod and anyway they think it's quite smart.'' She runs her own scooter but she's looking after this Vespa Rally for a friend. ''You need transport because there aren't any clubs in Beckenham.''

''I got into it because a friend was playing these Small Faces records and I looked at their picture and liked the whole look. You can't exactly walk into Top Shop and buy the original mod clothes so I go to second-hand shops and then alter things to the way I like them.''

[text partially obscured] wearing: a neck jumper from [...] skirt to [...] it in a Classics Shop for 75p [...] Hush Puppies £2 from [...] shop. ''I always wear white eye shadow, black cake [...] and never wear lipstick!''

[text partially obscured] explained [...] beauty in [...] Sean [...] an (19), an [...] technician from Streatham [...] at the time it was more fashionable than today and [...] my mates got into it as [...] He thinks Paul Weller is OK [...] wouldn't say he was [...] I like jazz and rhythm and blues and soul [...] mainly [...] Tamla Motown, Motown and [...] music. The music's more important than the fashion.''

He is wearing: a three year old Ben Sherman shirt (£3), trousers made by a tailor in Battersea (£25) and patent leather slip-ons from Brixton Market (£33). ''I don't think I'll be able to keep it up now - I'm unemployed!''

The thing with those sort of clothes, is that they naturally make you pose.
Gavin Gribbon

Clacton - 1985 -

Brighton - 1986 -

Photos: SMILER

Gavin Gribbon: The thing with those sort of clothes, is that they naturally make you pose. If you've got a nice fitted three-button suit you've had made for you, a nice button-down shirt and a tie, you stand, in that way, you stand in the stance.

Since the '60s, the real 'hip' thing to do was to wear a three-button jacket, have the two top buttons done up, and the bottom one undone, or alternatively to have only the top button done up... so that when you put your hand in your pocket, your jacket doesn't crease but the line stays straight. And when you stand like that, you look like a sculpture.

That's basically what you're trying to do; to make a sculpture of yourself.

MOD 'N' TIMES

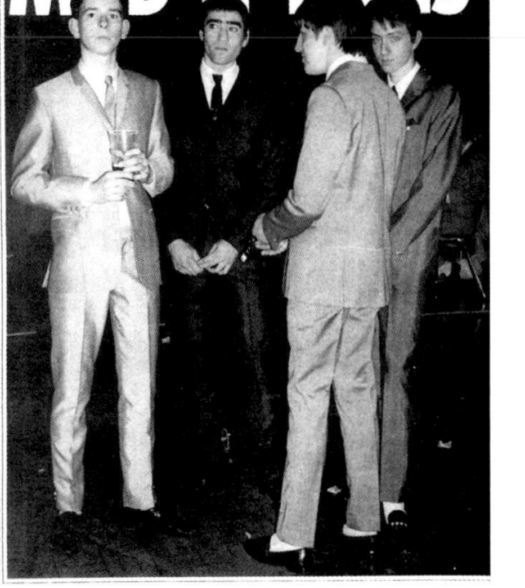

ROB MESSER: We were walking on Oxford St, when I got approached by this young lady, who was a photo reporter doing an article about the Mods for **Time Out**...

There are 'Mods' and Mods. Mods wear silk ties and handmade suits, bought in Jermyn Street or Saville Row, and wouldn't go near a Lambretta unless you paid them. And, 20 years on, they're still going strong.

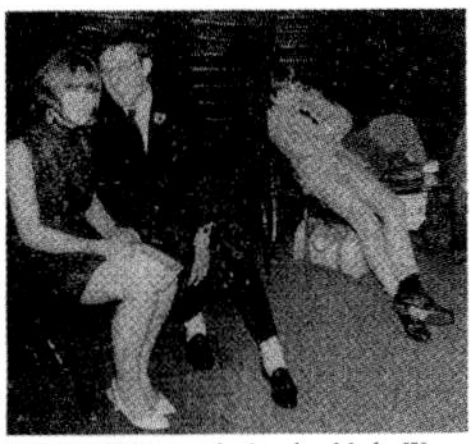

We are the London Mods. We are the King Pins of the circuit. We're older, taller and smarter than anyone else.

It's the Mods' night out and we are speeding our way to the 1985 National Mod Meeting, on the Six-Five Special to Peterborough. The coach is full of sharp young things. Everybody's speeding and the journey is a blaze of endless chatter, aggressive anticipation ('There'll be rucking tonight'), club news and deals and the continual comparison of suits, shoes, shirts and ties.

The rain drizzles interminably and the boys go through contortions in their seats, trying to change into the contents of their flash suit bags. The girls are dabbing and mopping at their make-up — another layer of pastel lipstick, another ring of eyeliner. 'I like your cardigan, Paul [he is wearing a beautiful, pearl-grey suede and cashmere number].' 'Oh this thing, it's my warring one — I always have trouble when I wear it,' he grins.

At last, we're heading for the doors in a bunched group; even I'm speeding now. The boys average 18, the girls are no older than 16: the atmosphere is like that of a school disco, especially as the venue is a huge gymnasium and the only bar packs up at 11pm. This is a disappointment for the 600 Mods who have come from all over Britain for this all-nighter. But at least there are two live bands (although both sound like punk groups) who inspire manic pogo-ing down the front.

The London crew I'm with sneer disdainfully. Live Mod music is notoriously bad — the best sounds are either black, dead, American, preferably a combination of all three. Later on, the four DJs do their best to coax as many as possible on to the dancefloor, with sounds as eclectic as vintage soul and the Specials. At times, the gym looks like a throwback to the '60s or a massive fancy-dress party; gaggles of girls sport Mary Quant cuts and original ski pants, and boys mill around looking older in their £200 suits.

It's now 3am and, apart from a few couples drooped passionately around the edges, most of us are still upright and outta sight. We've all been dabbing at the speed (rather than snorting the stuff, you stick your fingers in the packet and lick). There has been a minor scuffle outside with some 'scooter-boy scum', but most people have been greeting friends, sussing enemies or laughing at the baby 'plastic' Mods.

By Lindsay Shapero

A few fanzine editors are doing the rounds, but everyone's getting pissed off with queueing for the only soft drinks machine in the building. Paul, Jim and Chad think tonight's been a washout — they're disappointed with the amount of 'lower deck' (younger) Mods and can't wait to go home.

It's a very subdued crowd that slump in their coach seats an hour later. It's coming-down time, and no one talks above a whisper. Those still awake blame tonight's letdown on the Phoenix Set, two money men who organise both the national scooter runs and the all-nighters.

'They're out to commercialise Mod and rip us off,' complained someone bitterly. 'They're giving a good thing a bad name.' Not surprisingly, the London crew have been arranging 'pirate' runs and events for themselves.

As the coach races back towards London, the temperature plummets. I feel like shit, hope I die before I get cold. Next to me, a beefy Mod in a sharp suit is quietly sick. He's just relieved he missed his strides.

Our motto is adopt, adapt, appreciate. You can either be a face or a number — we're all fucking faces.'

Something good is always lurking underground and this time round it's Mods. Not the kids in parkas and two-tone Jam shoes wandering around Carnaby Street, but the 22-year-olds comparing prices in Jermyn Street, then slipping into Saville Row for some fabric. But this isn't a revival. For years pockets of Mods all over the city have been holding true to the ideals of their '60s predecessors. And none more so than the East/South-East crew, known as the Bow Street Runners.

The Runners don't publicise their riotous clubs, scooter-runs or all-nighters, some of which have been chugging along successfully for years. They get news through their own grapevine, in fanzines like *Right Track, Setting Standards, In The Crowd*. There's even a special slang combining Sarf London double-talk, 'Clockwork Orange' and '60s expressions: *Setting Standards* — 'A few of the trees were getting lary and I could sense a Newhaven-style ruck was about to go off. Unfortunately, it didn't, but a few of the Collier Row got a bit upset and were last seen ▷

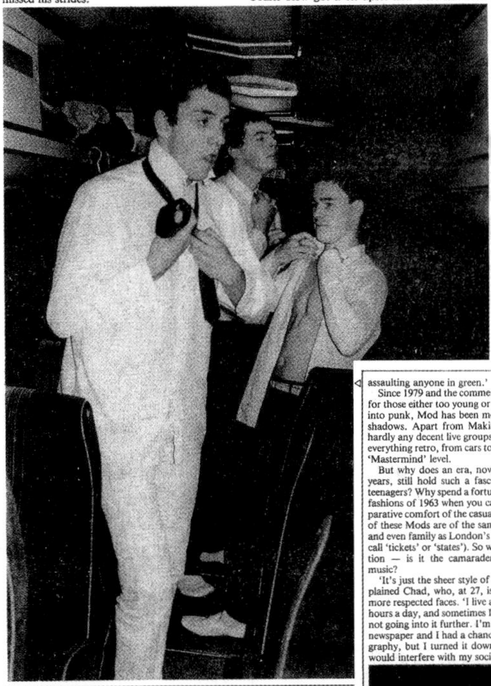

ROB MESSER: If you look at *Richard Barnes'* "Mods" book, you will see that most of the time they were not that smart... some are, but some are more 'casual' than well dressed. What we did was to take the best of the '60s, and create our style from the smartest details; we were in a way better than them.

◁ assaulting anyone in green.'

Since 1979 and the commercial Mod boom, fit for those either too young or too clean-cut to get into punk, Mod has been moving back into the shadows. Apart from Making Time, there are hardly any decent live groups, and knowledge of everything retro, from cars to clothes, is reaching 'Mastermind' level.

But why does an era, now dead for some 20 years, still hold such a fascination for today's teenagers? Why spend a fortune on recreating the fashions of 1963 when you can shop in the comparative comfort of the casual world? And many of these Mods are of the same age, background and even family as London's casuals (whom they call 'tickets' or 'states'). So what's the big attraction — is it the camaraderie, drugs, gear or music?

'It's just the sheer style of the movement,' explained Chad, who, at 27, is one of the scene's more respected faces. 'I live and breathe Mod 24 hours a day, and sometimes I can kick myself for not going into it further. I'm a printer for a local newspaper and I had a chance to get into photography, but I turned it down because I knew it would interfere with my social life.'

The Bow Street inner circle hail '60s Mods as the first true youth movement, dismissing Teddy Boys and their ilk as nothing but an oafish diversion. They also consider any Mod trend after '65 equally meaningless. 'As soon as someone tried to commercialise the Mod scene,' said Chad, 'it would change straight away to something different — no one could put their finger on it. Later on, though, it just got out of hand. Everyone thought it was about fighting on beaches with rockers, and jumping up and down to The Who. That was not the true Modernist movement.'

The real thing lounged in coffee bars chewing pills, never descending to the level of street-scrums for fear of their costly threads. The real Mods talked fast, could look after themselves and exhibited an amazing lust for life. It was when everything deteriorated into a dope-crazed haze that the true Mod scene fell apart.

But that past, obsessional attention to appearance spawned the traditional enemy — greasy, dirty biker boys. Nowadays, however, it's the Scooter Boy who must take the brunt of the condescending comments. 'Scooter scum', 'trees', 'greens' — all are terms of derision, for Scooter boys don't follow the basic ethic of sharp dress equals sharp mind.

'They are a complete bastardisation,' said Chad. 'All they do is ride scooters, which for me are nothing more than a form of transport. They used to hang around our clubs, which meant a lot of trouble, so we had to enforce the smart dress rule. They have absolutely nothing to do with us.'

Apart from Scooter Boys, Mods dislike casuals — surely, just one set of revivalist Modernists squaring up to modern-day Modernists. But the Bow Street lot don't believe they'll ever outgrow their own cult status, any more than they give away credit to their rivals. 'If you were to drop out,' said Jim, editor of *Right Track*, 'and put yourself into another cult, you'd be bored after two weeks. There's nothing with as much depth.' 'Depth' means knowing the difference between stepped and sloped trouser bottoms, plus having an encyclopaedic knowledge of music, from the usual Motown classics, through the history of R 'n' B, to uptown soul. In fact, anything up to the death of Otis Redding. Jazz, however, is beginning to creep on to the scene,

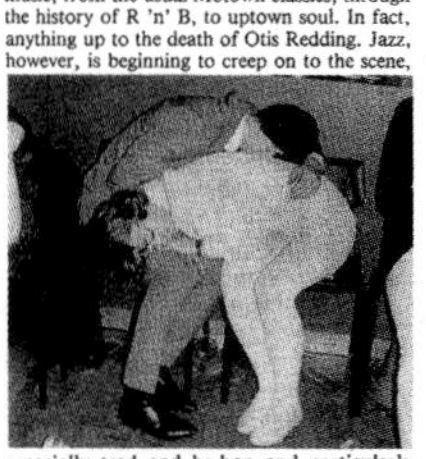

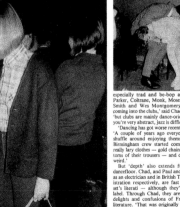

especially trad and be-bop and particularly Parker, Coltrane, Monk, Mose Allison, Jimmy Smith and Wes Montgomery. 'At last, it's coming into the clubs,' said Chad, who also DJs, 'but clubs are mainly dance-oriented and unless you're very abstract, jazz is difficult to dance to.'

'Dancing has got worse recently,' added Paul. 'A couple of years ago everyone just used to shuffle around enjoying themselves, then this Birmingham crew started coming down, with really lary clothes — gold chains across the bottoms of their trousers — and dancing got very weird.'

But 'depth' also extends further than the dancefloor. Chad, and Paul and Jim, who work as an electrician and in British Telecom's administration respectively, are fast becoming their set's literati — although they'll wince at that label. Through Chad, they are discovering the delights and confusions of French existential literature. 'That was originally brought in by a bloke called Beardley Pegley, who is one of my ideals,' explained Chad. 'The French image was really strong in the '60s because of all the French students in Britain, whose clothes were revolutionary at the time. Mods latched on to them and French literature went with it: there was Sartre — marvellous — and Camus, as well as Lawrence Ferlinghetti and that bloke Kafka. Then you had the beat generation with Kerouac, I've read all his stuff.'

'Unfortunately, it's the minority of Mods who think like us,' said Paul. 'Most of them are into live bands, mini-skirts and parkas, and bouncing around singing "We are the Mods" — all very embarrassing. There are good scenes around

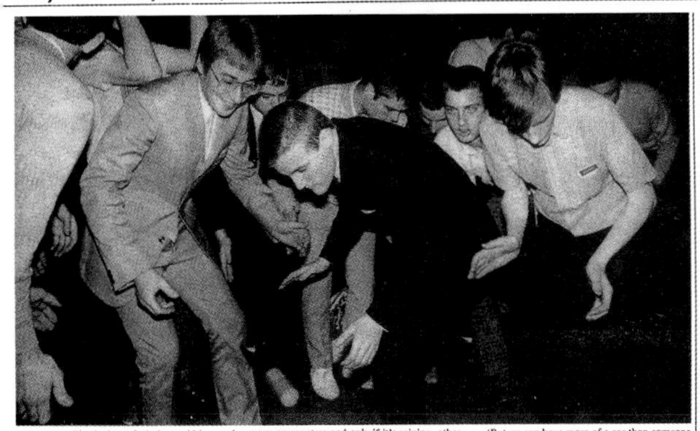

Coventry, Birmingham, Swindon and Liverpool, but too many are just sticking with it through the commercial side, believing what they read in *Smash Hits*.'

Again, there's that continual fear of commercialisation, which breeds mediocrity. And as an alternative to the much-hated Phoenix Set, the Bow Street Runners read the newsletter *Countdown*, part of Stiff's new, eponymous Mod record label. *Countdown* chronicles events, record releases, readers' letters and funny in-gossip: 'Once we finally gained admission to the golden water hole, we learned that Kev had been run down the night before by his mate, Jez, on his scooter. Apparently, Kev was thoroughly intoxicated at the time and lying face down in the middle of the road. His friend Jez came pop-popping along on his scooter and mistook Kev for a bin-liner, running over his prone and inert form in the process.'

As in the '60s, today's Mod scene is male-dominated. Girls are a secondary force, content with swishing their Mary Quant points in the background, leaving the boys to strut their peacock stuff. 'If you're a really dedicated Mod girl,' said Jim, 'there's a limit to places you can go without being pointed out as a Mod. Whereas if you wear clothes like mine, you can go most places and people are so stupid, they don't realise. They say things like: "Working a bit late, on your way home from the office?"'

And a true Mod will always look like a sharp worn on scooters and only if it's raining, otherwise a crombie is better. There's a whole range of specifics about what goes on at neck level. Tie pins are preferred to clips, and ties should be an inch wide, preferably made of silk, suede or knitted wool. Cravats are cool, as are either tab or button-down collars with gold clip-chains. Nearly anything in suede is coveted, Italian separates *de rigueur* and suits should always be made-to-measure.

Girls have a wider field to choose from, taking their influences from '58-'64. Mini-skirts are absolutely out, as are high heels. The best footwear is one-inch stacked shoes. Many girls make their own clothes from '60s patterns or, again, have them tailor-made.

'There's no such thing as an unemployed Mod,' said Jim. 'They just couldn't keep up with the scene.'

'I disagree,' countered Paul. 'I knew a bloke who was unemployed. He didn't have many clothes, in fact, he only had one suit, but that suit was always cleaned and pressed and he didn't look any different from anyone else. Dedication and effort can do it.'

There's much talk among these Modernists about dedication. For being a Mod is no easy task. Apart from the financial burden, there's the continual countering of Mod's bad image — just a bunch of kids in white winklepickers.

'The best part,' grinned Chad, 'is that older people have got stereotypes of what "youngsters" should look like. We're doing our own thing, but we're smart and neat, therefore, we're

'But we can have more of a gas than someone who's getting into trouble for being scruffy, with an openly rebellious attitude. Because we've got this nice front — veneer, call it what you want. They can't see what's really going on inside.'☐

EVENTS

THURSDAY

100 Club *Oxford Street, W1. Occasional Mod nights with live bands.*

Lords *Cranbrook Road, Ilford. Local Mod Club.*

FRIDAY

Crofts *200 Edgware Road, W1. Basement Club.*

SATURDAY

Solo Arms *Warren Street, W1.*

Ben Truman *Southwark Bridge. Pub meeting place.*

The Bizz *Tooley Street, SE1. Not 100 per cent Mod Club.*

SUNDAY

Sneakers *at the Bush, Shepherds Bush, W10. Best of the bunch.*

CONTACTS

Right Track Fanzine *Jim Watson, 25 Spencer Road, Seven Kings, Ilford, Essex, IG3 3PV.*

Setting Standards *Richard Franklin, 409 Green Lanes, Ilford, Essex.*

Countdown *Eddie Pillar, 34-38 Provost Street, N1 7QY (250 0398). Various Mod compilation al-*

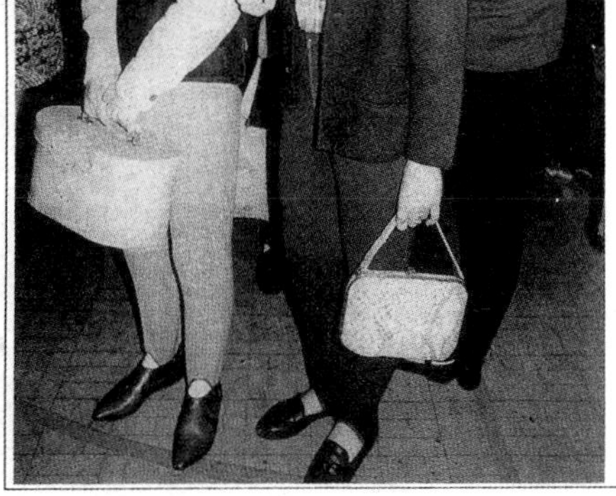

TIME OUT NOV. '85 Nº 797

THE ART OF DANCING...

Big Bob & Mick Wheeler in 1986

Gavin Gribbon: There is a book, made by a journalist called **Tony Parsons** , he wrote this novel in the early '80s, called "Limelight Blues"; the first three chapters are from the perspective of a Mod in the '60s, where he describes the crossover from Mod to *Hippies* in the late '60s. He is a Mod, quite fanatical about it, and he decides one night to go to a *hippie* club. And he's disgusted; *Hippies* dance from the waist upwards, when Mods dance from the waist downwards. It's the swing of the hips, and the movement of the feet that are the most important.

Nowadays people - in raves for instance, with their bloody 'Techno' - they don't know how to dance; they wiggle, like demented puppets...

Dancing is very important for a Mod, because it is a physical and sophisticated way to express yourself. That counts a lot when, as a teenager, you're trying to prove your identity to the rest of the scene. That's why each one of us shows his personality in the middle of the dance-floor; no more '60s dance style, everybody by the early '90s had found a more personal way of dancing, a signature for his or her own style.

The best moment in a party is always when you feel the music taking you, entering you with its rhythms, the beat of the bass, the slashes of the guitar, to the upper keys of the organ...

Personally, I couldn't understand any of that *Techno* shit; it was just noise to me!
The Author

...THE ART OF POSING

'Smash Hit' session - Photos: Andrew Catlin

Gavin Gribbon: Nowadays you hear on TV - for commercials for example - some tunes that we used to listen to, when we were on the mod scene, and nobody else knew them. Some of the music they now use commercially, was first ever played - since its release - to our generation, by people like **Toski** or **Paul Hallam**...

In some terms, that's great, because today we can turn back to people and say: "Yeah, we were fuckin' right!" In a way we were ahead of our time. On the other hand, you think: "But it's my originality, my culture..." You don't want to go out one day and realise that everybody in the street is dressed like you, has the same haircut and listen to the same records.

The author: That is part of the dilemma that this culture is fighting with, since its creation; you want to spread good taste of fashion and music all over the world, but at the same time you're killing any kind of individuality by doing that.

Rob Messer: Absolutely. It's like when you find a great record, and you want everybody to appreciate its quality. You play it at all the parties, until one day you hear it on the radio played over and over again... it's killing its value. Basically, commercialisation kills the myths.

Ian Jackson dancing at the Torquay *Untouchables* mod rally
- 1991 -
Photo:
Phil-Hip Beauvais

That's eventually what you're trying to do; to make a sculpture of yourself.
Gavin Gribbon

31

If there was one thing that I couldn't stand in the '90s: that must have been *Techno* and all that *House* music. I couldn't understand it! from the rhythm of it, to the hysteria that was sweeping Europe. I went to a *Rave* once, just to have a look, in 1991, somewhere in a forest; I thought I was lost in the middle of fuckin' aliens!

I remember quite clearly now... people at the time (late '80s/early '90s) didn't really make a difference; a *Rave* was nothing but a big party, whatever the music policy was, and some *Raves* would play *Jazz* instead of *Techno*...

There was a real drift, at this very moment in the general population, between people who enjoyed good music (mainly *Jazz* & *Funk*) and those who went to *Raves* to get drugged up and jump around on binary computerized drumbeats (ie: House, Acid, Techno... whatever the difference is).

I seriously hoped that the *Groovy* scene would win it out of the two camps (old school vs new school, if you like), but of course the 'Technos' were outnumbering us by one to ten thousand at least, so the sound of the 1990s will stay in history as dodgy mix generated by a machine.

The influence and the rise of Hip-Hop culture was also important during that decade; for the first time I saw Mods listening to French *Rap* (**MC Solar**, who launched his career with a rip-off of **Maceo Parker**...) because they were sampling original '60s *Soul* records (**Marvin Gaye**, etc...).

For my part I was a big fan of **US 3**, **Ronnie Jordan** (who coincidentally released "So What" from **Miles Davis** on the day of his death), because their influences were strictly *Jazz* (**Herbie Hancock**, **Quincy Jones**).

Eventually, **Brand New Heavies** and **Galliano** came to hold the flag, when **Jamiroquai** and **Arrested Development** went a tiny bit too commercial (for us), but for how long?...

Hip-Hop (and sampled music in general) seem to need to have a '60s connection in order to be taken seriously.

Paul Hallam: By the end of the '80s things were changing a bit, and maybe people were starting to look a little bit more like Mods; bands like *Wet Wet Wet* (I know, it sounds a bit sad) or *Curiosity Killed The Cat* were talking about '60s *Soul* records and they were talking with an air of authority. So all of a sudden it wasn't so much a taboo to be into '60s music, it had changed slightly.

from Top to Bottom:
*Tricia mcConnell, Elliot Winthrop, Mark Strange, Claire & Dom Strickland, Chris Penman, Angela Speakman.
Lowestoft - 1989 -
*Dawn, Danny, Chris, Lee Miller, Hayley, Angela Speakman, Vanessa, Phil Otto, Dave Edwards, 'Little' Sean.
Blackpool - 1989 -
*Claire Strickland.
Lowestoft - 1989 -
*'Putney' Sean, Phil Otto, Pat White, Tony Schokman.
Lowestoft - 1989 -

Photos: Dom & Claire Strickland

READING

HORSE & BARGE

MODERATION

CAP'n'GOWN

SMILER: Around 1988, the scene was beginning to split gently between two types of mod music. The scene was going towards playing more and more *Northern Soul*, with **Drummonds** for example (DJ *Rob Messer*) on a Sunday night, which was very nice and soulful, but not to my taste. I had been doing various nights at **The Cap & Gown**, in Reading, which turned into the **King's Tavern**; when we started the club in early 1989, the music policy was based on *UK Sue*, *UK Tamla*, heavy *British R'n'B*, proper *American R'n'B* and *Jazz*. *Soul*, apart from *Motown*, was probably the minor sound. And it would be packed; it got a very good name for itself, for a club on a Sunday night.

BOAR'S HEAD

King's Tavern
Photo SMILER

SMILER: A lot of Mods from London were coming every time, there would always be two car loads from Maidstone, which is a long way – *Lee Miller, Rob Bailey…* were there every week. We had people from Birmingham, Swindon, Bracknell, Chippenham, Winchester, Bournemouth, Fleet, Oxford, Basingstoke, Bristol, Newport in Wales… one night we even had a girl who turned up from Lytham (next to Blackpool). While *Drummonds* was practically a whole mod club, but they never had a dress policy, the *King's Tavern* was for Mods only, it was clear on the flyers. You would never get into the club unless you were a Mod; it got a reputation for having a complete mod policy. Hand-made gear, outside there'd be a line of original scooters and vintage cars, and we did all the original dances (the *Block*, the *Bang*) that had been seen since the 1960s.

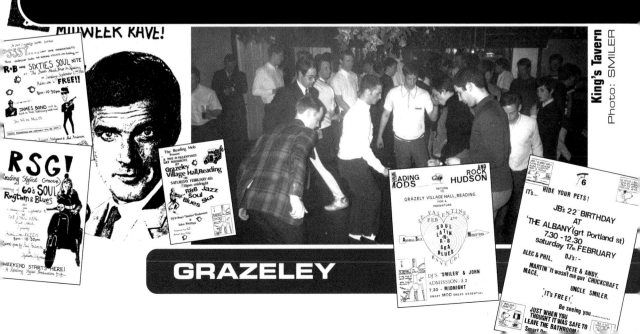

King's Tavern
Photo: SMILER

GRAZELEY

LONDON STREET

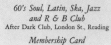

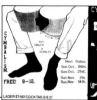

BUKOWSKI'S

Andy Preston
Photo: SMILER

THE 4TH DIMENSION

BRACKNELL

OXFORD

CHATHAM

NORTHAMPTON

COVENTRY

MAIDSTONE

LONDON

DRUMMONDS

SMILER: There wasn't a big scene in Reading, but I was DJing quite a lot in the South-East, in rallies, in London (at *Drummonds* on the Saturday night), Bracknell, Oxford… so I was quite lucky to get people from all over the place coming to my club. I remember some Spanish Mods, a big group of them, who were so disappointed in London because they were into *British Beat* and nobody was playing that sort of sound; they would make a point of coming to Reading every Sunday, just because they knew that they could hear it there. They were well pissed off with the London scene, because it got quite 'Northerny'.

The sad part is, when the *King's Tavern* finally closed in March 1991, I'd lost a lot of interest in it, because I was really getting more and more into the *Acid Jazz* music. I tried to re-open it two weeks later as an *Acid Jazz* club, but it only lasted for a couple of months; it couldn't get the momentum that it used to have in '89.

Rob Messer: We did use to play *Northern Soul*, but we used to play a lot of *R'n'B* as well; *Shirley* used to DJ there, because originally, *Drummonds* (in Euston) had started as a follow-on from *Sneakers* with *Paul Hallam*. He later gave it up, and *Shirley*, *Steve Coulson* (from Canvey Island), *Darren* (from Woodford) & me were running it; yes we used to play *Northern Soul*, but *Shirley* would play an hour of *Jazz* and *R'n'B*, so it wasn't *Northern Soul* only, but also a bit of *Latin, etc…*

Rob Messer: If the DJ before me was playing *Soul*, I would play something different; a bit of *Latin* or *R'n'B* or *Jazz*, and surely the people would be dancing. But after twenty minutes the dance-floor would go a bit 'flat', and you'd put a bit of *Northern Soul*; suddenly the place is 'buzzing' again. When the song comes up, they hear that beat and they're up, just go for it.

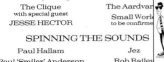

Phil Otto: This gig ('RnB Jazz Alldayer') was huge; it gathered at least 600 people. It took us at least six months to organise, and we barely made £80 after paying the bands & venue. So we decided it wasn't worth it; we wouldn't do it again.

Phil Otto: The 'Black Cat' productions (logo designed by *Dom Strickland*) was a sort of pre-*Untouchables* club, starting in January 1990. We used to gather around in pubs in *Carnaby*, every Saturday afternoon. We knew that there had been lunchtime clubs in the '60s, where people used to go during their lunch break. So we decided to have an afternoon club; which happened at the *Dublin Castle* in Camden. The first one made 67 entries, which wasn't bad for early-January. We wanted to have a live band each time. Within a month, when we got *Small World* to play, we made 100 entries. Then it was too small, and anyway it changed management after three months. From the 'Black Cat' it had become the 'Back Room' club (because it was at the back of the pub).

Phil Otto: On Saturdays it happened sometimes that we would play with **The Clique** at *the Dublin Castle* in the afternoon, get drunk, and then move the gear to *Drummonds* (on Saturdays, club run by *Tony Class, Rob Bailey, Smiler*, on Sundays it was *Rob Messer's* club) and play a second gig.

Please note: all flyers on the left page are Drummonds on Saturday.

Photography by Nick Knight

Styling and coordination by Simon Foxton.

30 YEARS OF PLAY ACTING

Ham it up! The theatricalities of dressing up have always gone in tandem with the clothes themselves — the art of the pose becoming synonymous with the art of selecting icons. Every youth cult since the war has adopted various stage-door mannerisms and dramatic stances that personify the outward projection of smugness, dissatisfaction, bravado and elitism. Strolling players, matinee idols, bit players and pierrots all. But don't be put off by any homogenized images — scratch the surface and the details come to light — as i-D shows here.

And though the styles may change and the music diversify, somehow the repertoire of poses remains remarkably similar. If the Teds of the 50s were the square root of all evil, then today's cults are the result of 30 years of musical and sartorial algebra. Yet the pose remains the same. Don't blink now!

'14-24' — British Youth Culture — Communications Through Commodities' is the last exhibition at The Boilerhouse's present site (it's moving to the east of London in the autumn), and it looks at the emergence of youth as a distinct economic category, from the great surge in mass culture which took place in the aftermath of the Second World War to the eclecticism of 1986. From the Teddy Boys to the Casual Boys — from I.D. tags to i-D Magazine.

Nick Knight and Simon Foxton were specially commissioned by The Boilerhouse to produce a set of photographs which embodied the major youth cults of the last 30 years — the results of which you can see on the following pages. To catch a glimpse of Nick & Simon's more modern exploits — The Preppy Casuals — look back at i-D No. 36 (May 1986).

'14-24' at The Boilerhouse, Victoria & Albert Museum, London SW7. 23 July-31 August. Opening times: 10-5.30. Weekdays and Sat. 2.30-5.30. Closed Fridays. Admission free (for psychos, winos and sociologists alike).

PHOTOGRAPHY BY NICK KNIGHT STYLING AND COORDINATION BY SIMON FOXTON ASSISTED BY ANDY KNIGHT AND CHARLOTTE WHEELER HAIR BY WENDY FROM SMILE MAKE-UP BY LYNNE EASTON FROM CREATIVE WORKFORCE LOCATION LIPSTICK STUDIOS, LONDON

Mr Paul 'SMILER' Anderson appears on the bottom right photo (next to **Eleanor Rigby**).

MODS: "Smile & stare: Mobility, cleanliness and asexuality. An upwardly mobile fashion victim's delight."

The **Phoenix Society** was soon replaced by the **Classic Club International** (CCI), still run by **Tony Class** to this day who organises a do at the Isle Of Wight every August Bank Holiday.

SMILER: Around 1989, I was DJing four times a week in London (coming from Reading), I was DJing in rallies with the *CCI (Tony Class)* – I was in their committee for two years, basically trying to change things from how they'd been. We all started to get quite disappointed because the scene was getting stale by 1990. The 'Manchester sound' was coming big at the time, bands like *The Charlatans*, *The Stone Roses*… and unfortunately quite a few Mods were going that way. So at certain rallies, records like *The Charlatans* "The Only One I Know", *Dee-Lite* "Groove's In The Heart"… all that was being played. But at the time we were pretty much still purists in our '60s sound, living in the 1960s, so we couldn't understand it.

Phil Otto: We had nothing personally against *Tony* or his rallies; in fact both *Smiler* and *'Putney' Sean* were *CCI* committee members. I also continued to attend his events in *London*, and I thought that the **Bizz** in Tooley Street (London Bridge), in its early days was a corker. A bit like an '80s youth club; a few *Punks*, *Skins*, Mods all mixed in together. *Tony* was good at what he did; it just wasn't what we wanted, especially for the rallies.

Paul 'Smiler' Anderson had been getting a lot of flak from *Tony Class* over something he had said.

Phil Otto

Hastings - 1995 -
Photo by the author

SMILER: In a rally in Gorleston, as I was DJing I remember shouting to the crowd: "Sod this *Northern Soul*, get some *R'n'B* down your throats!" *Tony Class* and a few other weren't quite happy, because I was a *CCI* committee member at the time; it didn't look good for public relations...

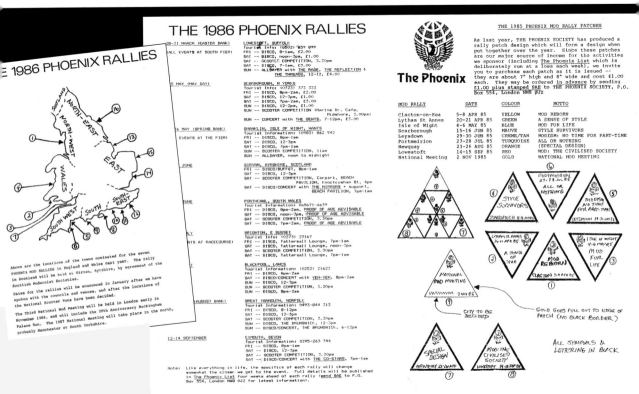

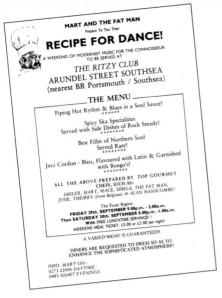

Rob Messer: I think *Paul Hallam* did two rallies in Hayling Island, and one in Clacton. But he got married, started having kids, so the mod scene wasn't his main thing anymore. I, along with **Mace**, started the **Rhythm'n'Soul Set**, the *RSS* which originally stood for *Rob, Steve & Shirley*. But *Steve* and *Shirley* were not really into organising rallies, so I did a first one in Littlehampton with *Paul Hallam* DJing; but I was pretty much on my own. Then *Mace* joined me, and we did Littlehampton several times, and we took on Hayling

Island because *Paul Hallam* didn't want to do it anymore. We did a rally there for New Year's Eve, which was the first time a rally was ever done during that Bank Holiday. You usually had Easter, Mayday, Whitsun and August; only four a year. So we decided to extend it to the New Year's Eve Bank Holiday, without knowing if it was gonna work. We eventually had two hundred people turning up, which was brilliant.

At the time there was no alternative to *Tony Class*, except us for at least two to three years. *Mace* & me did Felixstowe, Bournemouth, Chichester, Morecambe, Scarborough, Lowestoft, Great Yarmouth... quite a lot, until the *Untouchables* decided to put some alternative to our alternative. *Tony Class* was the commercial end of Mod; we wanted to be smarter, play the hippest tunes, the newest discoveries from the 1960s, proper Black music, and everyone was smart & sharp. But we soon got targeted as being snobs; there was a bit of arrogance in us, but we wanted to get the best Mods of the scene to come to our events, which were the places to be seen. Neither would we take the piss out of the new Mods in parkas & bowling shoes. We all started like that, and it's up to you afterwards to improve your image. And we lost money sometimes on hiring the places for our parties.

Phil Otto: We couldn't understand why the rally events had to end at 11pm, and we didn't like the membership cards, as we thought this was a little 'boy scout-ish', even though we did understand their purpose; keeping out undesirables. The music catered for too many factions of youth culture, the night before had ended with an hour of *Two–Tone* with all the *Skinheads* drunkenly jumping around while all the Mods looked on. This would have been fine if it had been a *'Ska Rally'*.

And so the conversation went on…

THE BEVS

Phil Otto and **Angela**, Claire's sister, who died in February 2003.
Photo: Dom & Claire Strickland

Claire Strickland: Angela and I DJed on the *CCI* rallies as **The Bevs** in '87/'88. *Tony Class* gave us our first spot at Lowestoft '87 ("Thanks *Tony* ") and we then got regular spots.

We played a mix and *Angela* was especially fond of *Ska* sounds. The other mod girls were really supportive of us but we still got a fair bit of flack for being like a female version of the two Tobys*. We DJed at Scarborough in the *Lemon Tree*, Gorleston in the fantastic *Ocean Rooms*, Hastings the next year and also *Drummonds* and *Circles*. When *Angela* went to Manchester university to study Paleontology, I carried on for a while, but it wasn't as much fun on my own. I think we were the only female DJs on the scene at this particular time. There had been *Sarah* before us but she'd packed in by then.

*The 2 *Toby's*: 2 DJs in the 1980s, having the same nickname, playing the set together.

Claire Strickland: A lot of Mods on the scene had nicknames; many were only known by these names. **Angela** and I were the *BEVs*, because we were sisters, had bright, bleachy hair and we always had a drink (bevvy). There are probably loads more, but these are the ones I can rember:

PUTNEY SEAN, CATFORD CHRIS, IRISH PAUL, MICK THE NICE, SMILER, CAMDEN COLIN, PRINCE CHARLES, WACKO JACKO, UNCLE WILLIE, NOJ, FLASH PETE, J.B., SPEED (London & Mansfield), TIGER JANE, GAMBA, RAB, STRIPER PIPER, CHRYSALIS, CHIN, H, TETLEY, CHIMPY, FLOPPY, WATFORD CHRIS, 'CHECK IT OUT' JOHN, SEX MACHINE, MINTY, BORING PAT, THE WORMS, GRANDAD SEAN, COUSIN CHRIS, THE TWINS, MAD SIMON, MAD PAUL, THE MONEY BROTHERS...

YOU PUT A *NORTHERN SOUL* TRACK ON, AND THE DANCEFLOOR IS PACKED; IT JUST HAPPENS. *ROB MESSER*

Photo: Nickie Divine

THE UNTOUCHABLES

SMILER: Around Spring 1990 we were in Bridlington; **'Putney Sean' Tracey**, **Phil Otto** and me admitted together that this wasn't the way we saw rallies. We talked about setting up our own rallies, which was a hard job; *Paul Hallam* had failed with the pirate rallies, *Rob Messer* and *Mace* had started the *Rhythm'n'Soul Set* events…

We were still quite happy, at the end of the day, to start our own set of rallies, even if there were only 50 of us who'd turn up, tailor-made *R'n'B* loving Mods. So a few days later we met up again; *Phil Otto* said that we should get **Rob Bailey** involved, because he was the favourite DJ of *Tony Class* at the

time. We had our meeting in the **Pontefract Castle**, in the West-End: **'Putney' Sean, Phil Otto, Rob Bailey, Andy Hynde, Dave Edwards, Dom Strickland, Dom Bassett, Jamie Rave** and myself. We were sat there discussing ideas; at the end of it *Dave Edwards* declined and said he'd help us out whatever we needed. *Dom Bassett* and *Jamie Rave* didn't seem interested and walked off. That was the start of the **Untouchables**. I came up with the name – after dubious ideas like "The Knights Of The Round Table" (!) - because obviously I love gangster movies, and at the time we all pretty much felt that way; we were quite well-known Mods, and we didn't wanna get, let's say infected by the *Manchester sound*. We really were into our '60s sound, that was puritanical.

Unfortunately, by the time it had all come about, I was already getting into *Acid Jazz*, and I started feeling a bit of a fraud, to be honest. I had started it, it was getting bigger and bigger, and I had less and less interest for it; it gave me the impression of a new *CCI*. It wasn't the vision we had first started with. **Maz Weller** joined in, **Dom Strickland** got more & more involved, but by then I must admit; I got fed up with it, really. The first official *Untouchables* do was

CLACTON 91

PRESENTING TOMMY CHASE
SAT 25   THE LORD NELSON

MOD/SIXTIES DRESS

7-1:30am £5

November, Saturday the 10th 1990, at the **Mildmay Tavern**, and we had decided that all the funds raised at this weekly club would pay for the next year's rallies. The first rally booked was in **Brighton, 1990 to '91 New Year's Eve**, and that was a big thing, but I wasn't focused on it, thinking of other things, and it had become bigger than I wanted to.

THE UNTOUCHABLES

NEWSLETTER

No. 1

Phil Otto: All the attempts in the past to do independent mod rallies had divided the scene, although they had improved the music content and were more true to the original mod ideals. We decided that we needed to heal divisions around the country and get people involved.

Phil Otto: We had a series of meetings in many places, and talked to all the main players that were interested. Our first rally in Hastings was a joint affair with *Mace* and *Messer*; unfortunately after a four hours argument over money, I vowed that I wouldn't work with them again, and the others felt likewise. This was a shame considering that members of the *Untouchables* didn't take a wage. A few perks perhaps, but this was nothing compared to the amount of work involved. The only rally that made money was the I.O.W and this paid for the other things we did.

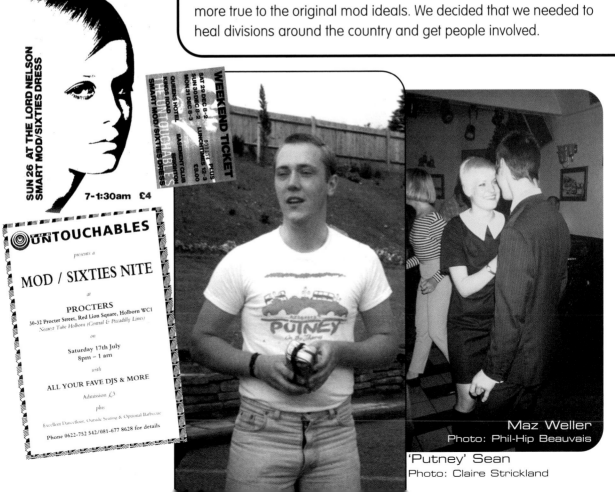

CLACTON 91

SUN 26 AT THE LORD NELSON
SMART MOD/SIXTIES DRESS.

7-1:30am £4

WEEKEND TICKET

QUEENS HOTEL
KING ROAD
THE UNTOUCHABLES
SMART MOD/SIXTIES DRESS

SAT 29 DEC 8-2
SUN 30 DEC 8-2
MON 31 DEC 8-2
LUNCHTIMES 12-3

THE UNTOUCHABLES

presents a

MOD / SIXTIES NITE

at

PROCTERS
30-32 Procter Street, Red Lion Square, Holborn WC1
Nearest Tube Holborn (Central & Piccadilly Lines)

on

Saturday 17th July
8pm – 1 am

with

ALL YOUR FAVE DJS & MORE

Admission £3

plus

Excellent Dancefloor, Outside Seating & Optional Barbecue

Phone 0622-752 542/081-677 8628 for details

Maz Weller
Photo: Phil-Hip Beauvais

'Putney' Sean
Photo: Claire Strickland

HASTINGS '91
SAT 30 AT THE TOP DECK BALLROOM £4
MOD/SMART SIXTIES DRESS   7-1:30am

My first rally

So we went to Hastings; two scooters, four fellas. **Phil Lesaffre** behind me, and our 'guide' **Marc Budoc** (accompanied by his passenger whose name I don't remember) who'd been there the year before. *Marc*, a guy from the *West Indies*, was older than us, coming from the early '80s mod scene; he'd witnessed the evolution of Mod in Paris. But he'd never grown up from then on really, since the age of fifteen, seventeen... a funny character anyway, hanging around on a *PX* with chrome panels covered with dodgy stickers, usually two hours late at any appointment. A mod *face* from Paris called *Doctor* told me that the year before *Marc* had come to Hastings on his own, to attend one of the first *Untouchables* rallies and had crashed after the do as he tried to impress everybody by doing wheelies on his scooter in front of the venue. He couldn't help it, he had to do it all the time, it was the big thing in France; to impress your mates, you'd do a wheelie at each crosslight. It would eventually ruin your clutch.

By 1992, I was a poor homeless wandering Mod in a less-stylish-than-ever ghost town that was Paris, but always very proud to hang out dressed in a three or four-button suit, always riding around on a *Vespa GTR* or *PX* with white stripes on the right hand side, still looking smart (or trying to) even without a penny in the world.

We decided to go to that rally in Hastings. We had no specific idea of what was going on over there in England, apart from the fact that it was England, so the mod scene should be alive somewhere, 'real' Mods should be there, somewhere...

The mod scene in Paris was by then at its lowest, agonising for the past four years at least. There were *faces*, getting older every year, like we all do anyway... who used to go to *Rob* & *Mace's RSS* runs, or *CCI* rallies, but for me it was a new thing; going abroad, on a scooter! which was quite a challenge; there was no shuttle yet, at the time. The ferry; a good hour at least, from port to port.

> The big fashion about tyres at the time, was that we would put 'Cosa' tyres on our *PX* model because they were bigger, providing a better grip on the asphalt, but you would need to add a couple of washers before each bolt, otherwise it would touch the exhaust.
>
> The other thing was: back in 1991/92, the English people had never seen a scooter with an electrical starter, which we had on each recent model of *Vespa* in France. So our big game was to start the scooter without kicking, in front of the club, and watch the disbelief on their faces.

in the U-K *by Enamel Verguren*

The other problem was: he was driving at 25 miles per hour - literally - so *Phil* & me managed to arrive at the ferry a good hour before him. Couldn't help it; we had to jump on the first one. For that, he never forgave me.

It was past midnight when we reached Hastings. Still I wouldn't have believed you could take curves at such a speed with a passenger on a 'P' range *Vespa*. Of course, when we eventually reached the town, the Do wasn't on the seafront like it was the previous year! How typical of *Marc* not to enquire beforehand where the venue was that year. So we found ourselves wandering on the freezing seafront - Easter Bank Holiday, what do you expect - until one o'clock in the morning, when I spotted a Mod leaving a club,

completely drunk, but still able to spot us at the same time.

It was at the **Crypt**, a little club not far from the seafront. The party was blinding, for us coming from 'no-Mod land'. I had to laugh looking at my mates getting changed in the cloakroom, when I just had to take my greens off and put a jacket on, to be ready to dance; personally it was more important, in order to keep any credibility, not to show myself half naked in the middle of a party... but well, I'm not here to judge. We had missed *The Clique*'s gig by one hour - that's when *Gilles Baillarguet* was their drummer - but we were there! The French connection, freshly arrived... we were in heaven, in the middle of the real *Faces*. They had a completely different way of dancing, even the

music was different from what we played in our clubs. But so good.

Eventually, at four o'clock, when the party had finished, we had to find somewhere to sleep. And O my brothers, I didn't have the connections I have now; when I go to any rally nowadays, I usually know at least one person in town who I can stay with... I developed over the 1990s a reputation for always having somewhere to stay during a rally, either some friend's family or a room to squat in. But then... it was absolutely out of question to waste our money on a hotel fee, we only had just enough for the petrol and a few beers, so three of us voted for that gap under the pier, while *Budoc* went for squatting some B'n'B... good luck to him. All I remember in the morning is the shivering waking me up; I hadn't even bothered taking a sleeping bag with me.

Breakfast on the pier; and what a sensation! In your suit, completely rough but living a real movie! A real mod life! For us being French, by completing this trip and being there, we had achieved what we had waited for all year, if not all our lives.

Something you don't forget. Ever!

I remember that the scooter competition didn't gather more than maybe ten scooters - including ours, though we didn't take part in it; were we too rough? I got quite shocked I must say, to see in the middle of them a *Lambretta* completely painted in the American flag! I couldn't believe it; this was England?... his owner left the competition quite pissed off anyway, 'cause he didn't win it.

After spending the afternoon with *Gilles* the drummer of *The Clique*, we couldn't wait to see the second night. We hadn't paid the entrance at the previous one, because we had arrived quite late... but this time *Maz* at the door would show no mercy. I don't know if *Budoc* had taken some *Speed* without telling us that night, but I would say that if he had, it certainly was not a drug for him to approach. He started dancing as soon as we entered the club, when nobody was yet on the dancefloor, and he couldn't stop, track after track. To a point that became almost ridiculous, quite embarrassing for us his 'comrades'.

That's where I heard "Psychedelic Sally" by *Eddie Jefferson* for the first time. We were aware that there was an *Acid Jazz* scene growing up, we could see flyers of the *Brighton Jazz Bop* mixed with the *Untouchables* flyers. We were curious about it, for the *Jazz* sounds that it was propagating... but some of the *Hip-Hop* vibes that it sometimes was mixed with couldn't be associated with the kind of pure mod music we were into at the time.

Obviously once again we hadn't planned our night ahead, but we ended up later on on the stairs in the corridor of a B'n'B. I know that *Budoc* tried to squat a room occupied by a guy we had met at the party, but it didn't really work by the sound of it, when we heard the guy actually screaming at him. We eventually got pulled out of our dreams when the landlady came to open the hotel, at 6.00am (two hours after we'd found sleep). *Lesaffre* & me jumped on my scooter and legged it; we knew that *Budoc* would spend about four hours getting ready in the bathroom, it wasn't worth wasting our time...

We were back in Paris by 7.00pm that day, when we received a call from *Budoc's* passenger telling us that they'd just arrived in Dover, waiting for the next ferry!

Sun 19th APRIL

12-3pm at The Crypt
scooter competitions & cruise

Sunday evening at

THE CRYPT

8-2am   £4.00

Scooters at the beginning of the 1990s were much less embellished with chrome and mirrors than they became later on in the decade.

Top & bottom:
*'Check It Out' John's scooter **(I.O.W -1988)**
*Guy Joseph's scooter **(I.O.W -1988)**
Photos: SMILER

Left:

Hastings - 1992 -
Photo by the author

By the end of the 1980s, the machines that the *Scooterboys* were riding were miles away from their original structure.

It had become more of a custom business than a mod-related hobby.

Saintes (France) *NSRA* Rally -1990 - Photos by the author

When we went to Hastings - Easter 92 - there was another rally at the same time, a *National* one, in Margate. We were curious, we had to see it. On the map in the ferry, the distance from Margate to Hastings seemed quite reasonable... lucky that we had good engines and good tyres at the time.

SCOOTERBOYS

After we'd arrived in Margate, by 5pm, we waited for an hour on the seafront, for *Marc* and his acolyte to turn up (if they'd caught the next ferry, hopefully...). I'd never seen so many *Skinheads* in my life! The seafront was covered; police vans cruising and stopping every ten yards to arrest pissheads doing wheelies on their over-tuned *Lambrettas*... I was wearing army greens on top of my suit, to keep myself warm 'cause I was driving, and a light beige scooter jacket, so I was still looking the business in the middle of that crowd, and my scooter didn't have extra mirrors or lights... but my passenger *Phil Lesaffre* was wearing a neat suit under a parka! One guy stopped to talk to us, and the little that we could understand was that if we had turned up at this rally a couple of years before, we probably would have been killed. The atmosphere was chilled out though. You could spot SHARP (Skinheads Against Racial Prejudice) and fascist *Skinheads* seating on the bench, next to each other and celebrating...

We were about to leave when *Budoc* and his mate arrived; they were really pissed off that we didn't wait for them - and I think to this day *Marc* has never really forgiven me. We eventually found the campsite, where a few of our compatriots had put up their tents. I saw at least 7,000 scooters piled up like in a scrapyard. All sorts, from 'naked' *T5s* to unbelievable choppers. By sunset, we headed for *Hastings*.

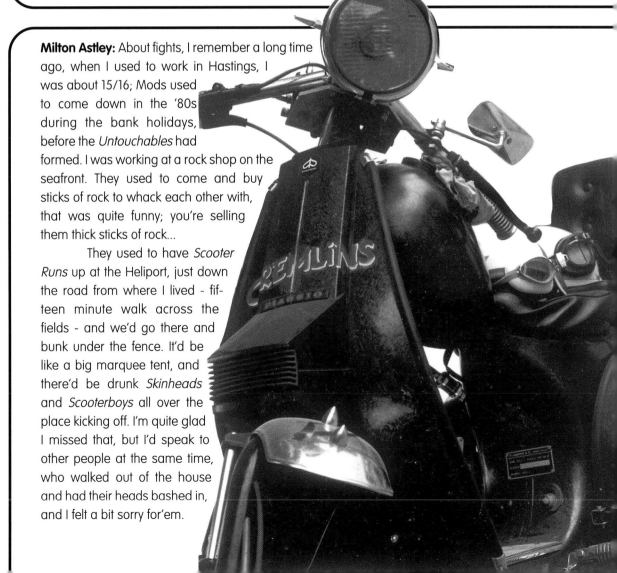

Milton Astley: About fights, I remember a long time ago, when I used to work in Hastings, I was about 15/16; Mods used to come down in the '80s during the bank holidays, before the *Untouchables* had formed. I was working at a rock shop on the seafront. They used to come and buy sticks of rock to whack each other with, that was quite funny; you're selling them thick sticks of rock...

They used to have *Scooter Runs* up at the Heliport, just down the road from where I lived - fifteen minute walk across the fields - and we'd go there and bunk under the fence. It'd be like a big marquee tent, and there'd be drunk *Skinheads* and *Scooterboys* all over the place kicking off. I'm quite glad I missed that, but I'd speak to other people at the same time, who walked out of the house and had their heads bashed in, and I felt a bit sorry for'em.

I've never had problems with the *Scooterboys*; if they're decent, they're the right bunch of people. Only a few elements, like anywhere else, can be trouble and it's mainly their attitude that is at the base of the argument; I noticed over the years that some of them would always try to make money by selling crap and worn-out stuff... when we - Mods - were much more inclined to give our spares away to other Mods. Most of the *Scooterboys* in this country have been Mods in the first place, and didn't like the scene, so they created their own laid-back environment, which I think is quite cool.

It is true that from their point of view, the Mods are too strict in their look and attitude, and they don't have anything new to offer; their fashion stays in the 1960s, and whatever is derived from it has the print of it, the 'Mod' stamp on it. Only the *Scooterboys* came with the idea of 'mutating' their machines, which created, at the same time, horror and laughter from a strictly mod point of view. But after all, who cares if they spend fortunes on chiselling every piece of chrome covering the engine of their scooters? At least we can acknowledge the fact that the job's well done.

Rob Messer: Maybe the *Untouchables* felt that we were playing too much *Northern Soul*, maybe they wanted a piece of the cake, I don't really know. I wouldn't say that they were jealous, but maybe there was a bit of that in there. *Rob Bailey* used to come to our do's, and literally beg us to DJ, so we used to give him a spot occasionally. It seemed to us that they were trying to steal our thunder a bit.

   When we cut ties with the *CCI*, we stopped going to their events, because we were running our own; if the *CCI* was doing a club in the North, we'd be doing one in the South, and vice versa. We weren't competing in the next town, trying to steal all his people. But when the *Untouchables* started up, they were directly competing against us, and we both suffered from it. I know that *Smiler* and *Rob* were still DJing for *Tony Class* at the time, so they were taking some of the *CCI* people, and some of our people. Unfortunately there were not enough people in the scene to split it three ways. Initially we did try to compromise with them, going as a partnership, and the first one we did (in Hastings) was half them/half us; but it didn't really work.

   We carried on with Clacton, twice a year, off-season, because we had the hotel venue and there was nothing on around February; so everyone was drinking and partying from Friday 'til Sunday, whatever the weather was.

Rob Messer and **Mace** carried on organising rallies in Clacton-on-Sea throughout the '90s, with, unfortunately, a poorer and poorer attendance.

WE'RE BACK!

The Rhythm & Soul Set proudly present a weekend of Modernist mayhem.

Friday 24th February (9-2) £2.00 &
Saturday 25th February (Allnighter) £5.00

MORE MOD MUSIC...

△Scooter-riding Mods arrive at Clacton in 1964.

High times at the Waverly Hall Hotel, Clacton-on-Sea, Essex.
Music from four decades of Mod, with D.J.'s including
Rob Messer, Mace, Dave Ingle,
Martin, Pid, Lee, Speed ... ickey
All the Hotel rooms ... 422716

FREEDOM *is the new sound*

Rob Messer: We were all getting older. Either some got married, some started to have kids... all in all, it affected their night life, and the scene of that generation slowly died out...

THE RHYTHM AND SOUL SET.
MEMBERSHIP CARD

rhythm, soul, jazz, beat, ska & fun!

NAME. *Paul Anderson*

SMART MOD DRESS ONLY!

THE MODEST MODS
WEAR THE GEAREST GEAR
& LISTEN TO THE
SOUNDEST SOUNDS
AT
Rhythm & Soul Set
DO'S
So for the best in
SOUL / Rn'B / JAZZ / BEAT
and Easter eggs
be at

THE
Erlsmere
HOTEL

24/32 Pembury Road,
Westcliff-on-Sea, Essex SS0 5DS

SOUTHEND

FRI / SAT / SUN
13/14/15 APRIL
8-100 am
with FREE lunchtimes
Weekend ticket £9

DJ'S · ROB · MACE
DOM · SPEED · TOBYS

plus live Rn'B from

The
IMMEDIATES
SUNDAY.

Rob Messer: The Porthcawl Runs, in the late 1980s, were the greatest week-enders. *Paul Hallam* used to DJ, the Birmingham lot, the Bristol lot used to be there... I tried to follow the buggies on the beach with my *Lada*.

SMILER: After *Sneakers* had closed down, a lot of us went to the Clarendon, but it was never the same. Then in June 1986, the film "Absolute Beginners" was released, and because we thought we had to try to learn a lot about *Jazz*, a lot of us started to listen to **Gilles Peterson** on **Radio London**; he had the 'Mad on *Jazz*' radio show, once a week. Obviously the following year, 1987, we were more sussed about *Jazz*, and *Latin* took over as well that year. **Tony Reynolds** - as a DJ - basically saturated the scene with it.

We started going to the **Electric Ballroom** - *Gilles Peterson's* night. **Dave Hucker** had a night at *Ronnie Scott* - upstairs - which was *Afro-Latin* stuff. There were Friday nights at the **Sol y Sombre**, *Latin & Brazilian*, and the **Purple Pit** - that's where we really discovered **Paul Murphy**. We started going to another of his clubs which was on a Saturday night - the **Purple PussyCat** - in Finchley Road; you'd see *Paul Hallam* down there, *Mick Ferrante*, you'd see **Jerry Dammers**...

Just a few of us being Mods; the rest of them were '50s *Jivers*, period suits, *Cadillacs* outside... but it just felt like an elite group, away from the mod scene.

> # I HAD LOST INTEREST; AND I FELT LIKE A FRAUD FOR STARTING THE UNTOUCHABLES.
> **SMILER**

Even though we still used to go to mod rallies, we didn't attend the mod clubs anymore. The *Jazz* thing took over; we'd go and see **The Tommy Chase Quartet** – THE *jazz* band at the time - at the **Café Loire**, where a guy called **Baz Fe Jazz** used to DJ. Compilations called "Jazz Dance" and "Jazz Juice" were released, which were brilliant. This is 1986/87, and that's how we learned about *Jazz*, by listening to **Gilles Peterson** "Mad On *Jazz*" on the radio, and there were **Paul Murphy, Dave Hucker, Russ Dewbury** – who ended up doing the **Brighton Jazz Bop**… a good variety of DJs who were making us discover new *jazz* tunes; I remember during the whole year of 1987, completely avoiding going to mod clubs.

Only once, on New Year's Eve '87, I was queuing up at *Gaz's Rockin' Blues*, and we couldn't get in, so I ended up down the *Bizz* club – mod nite. I really enjoyed myself there, I was going back to the mod scene, just for a night, but became a regular at mod clubs again. A lot of my friends didn't; there were ten times more clubs to go to in the *jazz* scene.

"Absolute Beginners" was in a way the reason for us to go back to our roots; when it got released on screen, it kind of put us under the spotlight and we felt that it was time for us to go onto the *jazz* scene. We all found – as Mods - that the movie was absolutely awful, but the book is fantastic; read the book, rather than watch the film.

RE-ELECT THE PRESIDEN

With **RE-ELECT The President**, there was a different label on each record, with a different president each time (*JFK*, *Carter*...).

Eddie Piller: I first met **Terry Rawlings** through **Tony Perfect** of *Long Tall Shorty* when I was looking for someone to design the **Well Suspect** compilation album cover. I had seen him around in the early days, places like *The Wellington* in Waterloo, but he'd dropped out of sight for a while... we met at a pub round the back of Carnaby Street and clicked. We shared a lot of friends, people like **Gary Crowley**, **Vaughan Toulouse** and **Tony Lordan**... *Terry* designed a great sleeve for the **Beat Generation and The Angry Young Men**. We got on so well, I eventually asked him to join me at **Extraordinary Sensations** (which had a small office in Dagenham at the time) and we just drifted into running **Countdown Records** together...

Countdown was a great laugh and we saw ourselves as making the Mods' last stand. The media had been so down on the mod scene since about 1980, that we saw the label as a two fingered challenge. The three of us (including **Maxine Conroy**) were given a budget to go and find stuff we liked. That was probably the only time that someone said to me: 'You've got good taste, go and find some bands.'

After a year under the wing of **Stiff**, we could see the writing on the wall: things were going downhill for them, and fast. An argument with **Island** (*Stiff's* main partners) saw *Stiff* kicked out of our shared office. *Countdown* went with them. It was good working out of the famous St Peter's Square offices. *Island* was always an institution to me and many other Mods because of the early *Reggae*, *Guy Stevens* and **Sue**... We relocated to Hoxton in the East-End of London. *Stiff* moved into an old fashioned warehouse off Hoxton Square but it was too small for us, so *Countdown* set up its own office in Provost Street, and my long association with Hoxton began.

Voice Your Choice was a club held by *Eddie Piller & Paul Hallam*.

After the unfortunate failure of **Countdown**, *Eddie Piller* started **Re-elect The President**, which became **Acid Jazz**.

Rob Messer: We didn't wanna go only to clubs that we were running, we wanted to discover other tunes, that's why we used to go to the **Purple Pussycat** (*Paul Murphy*) which was not a mod club. Twenty of us, in full mod gear, in the middle of one hundred people who would stare at us because we looked so cool. Sometimes he played some stuff that definitely was not in our bag, but if there was a decent tune, we'd be on the dancefloor showing to this crowd how to dance. We used to go to another *jazz* club opposite the *Astoria* on Charing Cross Road. The thing with *Jazz* is: the mod scene is not into all aspects of *Jazz*, it's got to be the right kind of feel. Some of it is too cheesy or too laid-back... it's got to be the right *Jazz* that hits the spot. That was the thing with *jazz* clubs; it could be boring the pants off you, and then suddenly you would have a series of ten records in a row that would be really cool and have the right vibes to them, and you'd go for it, after what you'd get back to your chair because the DJ would play some cheesy *Jazz* again. But going to these clubs dressed up as a Mod, you'd really look different, whereas going to a mod club you'd be pretty much dressed the same, a little smarter or not. Going to a non-mod club, you'd really stand out, but it's got to be the music you like.

Eddie Piller: As *Countdown* faltered I decided to set up a label on my own. I called it **Re-Elect The President** after an old *Vote Nixon* badge I had picked up in a junk shop. The name had a kind of ironic ring to it. I started with compilations; I continued the *Countdown* series for a couple of volumes and then released the debut from the Swedish *Mod/Psyche* band **The Creeps** and a re-released edition of *The Beat Generation*... They all sold well but I wasn't really happy. Mod, and more importantly my own perceptions on life, were changing. I was far more interested in the growing *jazz* scene of **Paul Murphy** and **Gilles Peterson** whose fresh outlook reminded me of what I was doing. *Jazz*, while still Mod, was so much cooler than what was going on in the mod scene. *Re-Elect The President* changed tack in mid-stream. I signed both **The James Taylor Quartet** and **The Jazz Renegades** to the label and suddenly I was moving away from *Garage Rock* and Mod into wholly different circles.

It started with *Gary Crowley*. As an old mate who had his own big-time radio show, I sent him a copy of the first *JTQ* single, "Blow Up". He played it for a few weeks until **John Peel** picked up on it. Radio was so different in those days. I was sitting in the bath at home when the phone rang. Cursing and without a towel I struggled to pick it up... "Hello, is that Eddie?... This is *John Peel*"... Blimey! *Peel* loved the record and wanted the band for a *Radio One* session. Although it was impossible – *Taylor* had emigrated to Sweden some months previously and had taken up classical piano. He'd firmly turned his back on the industry following the painful collapse of **The Prisoners**. *The James Taylor Quartet* had just been a one off covers session to record the "Blow Up" theme tune as a little single. He had told me that he wasn't coming back.

It took weeks of persuasion to even get *James Taylor* to think about returning to England. I had put off *John Peel* as much as I could and sensed that he was losing patience. These *Radio One* sessions were very hard to come by and it was only down to *John Peel's* persistence that *Taylor* eventually returned. By that time the single had already been in the top 20 of the *indie* charts for six weeks (and remained in *Peel's* tastemaker Festive Fifty for five years alongside some of the biggest records of all time). *Taylor* returned to London the conquering hero. Alongside the session with *Peel* I had managed to arrange a show at a gig at the top Soho nightclub **The Limelight**.

The event was a roadblock. Even *Patsy Kensit* turned up! *The James Taylor Quartet* were the biggest thing on the London underground scene in 1987 and so *Re-Elect* rushed out the "Mission Impossible" album to cash in on his success. The album eventually went silver and established the *JTQ* as the biggest draw on the new *jazz* scene.

Not far behind were *Re Elect's* other band *The Jazz Renegades*. A loose collaboration fronted by sax' genius **Alan Barnes** and *Style Councillor* **Steve White**. I knew *Steve White* through **Paul Weller** and **Mick Talbot** (the former *Merton Parka* and *Chords* session man) and having him on board gave *REP* some credibility with both journalists and the *jazz* scene. Although young, *White* was known as one of the best *jazz* drummers in the country, especially for technique.

With those two bands at the forefront of my promotional activities, it was not long before I hooked up with *Gilles Peterson*. He was the same age as me, a charismatic radio presenter at *Radio London* and an out and out *Soul Boy*. He had taken over from the legendary *Paul Murphy* when *Murph'* walked away from music and *Gilles'* weekly 'Mad On *Jazz*' show had become the lynchpin of the London *jazz* scene. *Gilles* sat on top of an expanded web, like a spider with his fingers in ever-so-many pies. He was part of the *Rare Groove* scene, he had a track record in pirate radio as a Jazz Funk DJ, he played at *Nicky Holloway's* 'Do At The Zoo' events. In short he was everywhere.

Mods were accepted in *Peterson's* world, along with refugees from the *Rockabilly* and *Swing* scenes, *B-boys* and *Rare Groovers*. Together they made a fascinating melting pot that mixed *Black* and *White*, contemporary and retro, and came out at the other end with something called **Acid Jazz**.

I was soon DJing the opening for *Gilles* at **The Wag** club on *'Jazz Monday'*. It gave me the opportunity to play my organ sounds and although *Bossa* and *Blakey* were the main sounds in London at the time, it wasn't long before the Hammond took its rightful place.

Peterson had a group of mates that used to hang out at his radio show. I was one of them and it was an exciting time. The people involved in the early London *jazz* scene realised that they were sitting on the cusp of something very exciting. There really was an atmosphere.

Gilles was looking for a new pad, so I introduced him to *Terry Rawlings*, from whom he rented his Thameside apartment.

Before long we decided to set up a record label together. He had the clout, and I had the experience and know how. Although I was still only 22, I had been running labels and dealing with distributors and exporters for six years. After much debate we christened the label *Acid Jazz*.

DJing in 1989

Courtesy of **Eddie Piller**

Nineties modernists photographed by Nina Schultz

Mark Lusty, Nick Aghadiuno and Guy Joseph (mentioned in the previous book) as well as John Cook, Kieran, James Taylor... feature on these photos.

I
f you thought mods ceased to exist in the Sixties, you're probably right. But a funny thing happened on the way to the Nineties – mod style emerged on the back of a number three crop and Duffers top, as last year's ravers turned into this year's modernists (p54). For all the old school mods who have issued death threats to new school modernists – this is not a mod revival. All it is is people dressing smart and listening to the best dance music of the moment. Which includes Deee-Lite (p46), winners of the best single and album of the year according to our contributors (p18), and currently wooing Europe after having hits in the UK and US (in that order). Note: just because Deee-Lite had their picture taken on a scooter, that does not make them mods. Meanwhile, Derek Jarman is in extraordinarily good spirits. On p60 he talks about the time a magazine printed his premature obituary, and about dancing in the street. Does this make him a mod? Probably more so than Massive Attack (p78), who John McCready argues are "Pink Floyd with bigger sounds and better drum patterns". As for the 16-page Review Of The Year (p10), it is obvious that 1990 was a year of reckoning for many: Mrs Thatcher, Vivienne Westwood, the poll tax, and youth cults with Gucci loafers, Adidas shell-toes, skinny jeans and sharp suits. As for 1991, just don't mention mods, OK?

Milton Astley: I used to be in the *jazz* scene at the time *Absolute Beginners* came out. There was *Modern Jazz* played in clubs like the **Wag**. *Gilles Peterson* used to do the **Soul Weekenders** in Barry Island. That must have been in '85, '86, when I was living in Hastings; we used to go to the **Jazz Rooms,** where you'd get *Jazz & Funk* beats. They used to play *Blue Note, Lee Morgan, Art Blakey, Horace Silver...* I got into that, and was collecting all the records, all these sleeves with these guys in their smart button-down shirts and tight collars, sharp suits

POST-MODERNISM

At the end of 1990, clubbers started to crop their hair and dress like mods. What do they think they're doing? And why? WARNING: THIS IS NOT A MOD REVIVAL...

This page: Kieron Hurley (front) of Acid Jazz records, student Bevan, 22 (right) and designer Mark Lusty, 24: "You must always be smart." Kieran wears Levi's Big E cords, Gucci loafers from Gucci, 27 Old Bond St, London W1, Wrangler Range coat; and Levi's cord jacket. Bevan wears Levi's Big E slim fit cords; top from a charity shop. Mark's trousers tailored from Eddie's of Wardour St, London W1; red top by Fenwicks of Bond St; jacket from American Classics, King's Rd, SW10; beads from Oxfam

Opposite: Photography student Amber, 18, with graphic designer Jon Cooke, 25: "The people in the clubs wearing mod fashions aren't dinosaurs living in 1965. Their perspective is modern, and they listen to Big Daddy Kane as much as Brian Auger." Amber's boots from Midas, Sloane Sq, London SW3; jacket from charity shop

SMILER: As 1991 progressed, I spent more time hanging around various *Acid Jazz* nights like the one at **Dingwalls**, and lost interest in the mod scene. There was too much bitching going on. Besides, you'd go to the *Mildmay Tavern* and there would be about eighteen people over there, on a Saturday night. I remember turning to *Dave Edwards*, and saying: "Now it just feels like the mod scene is like an orange I have squeezed all the juice out of." I got everything out of it, all I could have done, and that was it.

Main pic: Pete wears Levi's jacket from Chalk Farm market, London NW1; striped jacket by One-Legged Jockey; trousers by Voss; shoes by Johnny Moke, King's Rd, London SW10: "I don't really want to be associated with people who just seem to be living in the past. To me, mod is a set of values you adapt to modern life, not going round shouting, 'I'm a mod!'"

Top: Rachel Bayne, 22. Sixties roll-neck from charity shop

Below: Insurance salesman Nick Agadhuino, 24 (back): "It's all about having fun." Guy Joseph, 24, restores scooters: "Some of us aren't just bandwagon jumpers, we're sincere – we won't be with another fashion next year." Nick's suit by Eddie's of Wardour St, London W1; boots by Derber; Smedley polo-neck. Guy's suit tailored on Savile Row, London W1; Dexters American loafers from J. Simons, Russell St, London WC2; original Fred Perry from charity shop

SMILER: Around the same period, 1990/91, there had been talk of the *Acid Jazz* thing and the Neo-Mod movement, which, even though I tried to deny at the time, was still interesting for me. It felt really hard, because I still had this pure 1960s mod image, and yet at the same time I was fascinated with what was going on. A lot of my friends, who I had met through the early days, had moved onto that new scene but were pretty much looking like Mods.

Mention the word mods and Roger Daltrey kisses his American Express card, Paul Weller pretends he doesn't hear you, magazines think parkas and everybody else laughs. Probably youth culture's longest running joke, mods have had an image problem. What hasn't helped is that, strictly speaking, mods, as in modernists, only ever existed once. Every other mod revival since has been just that – a homage to the past rather than the present, populated by 16-year-olds with 20-year-old records and secondhand ideas. If mod is about modern style and soul, the only true mods of the Eighties were the casuals, in their Lois jeans and Gabicci tops, and with money in their pockets to spend dancing to Brass Construction at the weekend.

Over the past couple of years though, mutterings about mods have been heard in dark corners in clubs. Popular wisdom asserted that ravers were really mods in hippy clothes anyway, and it was simply a matter of time before they got their hair cut. Everybody thought it was a joke, started listening to the Manchester bands instead of acid house, and then people started getting their hair cropped and swapping their long-sleeved T-shirts for Duffer of St George tops.

"Ravers as mods? Without a doubt. Both are about living for the weekend, getting out of it and dancing. The word goes back to mods anyway." Eddie Pillar, owner of Acid Jazz records, is sporting a nifty goatee beard, Schott puffa jacket, striped Duffer top, straight-legged casual jeans and Adidas trainers. He's not a mod, although he used to be, and he will and does spend hours telling you why mod is dead but modernism isn't. For Eddie and many others, "mods were too insular and narrow-minded – they didn't like any music that wasn't Sixties soul, R&B and jazz, and never ventured out of their own little world". It took rare groove and acid jazz from the likes of Diana Brown & The Brothers and The James Taylor Quartet to convince him and other disillusioned mods that there was life after The Small Faces, and the fact that Barrie Sharpe (The Brothers) was part of the Duffers crew and James Taylor used to be in psychedelic/R&B band The Prisoners was more than sheer coincidence. The death threats from old school mods when Eddie stated his preferences in print simply affirmed his convictions.

Until this year, Eddie and his mates were an anomaly, neither mods nor modernists, following the redefinition and resurgence of the 'jazz' scene and ending up at Gilles Peterson's Talking Loud club every Sunday. And then they noticed that they were not alone. Yesterday's ravers were turning into today's modernists.

"At the time it happened, clubland was split between Charlie-sniffing casuals and people getting away from long hair. People started smartening up and latched on to the look that the Duffers had been selling. A lot of them don't understand what modernism is all about, though." Matteo should know. A teenage mod follower of The Jam, it took the club scene of the past two years to galvanise his enthusiasm once more, resulting in his club fanzine *Positive Energy Of Madness*. The new issue includes an interview with Paul Weller and The Beloved's Jon Marsh, a timely if unintentional inauguration of the new alliance. But as far as Eddie is concerned, you can blame Adidas shell-toes.

"The missing links as far as the fashion is concerned are the Duffers and Adidas. I got back into mod-style clothes through seeing a pair of shell-toes, and the stripy Adidas T-shirts are really Sixties anyway. What shell-toes did was show you that sportswear could look smart." The Duffers and, to a lesser extent, Michiko Koshino, provided a fashion impetus that crossed sportswear with Italian style and acid teds with mods. As far as the Duffers are concerned though, they've never done anything else. "We're doing the same thing we've always done," says Barrie Sharpe, "providing clothes for what we call a suavehead. All the original Sixties stuff didn't fit properly and it was made from materials like acrylic and acetate. We don't use crap materials. And as far as the designs are concerned – we're modernising them, that's what we're trying to do. People have got to realise that we're not living in the Sixties, we're living in the Nineties."

Someone who realised the dichotomy of listening to Sixties music in the Nineties long before the current vogue for modernist style is James Taylor, the Hammond organ player who inspired the Inspiral Carpets and The Charlatans as a member of The Prisoners, and has been trying to live down his mod past ever since. "Something has happened in the music scene over the last couple of years – drum machines and technology have taken a more important role. The geezer in the parka listening to The Small Faces is getting left further and further behind." Now into his fourth version of The James Taylor Quartet, the band have progressed from their Sixties R&B roots through acid jazz and into rap and house. "Our last UK tour in November really took us by surprise. I didn't realise we had such a strong following or that kind of following. We sold out every venue, and in London, Sheffield and Aberdeen I noticed all these people dressed really smart, but in places like Manchester, it was full of Charlatans and Inspiral Carpet fans – teds going nutty to modern R&B music."

The fact that Martin Blunt from The Charlatans used to be in the mod band Makin' Time and that Clint from Inspiral Carpets has rarely missed a James Taylor gig, is more than just coincidental. "The Prisoners were the first of The Charlatans/Inspiral-type bands, and they've been one of the most important influences on me," enthuses Clint. "But The James Taylor Quartet are delving into the future a bit now – what he's doing is the next stage, playing house music live. When I saw him in Manchester I was bowled over."

That James Taylor is finally starting to reap the benefits of his past is nothing less than he deserves. But he, like Weller before him, is at pains to distance himself from one thing. "Calling it a mod revival is a serious danger. You need a better word than that – 'cos it's to do with looking good and listening to the best fucking dance music around." Although, take note – at the recent Paul Weller Movement gigs, the official merchandise consisted of target T-shirts. There is definitely something in the air . . . ●

TEN ESSENTIALS FOR THE OLD SCHOOL MOD
Italian-cut mohair suit
Chelsea boots
Lambretta Li150
Fifties US fishtail parka (no badges)
Suedehead by Richard Allen
"All Mod Cons" by The Jam
"Sh'mon" by Mr Dynamite (on original UK Sue)
A copy of *Extraordinary Sensations* fanzine
A taste for cappuccino
Half a dozen blues or a gramme of sulphate

TEN ESSENTIALS FOR THE NINETIES MODERNIST
Duffer of St George winter collection
Gucci loafers
Late-night bus pass
¾ length double breasted leather mac
The Good The Bad & The Bubbly by George Best
"My Afro's On Fire" by The Outlaw Posse
"Killing Time" by The James Taylor Quartet
Arena
Guarana
½ an ounce of skunk
Straight No Chaser

Is this the last time we'll ever have to mention adidas shell-toes?

A POST-MODERNIST FAMILY TREE

The Jam
Paul Weller

The Merton Parkas
Mick Talbot

The Style Council (1)
Paul Weller
Mick Talbot
Steve White
DC Lee

Makin' Time
Fay Hallam
Martin Blunt

The Prisoners
Graham Day
Alan Crockford
James Taylor

The Daggermen
David Taylor

James Taylor Quartet (1)
James Taylor
David Taylor
Simon Howard
Alan Crockford

The Charlatans *
Martin Blunt
Tim Burgess
Jon Brookes
Jon Baker
Rob Collins

The Jazz Renegades
Steve White

Diana Brown & The Brothers
Finesse Dance Troupe
  (now The Pasadenas)
Jan Kincaid
Lascelles Gordon
Andrew Levy
Simon Bartholomew
Barrie K Sharpe
Diana Brown

The Prime Movers *
Fay Hallam
Graham Day
Simon Howard
Allan Crockford

The James Taylor Quartet (2)
Steve White
James Taylor
John Wilmott

The Brothers International
Jerry Dammers (simultaneous
  with Special AKA)
Diana Brown
Marco Nelson
Barrie K Sharpe

The Brand New Heavies (1)
Andrew Levy
Jan Kincaid
Jim Wellman
Lascelles Gordon
Simon Bartholomew
Linda Muriel

The Style Council (2)
Paul Weller
DC Lee (now in Slam Slam)
Marco Nelson
Omar (now solo)
Dr Robert (simultaneous
  with The Blow Monkeys)
Mick Talbot

The James Taylor Quartet (3)
James Taylor
Paul Francis
David Taylor
John Wilmott

The Young Disciples *
Marco Nelson
Femi Williams
Carlene Anderson

Diana Brown & Barrie K Sharpe *
Barrie K Sharpe
Diana Brown

The Brand New Heavies (2) *
Andrew Levy
Jan Kincaid
Jim Wellman
Ceri Evans
Simon Bartholomew
Lascelles Gordon

Galliano *
Robert Galliano
Constantine
Mick Talbot
Steve White
Linda Muriel

The Paul Weller Movement *
Paul Weller
Steve White
Paul Francis
Jacko Peake
Damon Brown
Will

James Taylor Quartet (4) *
James Taylor
John Willmott
David Taylor
Gary Crocket
Gary Haines
Paul Daley
Snowboy
Noel and Cornell McKoy

The K Collective *
Andrew Levy
Jan Kincaid

Heliocentric World *
Lascelles Gordon
Simon Bartholomew
Vanessa Darby
Joy Gibbons

Push *
Jacko Peake
Damon Brown
Will
Nicky Compton
Crispin Taylor
Ernie McKone
Mark Vandergutch
Osin Little
Conor Smith
Debbie French
Eddie Saunders

A Man Called Adam *
Sally Rodgers
Paul Daley
Steve Jones

*denotes bands currently in existence
*anks to Eddie Pillar, Dean Rudland and The Watch-Men Agency

Above: James Taylor, musician. "The fashion and the music owe a lot to hip hop – that's why The Outlaw Posse will be supporting us on tour next year." James' Golfmaster top, white Levi's jeans and black Levi's jacket – all from The Garage, King's Rd, London SW10; Dexters loafers from The Natural Shoe Store, 21 Neal St, London WC2

Main pic: Shop assistant Hailey Field and illustrator Ben Horner, both 23. "Christ! Just don't call me a mod!" Hailey's Levi's bought in the USA; boots from Midas as before; jean jacket from Chalk Farm market as before; jumper from Jamie at The Dispensary, Marlborough St, London W1. Ben's shirt from US thrift shop; medallion by Hailey Field

SMILER: In 1991, **Paul Weller** appeared on the *Jonathan Ross* show, and came out with the quote: "I am a Mod, I'll always be a Mod, you can bury me a Mod." All of a sudden, it helped me a lot to know that a person that first got me into being a Mod, was now involved with the *Acid Jazz* scene. It made me feel like it had all gone full circle; I really got into *Paul Weller* because of this *Punk/Mod* guy that he was first, and then there he re-appeared, he had evolved with his new material, and he was looking fantastically Mod, more than he had been for a long time.

He brought out "Into Tomorrow", which to me, if there was any life-changing anthem, would be it. On the same 4-track EP you had "Here Is A New Thing", in which some of the lines, meant personally, for having been so heavily involved in the mod scene (with the *Untouchables*) exactly how I felt at the time: "Gotta let go of the past..." It all said it to me; that's the right thing to do, that's the way things were going.

SMILER: I was going to **Dingwalls** on the Sunday, to 'Talking Loud', and to the **Starlight club**, which had a Do called 'Fez' on the Friday night. I'd be leaving the *Mildmay Tavern* when I was still DJing down there, and go to a club called the **Prohibition**. Going along to that, there was 'Jazz With Attitude' on Sunday nights at the **Milk Bar**, so I didn't wanna do my club in Reading anymore. There was a lot going on; *Jazz FM* started with **Chris Phillips** and **Jezz Nelson** a radio show called 'Something Else', showcasing a lot of acts. There was *Paul Bradshaw's* **Straight No Chaser**, which was THE *jazz* magazine, telling you what was going on, when all the mod fanzines had eventually folded. During some of the first *Untouchables* rallies in '91, I was wearing beads, almost rebelling against the thing I was part of; I was still part of the *Untouchables* committee, but as a DJ I started playing *funky* stuff (considering I had been an *R'n'B* DJ) and *jazzy* stuff... I never got to play my *Ronnie Jordan* or *Young Disciples* LPs – that I wanted to play - but I was playing a lot of early '70s *funky Jazz*.

Eddie Piller: There are lots of stories about how the name came about and as far as I remember it – the DJ **Chris Bangs** had been arranging DJ nights with *Gilles* under the name of 'Cock Happy'. The *Acid House* scene had been absolutely massive in London and the watchword "acciii-iddd" was ever present at every gig or party you went to. Mainly in an ironic way. *Bangsy* cut up a flyer for 'Cock Happy' with the words **Wah-Wah Funk and Acid Jazz** – we chose the latter as the name for the label. The name was actually ironic; we hadn't intended to release more than a few singles and then both move on. Because of the instant success of the first **Galliano** single, we had to review the situation.

Musically it was a meeting between Mods and *Soul Boys*. Early releases included the bongo madness of **A Man Called Adam** (who later spawned **Leftfield**), the *Be-Bop* of **Ed Jones**, the *Jazz Rap* of both **The Last Poets** and *Galliano*, the twisted *Disco* of *Chris Bangs* (who recorded under several aliases – **Extasis**, **The Quiet Boys**, **Johnny Dayglo**) and the whole thing was thrown together with irreverent madness and a healthy slab of '60s *Jazz* and *Latin*.

The instant success of the label was mainly due to the fact that *Gilles* had built up a massive scene around himself and a couple of other DJs, as well as the fact that *The James Taylor Quartet* had already ploughed their own furrow a year earlier with the massive hit "Blow Up". *Galliano's* single was re-released on 12-inch and sold 10,000 copies in a matter of weeks, and the label was fast becoming the new centre of cool for the media.

After a successful 18 months which saw releases by **Snowboy** and *Paul Weller*, *Gilles* had a change of heart. He had seen that the label was becoming something of a ghetto for retro *Funk & Soul* and he wasn't happy with the direction. I think that the mod thing was starting to take over and he wanted to leave. We split the label in two. He got *Galliano* and **The Young Disciples** (who had just completed their first demos for the label) and I kept **The Brand New Heavies** and *A Man Called Adam*. *Gilles'* new label was called **Talkin' Loud** and while he found a home at the major of *Phonogram*, I had decided to keep *Acid Jazz* fiercely independent. More success followed with the signings of **Jamiroquai**, **Mother Earth**, **Corduroy**, **D Influence** and a whole host of other, mainly retro sounding *Funk & Soul* bands. I even re-signed *James Taylor*, who I had been managing while he was signed to *Polydor*.

Letters

modern fantasy

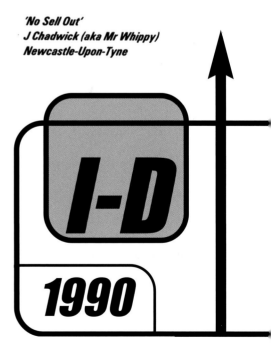

TO BE A MOD
OR NOT TO BE A MOD

THE UNTOUCHABLES

I THINK THEREFORE I AM
(GOING TO BRIGHTON).

All functions to be held at: Queen's Hotel Basement Club 1-5 Kings Road Brighton
Rooms are available at 15.00 per person per night.
Ring: 0273 21222

Milton Astley: Mod was for me a way to get a bit of an education. I've always been fascinated by the 1960s. All the stuff I learned from being a Mod, from the art of **Peter Blake** who introduced the target in his painting in 1961... to the cinema, the fashion, the music, the design.

Paul Lobb, Vanessa from Bournemouth, Trevor French and Matt Braim **- Hastings 1992 -**
Photo by the author

Rob Messer: Clubwise, I started 'Compared To What' with *Rochelle Piper* who was very much into *R'n'B*, back in 1994. At the time I was fed up with all those clubs playing *Psych'* sets; you wanna hear *Black music* at a mod club, and that's what we did: *Soul*, *R'n'B* & *Jazz*. Occasionally the odd white artist, like *The Artwoods* or *The Bo-Street Runners* who tried to be 'Black-sounding'; don't get me wrong, I love *The Small Faces*, but apart from the instrumen-tals ("Grow Your Own"...) they're a bit *Pop*. I like *The Beatles*, and *The Who*, but I don't wanna hear them in a mod club. I play that kind of stuff in my club 'Almost Grown' in Southend, but that's a different thing; it's not a mod club...

> ## Mod was for me a way to get a bit of an edu-cation.
> **Milton Astley**

SMILER: I carried on doing some *Acid Jazz* nights in Reading. My last ever appearance on the mod scene was with *The Clique*, DJing at one of their gigs in January '92, at the *Adelphi* in Hull, where I announced my retirement from the scene. A group of us went on holiday that same year – *Ady* from Bristol, *Matty* from Chippenham, and *Dave Brown*, we went to the Norfolk Broads - we'd all come from Mod and we all felt liberated, like we'd thrown off the shackles of the mod scene. All the music we were listening to were: **James Taylor Quartet, Galliano, The Paul Weller Movement, The Young Disciples**, '60s/'70s *Jazz & Brazilian*… and *Indie* bands like **5:30, The La's, The Revs**, early **Manic Street Preachers**… there were a lot of bands who had that kind of 1979 touch, and there were the 'Dance' bands like **Galliano, Sandals**… all the *Acid Jazz* stuff that was coming out was fantastic, mixed in with *Funk*. We were still Mods, but we were not restricted in what we were listening to.

I personally always thought that *Jazz*, from 1965 onwards, was the ultimate mod music, for its sophistication and its dancing abilities. Mainly if it's got keyboards in it; from **Booker T. & the MGs** (even if you can classify it as *R'n'B*), through *Ramsey Lewis, Jimmy Smith, Jack McDuff, Jimmy McGriff*… up to **Corduroy** in the 1990s, who were for me the epitome of *mod/jazz* music.

For a lot of Mods, it's not the case. *Northern Soul & R'n'B* are on top of the mod sounds. And for a very few others, it's actually *British Beat* and *Pop* that win the crown. It is quite amazing that one cult movement dispatches itself in such different tastes of clothes & music, but it has its charms as well; in a way its variety causes the scene to look more attractive.

Nevertheless, what characterises everybody in that scene is the expanding knowledge of each individual into quite an obscure part of 1960s music, up to these days sometimes. Whatever the specialisation is - from *R'n'B & Soul* to *Psychedelia*, travelling through *Jazz & Jamaican 'Roots' (Ska/Rock Steady/early Reggae)* Mods always know their best bit about a style in the panorama of 'cult & difficult to find' 1960s records.

It all changed a bit when the 'Acid Jazz' **wave appeared with** The James Taylor Quartet**'s early recordings, but still to this day, your music knowledge as a Mod is mainly covering the first or second half of the 1960s.**

> The mod scene itself had fragmented and become something I didn't want to be part of anymore; *Acid Jazz* came to comfort what we were into at the time.
>
> **Mark Lusty**

Reading Mods - Photo: SMILER

Mark Lusty: The **Solid Bond** parties were at the pinnacle of our mod career, if you like, during the *Acid Jazz* time; **Paul Weller** started to invite us to his parties, he must have done six of them, at the time when everybody was getting into the music business. And that was how you'd imagine the music business to be; everything was free, free bar... then he divorced *D.C. Lee*, and it stopped. They were fantastic parties; everybody who was somebody in the mod scene was there. *Weller* was re-launching stuff, in his **Paul Weller Movement**, and he invited me when I had been a *Jam* fan for all these years! He used to come to the office when I was working for *Acid Jazz*. He used to hang out with us for a smoke. We all had been Mods together, and we were working out a really good sound and really cool label; and *Weller* was involved in it.

Eddie Piller: In the 1980s, people like **Chris Bangs**, **Bob Masters**, **Bob Jones**, **Simon Dunmore**, **Jazzy B.**, **Norman Jay**, **Gilles Peterson**... wouldn't do regular clubs. In the mid-'80s, they would do warehouse parties, on-off parties; **Barry Sharpe** 'Family Funktion', **Femy Fem**, **Malcolm Nelson**... but there wouldn't be a club. In the late '80s, what happened was that our places started to find legal venues. So we had a night at the *Wag*, at the *Beat Route*, *Camden Palace* or the *Electric Ballroom*. Before that they were underground illegal DJs. Very different from how it is today. You couldn't choose to hear *Jazz Funk*, unless you knew someone who knew *Barry Sharpe* & his parties, you wouldn't hear *Funk* anywhere.

Norman Cummins -
Musician: RAW
Dog tooth hipsters
from Escape From
Havana, Kensington
Market, Campus
Italian knitwear from
Pierce and Angela
Brown, Archway 3,
Chalkfarm Market and
Chelsea boots.
Vocal part of the much
in demand funk combo
Raw. Previous
incarnations include
backing vocals for
Robert Palmer.

Cue Bill Cosby's def a
one for every location
the extreme, I-Spy, w

There's been lots of talk over recent months about the supposed emergence of the 'neo-mod'; of sta-press slacks and white 501s; of old style Adidas tennis shoes and polo shirts; of cardigans and jazz collections. But all this is anything but 'neo'. One only has to look at the seminal '60s television serial I-Spy to realise that.

I-SPY

Original Marks & Spencer cross necks, pyjamy jacket courtesy of Nick Talbot, slacks unknown source and black back quilters.

I-D THE BORN AGAIN ISSUE

Slam Slam with collaborators Dr Robert, Hector and Paul Weller, her latest single 'Something Ain't Right' was released on October 1st; the Album 'Free The

and red stripes on sleeve top from Escape From Havana, Kensington Market and Adidas Shell tops from Passenger.
hipsters.

PHOTOGRAPHY BY DONALD CHRISTIE AND NICK KNIGHT
STORY BY THE WATCH-MEN AGENCY

earing 501s, Adidas suede top and tennis shoes; Robert Culp's halting sense of irony and wit, in double def sports shirts and golf sweater
y competent spies and soul brothers had a perspective and style all of their own that went way beyond the boundaries of time. Radical
e seasons (from 1965 to 1967), was the first ever TV series to feature black and white co-starring actors. Travelling under the guise

I-D magazine
Nov. '90 - N° 86

Richard Okon -
Photographer.
Original US Levi 501s,
John Smedley from
Woodhouse. Loafers
from J. Simons and US
check jacket from
American Classics.
Richard 'Young Rich'
Okon is recently back
from New York, with
uncensored tapes of
Muslim discourse, the
contents of which
have not yet been
made public.

professional tennis player and sidekick, the global adventures of US Government agents Culp and Cosby (the antithesis to the 'Men From UNCLE' in more ways than one) are li
with mishaps and misrepresentations, a world where the bad guys are not always bad and where the best man doesn't always win. Sure, Scott was nowhere to be seen o
opening credits, and agreed, he never got the girl, despite being multilingual beyond belief; but in a time of apartheid in the Southern states, of racial inequality throughout the U

SPY

John Cook - Graphic Designer.
Wrangler 'rope-bottom' cords from Escape From Havana,
Kensington Market, crew neck from Cenci, and suede
Gucci loafers.
John 'Cookie' Cook is firmly in the creative camp of the
group. A graphic designer, responsible for most of the
highly acclaimed acid jazz visuals and sleeves.

Glorie Athow - Administrator
Original US Levi 501s, Schott's sleeveless jacket, T-shirt
from Oxfam and ankle boots.
Glorie by name and Glory by nature - archetypal hippie
chic - reputed to have enough Gucci and Timberland to
keep them in business for a year.

Steve White - Musician: Steve
White Quartet.
'Campus' 3 button long sleeve polo
shirt from Escape From Havana,
Kensington Market, Levi Classic
'cords' and hush puppies.
Do not be fooled, White's calm
persona is but a foil - he is a mean
sticks man and should be watched
at all times. (A Certain Kind Of
Freedom compilation album,
Polydor and Jazz FM Jazz Festival
in November).

Kieran Hurley - Label Manager Acid Jazz.
Original Wrangler 'rope bottom' cords, Campus Italian knitwear from Escape From Havana, Kensington Market and chisel toe boot.
His dislike of clubs is notorious, so too are his under cover weekend exploits in Brighton. He drives a 1964, right hand drive Spider convertible, colour red.

I-Spy had a certain
even to this day m
to get their heads
be involved in the
Spy deserves a con

But until now, th
kept secret, a signa
handful of people
fraternity hand sh
code, you have
anywhere near
collaborators, how
their intelligence
vers available prin
then only for a rela
time, is nothing l
exercise in itself

a car boot sale in Penge, a sports shop in Cardiff - uncovering the sources relied on luck, a lot of leg work and word of mouth. Gradually, however,
reliable outlets are beginning to appear: notably the Crazy Clothes Connection in Rye Lane, south London and Escape From Havana, Kensington
Other sources remain pretty much close to their chests... this message will not self destruct...

Andrew Levy - musician: Brand New Heavies/X-Collective.
'Anthony Turner' shirtjacket from the 'Killer' collection and original hand made sta-press trousers.
Andy, with his partner (Jan Kincaid) have been rumoured to be the Steely and Cleavie of the British funk scene. Andrew is the thumping bass player for the Brand New Heavies.

Group shots taken during the regular monthly Hardtimes club night at The Pyramid Arts Centre, 10/16 Ashwon St. Dalston. The next Hardtimes event is Saturday 27th October.

SPY

SMILER: The other thing was that in '90 I split up with a long term girlfriend. At the time there were hardly any girls in the mod scene, it was very incestuous; if you hadn't been with her, maybe your friends would have been with her. Then you would go to an *Acid Jazz* club, where there'd be girls, who actually looked *moddy*; mainly at the **Fez** club in *Paddington* where you'd see people you knew from the mod scene. *Paul Weller* used to go there, *John Cook*... a lot of Mods used to go there because the mod scene was so stale, and the *Acid Jazz* scene was on & up. It was an evolution to me.

jazz & OTHER ASSOCIATED MUSICS FROM BE-BOP TO HIP-HOP

Opening at Bukowskis (basement)
Street, Reading. Entry Free
day July 12th 8pm – Midnight

steps ahead

ACID JAZZ
ALL IT WAS TO ME: MODERN DAY 'MODERNISM'.
SMILER

SMILER: I could understand that I felt I let some people down, because I was so involved. But at the same time, I couldn't fool myself; I was doing what I wanted to do, I felt free. I remember selling all my hand-made shirts, hand-made suits and trousers... to *Mick Ferrante*. By then I was wearing more casual gear, Italian *Gabicci* tops, *Duffer of St George*, *Paul Smith* trousers, *Patrick Cox* loafers, *Adidas Gazelles*... though I was always seen in a suit on the mod scene; so it was lovely to go out and feel a bit more liberated at the time. It was still pretty smart.

It pissed me off because you'd leave the mod scene - the club scene - and people would start rumours of seeing you badly dressed... it was rubbish, never the case. And you'd be accused of blowing out, but I never saw it as blowin' out; I saw it as modern day Modernism.

A SOUL JAZZ PRODUCTION

FREEDOM JAZZ DANCE

DANCE JAZZ EVERY SAT. 9-3AM
AT PROHIBITION
9 HANOVER STREET
ADM. £5, £2.50 B4 10.30
DJ's STUART & ALEC OF
SOUL JAZZ RECORDS
& PETE THE LODGER

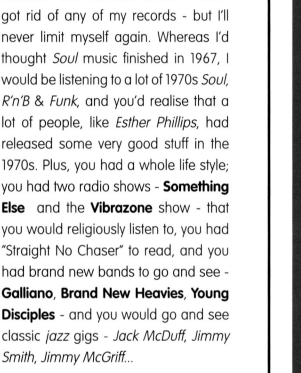
SMILER: I love the retro scene - I never got rid of any of my records - but I'll never limit myself again. Whereas I'd thought *Soul* music finished in 1967, I would be listening to a lot of 1970s *Soul, R'n'B* & *Funk*, and you'd realise that a lot of people, like *Esther Phillips*, had released some very good stuff in the 1970s. Plus, you had a whole life style; you had two radio shows - **Something Else** and the **Vibrazone** show - that you would religiously listen to, you had "Straight No Chaser" to read, and you had brand new bands to go and see - **Galliano**, **Brand New Heavies**, **Young Disciples** - and you would go and see classic *jazz* gigs - *Jack McDuff, Jimmy Smith, Jimmy McGriff...*

DUFFER OF ST GEORGE

Eddie Piller: It started as a stall in Camden market, and they opened a shop in Portobello Road, designing mod clothes for young people; good material, good cuts influenced by '60s patterns. They are now one of the biggest fashion houses in Europe, but at the time they were almost exclusively for the post-Mod & *Rare Groove* scenes.

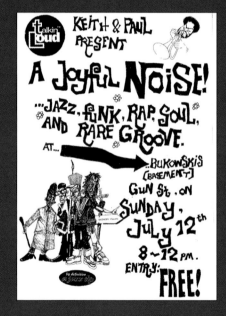

> # The mod scene had moved on to Acid Jazz.
> **Mark Lusty**

The Brighton JAZZ BOPs were to me the new rallies. SMILER

SMILER: The Brighton **Jazz Bops** were to me the new rallies, organised by **Russ Dewbury**, who had been involved in the *jazz* scene for years; you'd see tons and tons of ex-Mods, a lot of them still looking the same, but you wouldn't see them at rallies. They were at the Brighton 'Jazz Bop', at *Notting Hill Carnival*... you would go to 'Good Times', *Norman Jay's* stage, around that period of time, and you'd find people you knew from the mod scene. These events became to me the new rallies, kind of substituted it.

Having been involved with the *CCI* and the early *Untouchables*, it felt like a job; going to rallies, helping to organise them, DJing... whereas I would just be a punter at the *Acid Jazz* clubs, and I'd be loving it. It was like a brand new mod scene for me.

BRIGHTON JAZZ BOP

'Little Milton' & Charlotte - Photo: Milton Astley

HARRY PALMER

Mark Lusty: We always used to buy clothes, *Mick Ferrante*, me and a few others, since 1982. At that time you could go around London, find any 'oldish' looking shop that generally had old stocks from the '60s in their back room, you could befriend the old man... but you had to travel for miles to find those shops. From the early '80s to the early '90s, you could find stocks going back to the '50s, that had been on the shelves since then and never been worn. A lot in the East-End, or in some basements around Carnaby St. You would buy the whole stock for virtually nothing, all brand new shirts in bags & boxes. Fantastic clothes that led us to form a little community of cloth dealers with *Greg Fay*, *Mick Ferrante* & myself. *Mick* had the nick-name of 'Mick the shirt', at some point. You used to just bring the clothes down to the club, when you think that there weren't really at that time any vintage cloth shops like we have now. There was only Camden market on a Sunday, and Portobello on a Saturday, and then they'd have been fairly well worn. On the other hand, the stuff we'd find would be brand new, never been worn. And they'd all be one-offs, so you would keep the best shirts for yourself. We found stocks of *Denson* shoes; they were not really considered cool in the '60s, because they were massively produced and would be the equivalent of a cheap shoe manufacturer nowadays, but when they came back in the '80s/'90s, evidently they became cool because they'd been designed specifically towards Mods.

Chilling out into the 1990s - Photo: SMILER

- Shirt designed by Katy Stephens - Photo: SMILER

Milton Astley: Katy Stephens, who died just a few years ago, used to design fantastic shirts; giraffe collars, butterfly cuffs, fly fronts...

Mark Lusty: At the end of the '80s, I had so much stuff that I wanted to have a shop. I had an office in Elephant & Castle, where I used to have appointments with lots of bands to sell them clothes, but not enough to earn a living; I wanted to take it further and open a shop. At that time, *Eddie Piller* had started the *Acid Jazz* label and had signed a band called **Sandals**, a really cool *hippie* band, a bit like *Leftfield*, ahead of their time. Part of their recording contract was that *Eddie* had to take on the lease of a shop, then in the *Trocadero* (West-End), and I was supposed to supply it with clothes. He brought me in to be their only supplier. I was very much interested, because working on the side of Mods and the *Acid Jazz* thing at the time, it had become important to the people I was hanging out with; the mod scene had moved on to the *Acid Jazz* scene. *Acid Jazz* came to comfort what we were into at the time, so to be involved in it was fantastic.

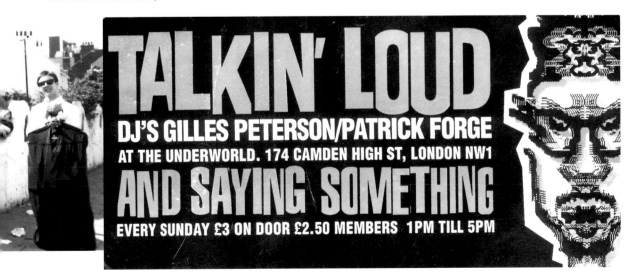

FREE SPEECH presents

COURTNEY PINE
REGGAE BAND
plus support EVA-LUTION

JAZZ AT DINGWALLS

MIDDLE YARD CAMDEN LOCK LONDON NW1

THURSDAY 21ST JULY

DOORS 8.00PM TICKETS £12

CREDIT CARD BOOKINGS 081 341 4421
OR FROM RHYTHM RECORDS CAMDEN TOWN
JACKSONS LANE N6 HONEST JONS W8
...ONGO LEXINGTON ST W1 MOLE JAZZ N1

Sunday 12th December 9... 7 til 2am
talkin' Loud at the Fridge Presents
THE BRAZILIAN CHRISTMAS PARTY
Performing live and Direct from Brazil
JOYCE
DJ's GILES PETERSON / PATRICK FORGE / JOE DAVIS
£8 adv £10 on door 7PM-2AM
SUNDAY 12th DEC '93 The Fridge
Townhall Parade /Brixton SW2
NO 1039

Street Style

Mark Lusty: But unfortunately, the shop - **Harry Palmer** - never happened, despite the fact that we had a lot of people involved; *Duffer of St George* (*Barry Sharpe's* label, quite big since then), *Paul Smith* were interested, *Brand New Heavies* as a band were following us, and a lot of Mods who are heavily in design & fashion now, *Marc Powell* who was quite a key player in the West-End (he had a *jazz* club called 'Violets' that we used to frequent)... the shop had become a big melting pot, but due to Westminster council, nothing happened. We did carry on though, through mail orders and the *Acid Jazz* label. We developed a company called *Space Head*, so the shop did come through eventually, but never like we wanted it to be.

Mick Ferrante: The pinnacle of my career was that I got involved with the *Victoria & Albert Museum*, in '95. They had a *Street Style* exhibition, they were collecting a lot of stuff and they needed someone to help them out. So I told them what to buy and what not to buy, I gave them my professional opinion, and they used and misused it, but it was a very successful exhibition. I helped them in the book as well. So I took my Mod understanding into my career.

Hastings - 1995 - Photo by the author

Milton Astley: I was lucky I met *Mick Ferrante*, who really taught me what to wear; he was always trying to sell clothes. Once at the Isle Of Wight, he didn't want to be charged for having a stall in the venue during lunchtime, so he was flogging shirts from the back of his car, until the police came and asked him to stop.

The Manchester sound (*Charlatans, Happy Mondays...*) was something that I could appreciate at the time, but never associate with the mod scene, or with any mod sound to my knowledge.

Their attitude was cool, and their dress code was sometimes similar to casual Mod; but their music was far too *funky*, and far too remote from the *punky* essence of mod *Revival*, or the beats of early *R'n'B*. If their early stuff was spotless (*JTQ...*), their later releases were kind of inaccessible for us.

Grunge kind of started alright with *Nirvana* (almost *Psychedelic*, in a way) but ended up in a mixture of dodgy *HardRock/Punk Metal* noise! Their look was appalling anyway...

Street Style exhibition (at the V&A - 1995): All the trends & fashions since the late 1940s were represented on mannequins... gathering amongst others: Mods & Rude Boys.

The 1990s not only brought out *Techno & Dance* music that was made without instruments, it also introduced the technique of *sampling*. I don't have a problem with it when it's well used, the only cloud being that it led a whole generation to ignorance; people started thinking that they were listening to the original stuff. So the kids believed that *Galliano* was putting out genuine stuff, when actually they were sampling some of *Booker T & The MGs* first album (with "Stoned Again") or *Jackie Mittoo*'s "Totally Together". And I have a problem with that. What Mod is about, in our days, is to know as much as you can about music, if not everything; the ignorance of the masses is what separates us from them.

Paul Lobb: I think that if the 1990s were much less violent than the previous decade, the reason is because of the emergence of the **Ecstasy** pill. As soon as people started taking that drug, fights suddenly disappeared. It came to a point where you couldn't find anything else at a party.

Leonie and her boyfriend at the time, *Paul*. They were the only ones in the scene who, like me, used to take their scooter to go to any night out in London. The difference was that they didn't drink...

London 1994: A beautiful summer; the best since 1963, they said. There wasn't this violence of the '80s anymore; everybody was cool. I remember riding with my old *Vespa* on Shaftesbury Avenue, one morning, and seeing this tough *Biker* on the other side of the street, on a massive three-wheeler, German chrome helmet on... the real *Hell's Angel* by definition. We looked at each other, and we smiled at each other. Just an honest, respectful, sincere smile. I was glad to see somebody in the middle of the crowd, who stood out, for his ideal. Maybe he was thinking the same when he saw me. Two islands left in the middle of a society where personalities are fading away...

Kevin Walker - **Brighton 1999** - Paul & Leonie - **Carnaby St 1994** - Photos by the author

Kevin Walker: I was coming back from a club at night, in the middle of nowhere - I lived in Littlehampton - on my *Vespa*, when I ran out of petrol. Luckily, I always carried a jerrycan on my scooter, so I stopped, just in front of a petrol station - which was obviously closed because it must have been four in the morning. As I started to refill my tank, I heard behind me quite a famous rumbling noise that usually signifies the arrival of big motorbikes, and in numbers. I turned around, fuck me! About ten or fifteen *Bikers* on their *Harleys* starting to circle around me. "Hey kid, you're alright? Do you need some petrol?" They were cool, after all. I was like: "No no, thank you, I've got some, thanks..." I could hear the girls sitting behind them, shouting: "Kill the bastard!" I just waited for them to leave, before I started my scooter and went on.

Milton Astley: I moved up to London, got a job in the *Dorchester*; I used to go to *Ronnie Scott* all the time, to see *Georgie Fame*, all sort of early *Modernists* - that type of Mod. Then I got into *Acid Jazz* as well; I went to *raves* and other clubs, but I wouldn't go along with all the *Acid Jazz* thing. I used to to enjoy it, but it got more commercial, so I started getting back into the more purist stuff; the same things I used to listen to when I first got into it, which brought me onto the mod thing. More *R'n'B* and *Soul*, and that was it; that was more my sort of music. That was around '94, '95. Loads of us would go to the rallies, and we used to meet up every Saturday afternoon just off Carnaby Street in the *Modesto Coffee Bar*. I got a *Lambretta* and *Luke* had one as well, *Steve* had a *GS*... six or seven of us who used to meet up every Saturday on the scooters, going to *Textile King*, getting materials, then going to *Charlie*, getting stuff made, living the real mod lifestyle all weekend. It was good fun.

Eddie Piller: Keb Darge is one of the best *Northern* DJs & dancers I've ever known. He invented **Deep Funk**. His impact came when he decided that there was a market for *Funk*, after the *Acid Jazz* scene had finished. *Acid Jazz* went for *Trip-Hop* & *New Jazz*, which is a mixture of German *Latin House* shit; so people into *Soul* went back into *Northern Soul*. *Darge* thought that there was a market for people who like *Funk*, and his 'Deep Funk' thing was the last good thing to happen to *Black* retro music.

Acid Jazz was an option, but missed the chance to become my choice, as far as I was concerned. By the late 1990s, it had all turned into *Hip-Hop*, and unfortunately had nothing to do with the mod scene anymore.

On the other hand, you had the '*Funk* option' which was offered by **Keb Darge** and his clubs. Suddenly, by the end of the '90s, we had decided to go to **Madame Jojo's** every Sunday night.

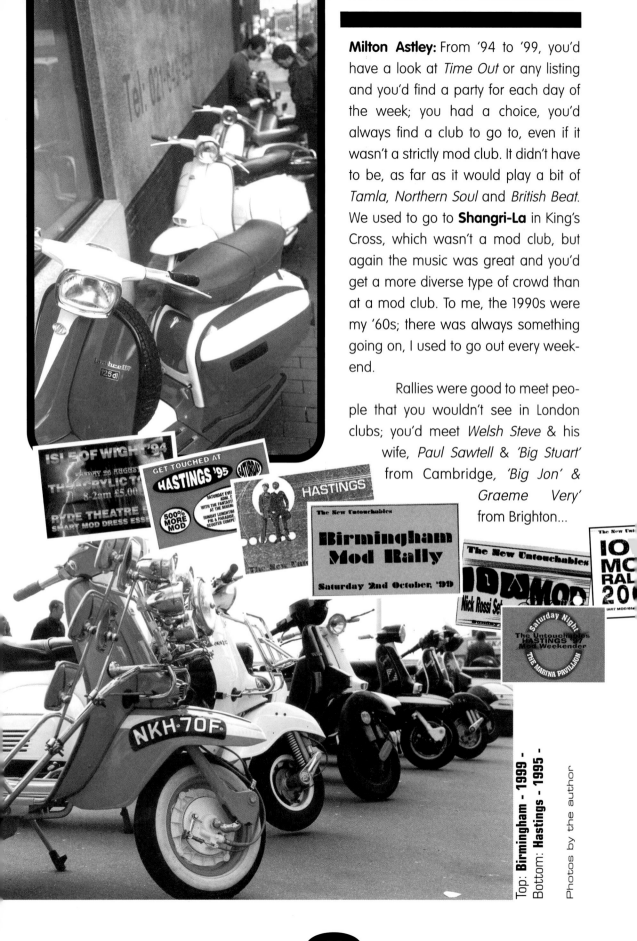

Milton Astley: From '94 to '99, you'd have a look at *Time Out* or any listing and you'd find a party for each day of the week; you had a choice, you'd always find a club to go to, even if it wasn't a strictly mod club. It didn't have to be, as far as it would play a bit of *Tamla*, *Northern Soul* and *British Beat*. We used to go to **Shangri-La** in King's Cross, which wasn't a mod club, but again the music was great and you'd get a more diverse type of crowd than at a mod club. To me, the 1990s were my '60s; there was always something going on, I used to go out every weekend.

Rallies were good to meet people that you wouldn't see in London clubs; you'd meet *Welsh Steve* & his wife, *Paul Sawtell* & *'Big Stuart'* from Cambridge, *'Big Jon'* & *Graeme Very'* from Brighton...

Top: **Birmingham - 1999 -**
Bottom: **Hastings - 1995 -**

Photos by the author

DON'T MISS THE

MOUSETRAP MOOD ALLNIGHTER

SAT 25 JANUARY
PLASTIC SURGERY
FROM TOP DISC SPINNERS
SPEED, CATFORD CHRIS, SHINZO,
NICK HUDSON, KARL FLAVELL,
SCOTT (QUINTESSENCE)
AND DR ROBERT.

SURGERY BEGINS AT 10PM - 6AM
ADM £6

AT JACIS, 259 SEVEN SISTERS RD, FINSBURY PARK, LONDON

OPERATING THE FINEST TUNES EVER IN FUNKY HAMMOND GROOVES, FREAKBEAT, N.SOUL, RHYTHM & BLUES, GARAGE, PSYCH, SOUL JAZZ, AND AUTHENTIC JAMAICAN SOUNDS FROM THE 60'S

Claire Strickland: The **Mousetrap** all-nighter was actually *Rob Bailey's* club, not an *Untouchables'* do.

THE UNTOUCHABLES
22 GAMBOLE ROAD, TOOTING BROADWAY, LONDON SW17 0QJ
TEL/FAX: 0181 672 7581 or 0181 677 8628

BOOGALOO IN BOURNMOUTH
Mod Rally 10-12th April
All events held at The Balmoral Hotel
11-13 Kerly Road, Bournemouth

Friday Night 9-2am
The weekend starts here
Hot Mod Hits from our guest DJ's

Saturday Night Live 8-2am
It's a big 10-4 for
Convoy
plus hard ass Mod sounds
& prizes for groovy dancers

Sunday Night Showdown 8-2am
Keep your wits about you for
The Hoodwinks
plus our Untouchable DJ's taking you to a
climatic finale (orgy upstairs afterwards)
All afternoon do's held at The Balmoral
Hotel, scooter comp/cruise 2pm
Sunday outside hotel. If you would like to
stay at the hotel please ring them direct
on 01202 551186 and inform them that
you are coming to The Untouchable
weekender to get a discount on rooms
More details on the next page

Milton Astley: If there really wasn't nothing on, you'd go to the **Monarch** in Camden. As well as mod clubs, there were clubs where Mods used to go.

In my opinion, the main clubs in the 1990s were:

- **Mousetrap** monthly all-nighter, in Finsbury Park to this day, existing since 1991, organised by the *Untouchables* in the beginning. The first time I went there, when I arrived in London (Summer '94 that was), I danced so much that my suit was soaked with sweat; I went to grab my cigarettes from my inside pocket, they looked like they'd fallen into a pond...

- **Blow Up**, every Saturday, started in Camden, at the *Laurel Tree*. On two floors, with DJs *Andy Lewis, Paul Tunkin & Ian Jackson* + the *Karminsky Experience*. The best music ever. I remember seeing *Ian Jackson* dancing on the little stage that they had downstairs; he couldn't stop, he would dance all night. But the venue was too small for the attendance, and besides it was Camden, so you would have a mod crowd going regularly over there, as well as a big bunch of wankers & tourists.

- Even if Mod was trying to escape from its mould of *Soul & R'n'B*, turning by the early '90s towards new sounds supplied by *Acid Jazz*, *Talkin' Loud* or *Indie* music, we still used to attend the **100 Club** every month at *Ady Croasdell's Northern Soul* Allnighter.

6T'S
RHYTHM' N'SOUL SOCIETY

In 1995 a band called **Mickey Finn & The Blue Men**, who'd had their time of fame in the 1960s, had a track re-released: "Ain't Necessarily So". I met **Mick Stannard**, their original bass player, at the Isle of Wight in 1994; he was still the same *Face*, same attitude since the '60s...

SPECIAL EDITION

'Big Stuart' (friend of *Paul Sawtell* in Cambridge), like *Mick Stannard*, was a Mod in the '60s who came back to the scene in the mid-'90s. They both had beautiful scooters; chromed mudguard & panels... just to hang out with them made you look cool.

The '90s were my '60s.
Milton Astley

THE SANDALS & TONGUE KUNG FU

Eddie Piller: I signed **A Man Called Adam** very early; they were a seven-piece *Be-Bop* band at the beginning, a Mod band playing *Jazz*. They split into **Leftfield** and **The Sandals**; they were all ex-Mods into *Jazz/Beatnik/Lounge/Psychedelic*.

The Sandals ran **Tongue Kung Fu** in Covent Garden, the most successful club in London at the time; 400 people every week. Playing *Psych & Easy Listening*... they really paved the way, they opened people's mind.

Night Train used to be an Untouchables' do on a Saturday, like *Blow Up*, just 'round the corner from it (Mornington Crescent).

NIGHT TRAIN
EVERY FORTNIGHT ADM. £4.00 PUB PRICES

SATURDAY JULY 8th
LIVE ON STAGE
THE ADVENTURES OF PARSLEY

SATURDAY JULY 22nd
LIVE ON STAGE
CASUAL

THE HIPPEST MOD CLUB IN TOWN
TWO ROOMS COVERING THE FULL SPECTRUM OF MOD SOUNDS PLUS LIVE BANDS

NIGHT TRAIN
SATURDAY 9-2am ADM.£4
YOUR CONDUCTORS FOR THE NIGHT ARE:
DAVE EDWARDS*ROB BAILEY*DOM*CATFORD
CHRIS*SPINNING ANYTHING MOD FROM 1960's TO 1990's
AT THE ALBANY, GT PORTLAND STREET, LONDON W1
(NEAREST TUBE GT PORTLAND ST.)

3rd FEBRUARY
THE KYND

2nd MARCH
THE AARDVARKS

31st MARCH
KNAVE

Milton Astley: We used to run a night called **Pit Stop**, at the *Red Rose* on Seven Sisters Road near Finsbury Park, on a Saturday, sort of warm-up to the *Mousetrap* allnighter, with **Stevie Cox (Emma Silk**'s boyfriend - *Emma* became a tailor in the scene) whose dad was an original *Skinhead* from 1967 (who had probably the best collection of *Rock Steady* in the country). He used to DJ for us and we used to get a crowd of 'Trojan' *Skinheads* coming.

During the mid-'90s, you would go to two or three clubs in one night. Mainly when the *Untouchables* split up; you would start in an *Untouchables* club, then go to one of *Rob Bailey's* nights, and if you were still awake you would go to **Blow Up** (after it had moved to the *Wag*) at four in the morning for a couple of hours.

Hastings - 1995 - Photo by the author

THE BLUE NOTE CLUB (Hoxton Square)

Eddie Piller: I bought it in '94. I just had an idea; I wanted a small nightclub that wouldn't play *House* music. There was no club in London that didn't play *House* music. We had *Asian* music on a Monday with **Talvin Singh**, *Drum'n'Bass* on a Sunday with **Goldie**, *Funk* & Mod with 'Magic Bus' every Friday; Saturdays were rotations; we had 'Cold Cut' from **Ninja Tune**, 'Dub' with **Aba-Shanti**, we did live nights with **Ocean Colour Scene** and **Ian Brown**... it was just a *Non-House* club, and even when *House* DJs like **Andy Wetherall** and **David Moralis** came to the club, they didn't play their normal *House* set.

Caspar de la Mare: I used to go to 'Wendy May's Locomotion', that's how I got to know **Andy Lewis** - through *Wendy* & *Stuart*. It started life at the *Town & Country Club*, which is now the *Forum* in Kentish Town. The management screwed it a bit, so they moved to the *Underworld* in Camden; it was one of the longest clubs in London. Then *Andy* started 'Blow Up' at the *Laurel Tree* in Camden, which he called 'Londinium', but there was another club called that. It started as a proper mod club upstairs (downstairs was a gay bar), and if you weren't there before 9.00 it would be sold out. *Andy* met the **Karminsky** brothers at the *St Moritz*, and offered them to play downstairs as well.

Get Touched!

HASTINGS EASTER BANK HOLIDAY 5-8 APRIL '96

ALL NIGHTTIME EVENTS ARE HELD AT THE MARINA PAVILION, LOWER PROMENADE, MARINA, ST LEONARDS ON SEA

FRIDAY 9-2am WEEKEND STARTS HERE! £5

SATURDAY 8-2am COOL FRENCH BEAT WITH DUTRONC £6

SUNDAY 8-2am SMALL FACES SET WITH MUSTN'T GRUMBLE PLUS YOUR USUAL RALLY DJ's & GUESTS

SATURDAY & SUNDAY LUNCHTIMES AT THE PIG & PARADISE, HASTINGS SEAFRONT NEW DJ's TWIDDLING HIP SOUNDS, RECORD & CLOTHES STALLS

PRIZES FOR SCOOTERS & CRUISE AT 3pm SUNDAY OPPOSITE PIG & PARADISE

DRESS SMART FOR EVENING EVENTS

FOR MORE INFO. RING 0181

I was desperately skinnt that year - Dec. '95; no job (on the dole), had just moved in with the girlfriend to a new flat... I didn't have a penny to the world to spend over Christmas that year; real misery when I think of it, not especially a good period to remember. So I tried to exercise my talent as an illustrator - that was my job then, I used to draw book covers for a little publisher; I grabbed my pencils & brushes, and went on portraying loads of music *Faces*; *Marriott* of course, *Weller*... couples on scooters, fictitious '60s advertisements for rare foreign scooters, etc.

My idea was to take those drawings to the New Year's Eve Rally organised by **The Untouchables** in Eastbourne, and to sell them framed during the afternoon session. I had the lift sorted out with **Paul Sawtell** and his mate **'Big Stuart'**, and I had the possibility to stay at **Louise Howlett**'s parents for the duration of the event (3 days). My girlfriend was to stay in London - we couldn't afford to be two on that trip - where she spent the festivities with our neighbours. Pretty sad, but I didn't know if I'd make any money out of these drawings, if I could support the both of us...

We arrived in the afternoon of the first day, in a stormy and miserably damp and cold Eastbourne, empty as usual, and we didn't stay to admire the assets of the town & seafront; we headed straight to *Paul Sawtell's* B'n'B, where he got ready for the night. I was ready myself, being dressed up since the morning; I couldn't be bothered then, to have an outfit for the trip, then get into my suit... but *Paul*, he even had a mini-iron (the travel' model) just in case. I wonder now, if he didn't have a mini-ironing board with him in the car!

I.O.W - 1995 - Photo by the author

Rallies were good to meet people that you wouldn't see in London clubs.

Miltom Astley

THE UNTOUCHABLES NEW YEARS EVE '95 PARTY

Paul Sawtell and Louise Howlett
Hastings - 1995 -
Photo by the author

Just to walk from the B'n'B to the pier - where the party was - seemed nearly suicidal; there was no parka warm enough to really protect you from that icy rain! We didn't wear parkas anyway, crombies and macs instead. Well, that is not the point - the point is: that year, a good contingent of the Parisian mod scene had decided to make the effort to come to that Rally especially, which was a surprise to me, for I didn't expect to bump into them on the first night. The **Gambetta** lot; *Docteur, Budgy, Stan & Virginie...* and the *StGermain-En-Lay S.C.* were there, at the bar when I entered the club. As usual, those French Mods were coming with a new asset, in terms of fashion; it wasn't the first time Mods from a different country - or a different town - would turn up at a Rally with a set of clothes that was typical of their lot. And that was part of the charm of those gatherings: we would look around, and learn from each other. Same with the dancing. We most certainly did end up, *Louise* & I, at their B'n'B after the party - which would finish at 2am (!) when everybody would still be buzzing with *Speed...* a very chic hotel with many rooms, where the fun would go on, as the Frenchies were occupying a whole storey.

The next day I went on the mission of trying to sell my frames at the afternoon party, in the same venue at the end of the pier. Surprisingly **Maz Weller** came to buy about £30 of drawings that day and complimented me on my art, which was most heart-warming for me. I'll never forget it, thank you *Maz*! I remember as well two young Mods, dressed in bomber jackets & Sta-Prests, who would buy a little thing at each stall...

Pat Lee aka 'Irish' Pat
I.O.W - 1997 - Photo: Nickie Divine

Paul 'the hairdresser' (before he became a *Skinhead* in the late 1990s), 'Tiger' Jayne and Tina Vaughan

Photo: Dom & Claire Strickland

untouchables present
ISLE OF WIGHT **MOD RALLY**
25th-28th AUGUST 1995

ALL NIGHT EVENTS TAKE PLACE AT THE FABULOUS
RYDE THEATRE
LUNCHTIMES ARE ON THE SEAFRONT AT
THE KING LUDD

FRIDAY EVENING 8.30-1.30am £5
THE CLIQUE

SATURDAY EVENING 8-1.30am £6
LOS FLECHAZOS

SUNDAY EVENING 8-1.30am £6
THE 100 MEN

SATURDAY & SUNDAY LUNCHTIME 12-3pm

SATURDAY AFTERNOON MOD CUP
DRUNK FOOTBALL MATCH 3pm

SCOOTER COMPETITION & CRUISE MIDDAY ON SUNDAY
OPPOSITE KING LUDD

WEEKEND DJs INCLUDE ROB BAILEY * PID & LEE *
MARK ELLIS * SPEED * MICK TAYLOR * CATFORD CHRIS
* DOM * IAN JACKSON

ALL EVENING EVENTS ARE STRICTLY
SMART MOD DRESS ONLY
FOR MORE INFO RING THE UNTOUCHABLE HOT LINE
0181 672 7581

TOURIST INFO. & ACCOMMODATION TEL: 01983 562905

THE SUAVE GENERATION

UNTOUCHABLES PRESENT

IN LEEDS ON SATURDAY 18th FEBRUARY '95
WITH SPECIAL GUESTS LIVE ON STAGE
THE ACRYLIC TONES

SPINNING THE GROOVES DJ's ROB BAILEY & PUTNEY SEAN (LONDON)
TEASING YOUR TOES WITH LOCAL LADS MARK ELLIS & LEE MILLER

AT THE WEST INDIAN CENTRE, 10 LAYCOCK PLACE, CHAPELTOWN, LEEDS 5
ADM. £5 8-3am(ish) SHARP CLOTHES & SHARP DANCING ESSENTIAL

COACH FROM LONDON WITH PICK-UPS ALONG THE WAY
FOR MORE INFO. RING THE UNTOUCHABLES ON 081 672 7581

untouchables present
LOWESTOFT MOD RALLY
14-17 JULY 1995

ALL EVENTS TAKE PLACE AT THE
SENSATIONAL
BLUE NOTE NIGHTCLUB
CLAREMONT PIER, ESPLANADE, LOWESTOFT

FRIDAY EVENING 9-1.30am £5

SATURDAY EVENING 8-1.30am £5

SUNDAY EVENING 8-1.30am £5

SATURDAY & SUNDAY LUNCHTIME 12-3pm
NIGHTLY SPINNING THEIR FINE SOUNDS
MARK ELLIS SPEED RECORDS ROB BAILEY
GRAHAM CLOSE PID

SATURDAY AFTERNOON MOD CUP SOUTH
FOOTBALL MATCH
SCOOTER COMPETITION & CRUISE SUNDAY
SUNDAY AFTERNOON

WEEKEND DJs INCLUDE ROB BAILEY
PID SPEED MARK ELLIS SPEED
MICK TAYLOR CATFORD CHRIS

ALL EVENING EVENTS ARE STRICTLY
SMART MOD DRESS ONLY
FOR MORE INFO RING THE UNTOUCHABLE
HOT LINE 081 672 7581

TOURIST INFO. & ACCOMMODATION
TEL 01502

That as well, was quite heart-warming, to know that new blood was coming to the scene. All together I must say, despite the financial situation, it was a fantastic time I was witnessing at this Do. I would say, much later in my life: never take a girlfriend to a Rally, try to find one there; it's much funnier.

On the way back to *Louise's* house, the shops were buzzing with people; it was a Saturday, *30th of December*, and a detail, that is so characteristic to Great-Britain, came to my attention: a Scottish guard was playing bagpipes at the entrance of a supermarket. I personally love the sound of this instrument, and even if a lot of people find it 'cheesy', I think that there only is one place in the world you can see a Scottish man playing it, and that's what makes the charm of this country.

Of course I spent all the money I had made in the afternoon on the forthcoming night, and once again we ended up at the French place. **Skooby**, a band that I had never seen before, had given us a fantastic gig, so good that people were dancing in front of the stage; I had never seen such a reaction of the public (not since *Ready Steady Go*).

The main night was still to come. For this occasion the French lot had brought with them some Champagne, and I think there were about 45 bottles for only fifteen of us. We were drinking pints of the stuff! They didn't stop opening bottles for the whole party; I must say that we did it in style, that night.

The shame about this night though, was that it had to finish at 2am, when we could hear the noise of another party (*Techno* music) in a room down the stairs - which was probably going on for the whole night! It didn't stop *Louise* & myself from turning up at the same hotel as the night before, where - once again - the party was getting frantic on the French floor. I didn't find it very difficult to have the doorman let us in, taking on an even worse accent than usual, and we arrived in an over-heated place. In both senses of the term; the temperature was probably 40°C more than outside, and the atmosphere in the rooms was steaming. Now, the bubbles of Champagne were kicking in our brains, and of course we had the 'obligatory' spliff, which didn't help. *'Docteur''* was going mad, running from room to room and pulling the beds out, throwing mattresses and messing around with everybody's suitcase... he even tried to throw the TV through the window, but then he realised that he had to stop.

As I said, I never say no to a smoke, but this time I should have. After the first 'bong', I felt the need to open the window for a bit of fresh air. We were at the fourth or fifth floor, so when my puke reached the courtyard, it made quite a typical splashing noise. I got sicker and sicker, to a point where they had to place a plastic bag on my face, with the handles holding 'round my ears, like these bags you feed horses with.

Of course they had to carry me down the stairs, where the janitor was quite suspicious and ready to call for an ambulance. They drove us back in their van, *Louise* and me, to her parents, and I fell straight like a ruler on the bed without even thinking of trying to undress. I think they took my shoes off though.

The next day I had a lift with *Paul Sawtell* and *'Big' Stuart* back to London, but you wouldn't hear me in the back of the car... believe me, I'm a connoisseur; Champagne hang-overs are the worst ones.

Milton Astley: To do the mod thing properly used to cost you money; by the time you've paid for your clothes... especially rallies. I could never have a proper summer holiday, when I was doing three or four rallies a year. Each rally was costing me about £300/400.

Even the average night out; you'd meet people at the pub first, spend £15/20 before going to the club. Then you'd pay around £6 to get in, score some *Speed* which would probably be a tenner, plus another £20 on drinks, especially if it's an allnighter. On top of that I wouldn't wait for the first tube, so by 5.00am I would have enough and jump in a mini-cab that cost me roughly another £15 or plus. So all together, you'd end up spending a good £70/80, without really caining it. If you do that on a Friday night, then do it again on a Saturday night... to eventually end up at Camden market on a Sunday lunchtime and go to the **Elephant's Head** where *'Old Man' Shaun* and *Rob Murphy* used to DJ. Then you'd go to the **Big Club** (*Alan Milliner* aka *Dr Strange*) in Tuffnell Park to see a gig.

FRAT SHACK
AN ALTERNATIVE TO MOD NIGHTS.

I vividly remember the **Frat Shack** allnighters. They were more of a *Rock'n'Roll* thing, mixed with *Bossa-Nova* and '60s *Garage Punk*, but you would always spot a few moddish groups hanging around at any of these parties. Organised by **Josh Collins**, whose girlfriend **Babzotica** was a tailor and had a boutique of outrageous '60s clothes, and **Liam Watson** (who was in charge of the **Toe Rag** recording studio - nearly all the bands on the '60s scene went to record over there).

We wouldn't only go to mod clubs; there was so much going on at the time... you had a real quality of choice during that decade.

The **St John's Tavern** was also a cult venue, situated on Junction Rd near Archway; hundreds of bands played there from the late '80s to the mid-'90s. But one that you'd never miss, or that you would see at least once, was their resident combo: **Thee Headcoats**, originally *The Milkshakes*, and their girlfriends *Thee Headcoatees*.

I used to take an acid each time I would go to the *Frat Shack*. **Alan Milliner**, who was DJing at every party, was absolutely blinding; the music he played - a mix of '60s soundtracks and *Boogaloo* - used to make me trip completely. He used to hold the records in his mouth while he was DJing! Quite outrageous, knowing the value of his gems...

The problem was that it quickly became too popular; eventually too many people would turn up, and even venues as big as the *333* in Old Street were too small for it.

'60s GARAGE PUNK SPECIAL!

The Sires • The Nuthins • The Disturbed • The Elecric Fayre

Thursday 17th October 1996
First band on stage 8.30pm
Entry – £3.50 only!

The Western Room, St John's Tavern
Junction Road, London N19
Nearest Tube: Archway

For further information:

As well as mod clubs, there were clubs where Mods used to go to.

Milton Astley

STOMP, SHOUT, WORK IT ON OUT AT

THE HIDE☉UT

MONKEY, WATUSI, SHAKE AND SHIMMY TO BEAT, R&B, GARAGE-PUNK, AND INSTRUMENTAL ROCK'N'ROLL

SATURDAY 23 MARCH • 9 TILL LATE
ADMISSION FREE BEFORE 11PM, £1 AFTER
Upstairs at The Barley Mow, Rivington Street EC1
(Corner Rivington Street and Curtain Road)

The Hide-Out was not a mod club, more of a '60s *Garage* night, organised by Liam Watson & Ben Olins.

Speed was, of course, the ultimate 'plus' to any night out for a Mod since the '60s; from French **Blues** (*Dinintel*) & **Dexedrine** to **Base** and **Pink Champagne**, a mod night couldn't be so-called, without the sparkles of joy and energy - mixed with alcohol - given to you by the induction of these substances.

The following lines are taken from various quotes, from people who will understandably want to keep their confidentiality; they are not, in any case, a valid testimony of their veracity.

*At some point, I couldn't go out or enjoy a party without my *Speed*. It was *Speed* before alcohol, *Speed* had become more important than anything else! I used to take some, nearly every day, at the pub I would put a bit in the beer of my mates... there were 101 reasons to take the stuff. That's what you call a "Speed Freak". However, it became quite tiring after a few years, and I got sort of immune to it; I couldn't feel it anymore.

*Problem was: when it came to shag a girl... in medical terms: impossibility to get a 'proper' hard on, added to a very little chance to come before an hour.

*The *Ecstasy* that appeared in the early '90s became more and more popular as it became cheaper, and I'm afraid, had slowly replaced our usual uppers by the end of the century. The consequences were probably the same as the commercialisation of the *Acid* in California in the '60s; everything turned *Flower Power* in the mod scene, the clothes, the music, the dances...

* *Speed* is not as bad as *Coke*, or alcohol, or even cigarettes...

*Once I spent 11 days in bed, after taking some *Speed* for one week non-stop, day & night.

*I used to get in for free anywhere; a little wrap to the dog at the door of the club... sometimes I felt like *Al Pacino*; sat at a table, surrounded by gorgeous women, facing a queue of people coming up to the doctor, to get their little remedy.

* *Pink Champagne* was really good. Compared to *Blues* pills that would give you a bad come down leading to a depression, the pink powder we used to get in the '90s once got me awake for three nights in a row, and I still was able to walk, talk... I eventually used it for working at night; the concentration it gave you was fantastic, as with *Coke* it was impossible to concentrate.

*A very good friend of mine (who had invented this trend actually) and me, were the only two guys on the scene who used to sell *Speed* in wraps made out of porn magazines; so you could be seen licking it at the end of the night.

As *Acid* went onto spoiling the new generation of Mods toward the end of the 1960s, we could almost today see a parallel with the spread of a new drug called *Ecstasy* by the end of the 1990s. The reason is: it became so cheap that it popularised itself to all the scenes of the youth culture (ie. only connected to *Techno* music and *Rave* parties in the early 1990s, it was fairly expensive back then).

Speed (though it can have some after effects) is not a passive drug; you take it to stay awake in the first place, and to enjoy each minute of the night. It stimulates your brain for a few hours, and will eventually promote you to a stage where you will communicate - in a full loving mood - with everybody at the party, spreading new relations with people who are - or not - on the same level.

Ecstasy (or *Acid*) has never done that for me; on the contrary, I would stay 'blocked' on my chair, head in my hands for hours, wondering why I took that shit and most probably promising myself (like each time) that I'll never do it again. *Magic mushrooms* have definitely a better buzz, but it still is a *hippie* thing.

Unfortunately, *Speed* also can have a second effect; anxiety and stress might be inclined to take over sometimes... insecurity, fear of the unknown, mainly when danger is around (when a fight is about to kick off) or only by walking alone in the street, without your crew, which in the 1980s was a permanent challenge in itself. So beware of the side effects.

Also, after taking the stuff for many days in a row, you start babbling forever and that can be quite boring or embarrassing for your surroundings. I remember this guy who couldn't stop talking bullshit, hours after hours... just waffling, saying whatever was coming through his fucked mind.

Eventually, the state after the *Speed* has stopped having an effect, better known as 'come down', can lead to a massive depression, as with the 'Blues' (so-called for their after-effect) that we used to take in France; after a whole week on the stuff (about 30 pills a day at the end) I ended up 'crying for my mother', all alone in my flat. Whereas *Dexedrine* is strange; it works by waves... one minute you're on top of the world, the next you feel normal again, and then back to buzzing.

I tried everything when I was a teen-ager: sniffing *glue* (to start with), smoking *hash & grass* (like everybody), snorting *heroin & cocaine* (too expensive), gobbing *amphetamines*, *acid & mushrooms*, even stronger *hallucinogens*... and guess what? *Speed* won the crown, as far as I can remember. *Speed* puts you in a state that you'd wish to reach for your entire life! It makes a 'superman' of you, someone that everybody likes and admires, a social party-goer kind of 'beast'; in other words a Super-Mod.

"I FEEL THE NEED...
FOR SPEED!"

Background: **Hastings -1995 -** Photo by the author

MEL○DY·MAKER
PARKA LIFE

GERMANY DM 5.30/SPAIN

NOVEMBER 19, 1994 75p

Touched by the hand of

MOD

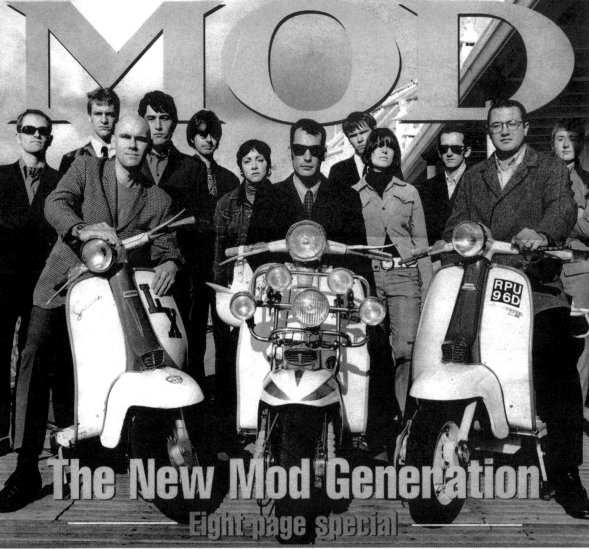

Mods r'us – Photographed by Pat Pope

The New Mod Generation
Eight-page special

THE STONE ROSES That new single at last
HENRY ROLLINS The Black Flag diaries

NEW ORDER ★ URGE OVERKILL ★ STEREOLAB ★ JESUS LIZARD ★ VERUCA SALT
HOLE ★ LUKE GOSS ★ PHIL DANIELS ★ PAVEMENT ★ DA BRAT ★ PATRICK PRINS ★ METALHEADS

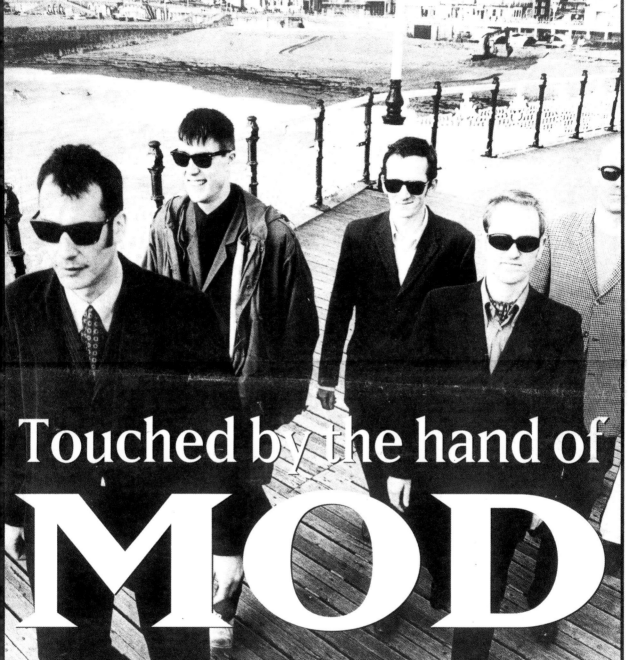

Touched by the hand of
MOD

Anyone who witnessed Blur's 'Alexandra Parklife' show will immediately have recognised the signs. **MODS ARE BACK.** There's no escaping it: The (Second) Mod revival is officially on. Crusty, grungey slacking is dead, long hair is out. A new, slimline, tailored chic has taken over the fashion and club scenes, and has influenced almost all of 1994's brightest Britpop stars, from Blur – whose fault the whole damn thing may be – and Elastica, to the NWONWers. In

this eight-page special, we look at the history of Mod, check out the great Mod icons and classic anthems, examine the Blur connection, find out where to be seen, what to wear and where to buy it. We also talk to the new ace faces of the New Mod Squad – Menswear, Thurman and Mantaray. And on page 43, in a Rebellious Jukebox special, Mod icon and star of The Who's 'Quadrophenia' movie, Phil 'Parklife' Daniels talks about the records that put a shine on his scooter

Paul Weller, Oxford 1984

Touched by the hand of
MOD

KEVIN PEARCE, author of Mod Bible, 'Something Beginning With "O"', tells you everything you wanted to know about Mod but were too uncool – too un-Mod.

They would be totally outraged by the received notion that Mod's all about parkas, target T-shirts, The Who, The Small Faces and Union Jacks. If you must mention any of the original Mod-associated groups, at least look a little further for those who, in their own way, briefly and spectacularly soared past the establishment outfits.

The Action in many ways were the ultimate Mod group. They artfully perverted the new soul sound, while singer Reggie King was a showman of substance and style with a voice so extraordinarily sweet and smooth and a haircut to match.

The Creation, meanwhile, were more into experimental noise and abstract arguments, with Eddie Phillips' guitar producing poetical phrases which matched the group's pop art propaganda. "Our music is red with purple flashes," they said as they ceremoniously set fire to action paintings during their live performances.

for a while and an important learning process for many. It was also a time when people like Creation's Alan McGee and Acid Jazzateer Eddie Piller first flexed their creative and entrepreneurial muscles.

Contrary to popular opinion,there were even some great Mod groups around at the time, particular the Zola-quoting Purple Hearts and the Killermeters who were fronted by an extraordinary Eric Cantona clone. However you were just as likely to see Mods out buying 45s by the truly inventive groups of the time like Scars, Joy Division, Delta 5 and The Gang Of Four.

By far the best group of the time were Dexy's Midnight Runners, who were totally obsessive, very successful and very strange, and you can't get more Mod than that. Led by the heroic Kevin Rowland, Dexy's produced a series of records which for pure vision and intensity leave the likes of the first Clash LP and Side Two of Van Morrison's "Into The

Mod Icons

1. JAMES BROWN

Popularly and tediously known as "The Godfather Of Soul" in much the same way that Bruce Springsteen is known as "The Boss". James Brown was The Godfather Of Soul. And, thus, he is still revered by mods for pretty much inventing that funky, strutting Mod sound. When listening to JB, chewing gum and wearing sunglasses is almost involuntary. Lose points with your new Mod friends immediately by getting him confused with James Brown, the editor of Loaded magaz

2. WILSON PICKETT

Another soul/R&B god, whose "In The Midnight Hour" was and is a anthem. Looked cool, stayed cool. Lose points with your new Mod fri immediately by getting him confused with Flying Pickets.

3. PETE TOWNSHEND

By his own admission closer to a beatnik th a Mod – he attended art school, was midd class, drove a flash American car and smo dope – Townshend nonetheless defined M for many kids out in the provinces who cou get to the ultra-hip west London Mod clubs And, in "My Generation", "Substitute", "Anyway Anyhow Anywhere" and "The Kids Are Alright", he summed up the Mod experience perfectly.

4. STEVE MARRIOTT

Singer with The Small Faces, and possibly the greatest white soul sing history. Unlike The Who, The Small Faces were genuine 24-carat Mo and Marriott's front-room-curtains-styled centre parting is still imitate many new Mods. And Bobby Gillespie.

5. CHAS FROM "PERFORMANCE"

Sharp-suited gangster in fantastically violent Nic Roeg movie. Made in 1969, the film missed the first round of Mod, but Chas' cool threads and habit of carrying items with which he might defend himself in case of attack have found favour with the harder end of new Mod culture. Lose points with your new Mod friends immediately by getting him confused with Chas out of Chas'n'Dave.

6. DAVID HEMMINGS

Star of "Blow Up", the awesome Swinging London thriller from which Camden's new Mod nerve centre takes it name. Hemmings is popula mainly with those into late-Mod fashions (gingham shirts, Chelsea bo

Touched by the hand of
MOD

Supermod, Superficial

SARRA MANNING investigates the precious world of Mod fashion

I LOOK PRETTY YOUNG BUT I'M JUST BACKDATED

IN 1963, The Beatles invented sex. The Sixties also saw the creation of the teenager and the birth of Mod. Throughout the Fifties and Sixties, England luxuriated in a post-war economic boom. For the first time, young people had a disposable income and were desperate for something to spend it on.

There were various youth cultures, from the grease and grime of the teddy boys to the intellectual glamour of the beatniks. The Mods took elements from both of them. From the teddy boys they acquired an obsessive attention to fashion detail and from the beats came a minimalist sense of style. Merged together, the main tenet of Mod was to look sharp.

Just as the Mods pilfered from cultures, so they reacted against them. Compared to the louche flamboyance of the teddy boys, the mods rejoiced in miniaturisation. Shirt collars and trouser hems were narrow, suits were slim-fitting and hair neatly styled. They spent their shillings on the latest Italian fashion, be it clothes or scooters. Looking sharp wasn't just a question of money but a fanatical series of dos and don'ts; the wrong trouser hems could swiftly make you the object of ridicule. If they were 14 inches, then only half between hem and shoe was allowed, whereas if the swing of your pants was 15 inches, then a one inch gap was necessary. Hmmm, there couldn't have been much on telly on the Sixties.

By the time the first Mod revival happened in 1979, times were harder. Thatcher had just come into power after The Winter Of Discontent and unemployment was on the rise. These hard times was reflected in the more grubby incarnation of Mod which was an off-shoot of punk. The grubby khaki of the parka was a million miles away from the clean lines of Italian tailoring.

Pics: Joe Dilworth

WHICH MOD?

MOD this time round is a lot more complicated. After 30 years as a youth culture there is no such thing as a definitive Mod. There's your garage Mod with his pointy toe Cuban heels and psychedelic shirts; there's your Acid Jazz Mod with his sideburns and white hipsters; there's your ska mod in his slim-fit, button-down Ben Sherman and bowling shoes and your Blur Mod in his Adidas tracksuit top and trainers. Not forgetting your Mixer Mod, your R&B Mod and your Northern Soul Mod. In 1994, mod is mix and match. Even your most hardcore Mod will concede at least four different categories.

Lovable faux cockney urchins, Blur, are held responsible for the current Mod mood but rather than a cause, they're more of an effect. Mod has always been a reaction against the prevalent social style, a zeitgeist of political fashion. Just as previous Mod scenes have reflected times of either great economic wealth or disparity, Mod '94 owes its existence to what's gone before.

Grunge, with it's man-I-just-got-out-of-bed-had-a-quick-sniff-of-my-T-shirts flair and crusty's walking rubbish tip rags, may have embodied elements of hard times chic but aesthetically they're not very appealing. Mod has reacted against slacker musically and sartorially while nodding to NWONW skinny-fit sportswear and the new glam elegance. Both looks exude a certain Englishness.

Mod clothing is sharp and characterises a personal pride that's sorely lacking in flannel shirts and combat trousers. Male fashion can be so staid but Mod is a good excuse to dress up without feeling like a ponce.

Owner of Brighton Mod stylists, Jump The Gun, Adam sees the new Mod scene as a product of its time.

"Pelt's only become Mod because people are going back to traditional British values since the Stussy thing and all the American influence. People want to go much more towards British ideas and the Mod thing is just so typically English and aggressive. The Seventies revival of Mod was very different from the Sixties. This time it's very new. Also, people want music to be more political and aggressive – and it is."

HIS CLOTHES ARE LOUD, BUT NEVER SQUARE

BEFORE you throw your hands up in despair and claim you're neither political or aggressive, you just like the cut of the Mod cloth, remember that Mod means modernist. It's about looking forwards. So if a tailored mohair suit (three button of course) is going to make you feel like a recalcitrant five-year-old child dressed up for a wedding, remember that with so many Mod looks around it's easy to find something to suit your personal style and wallet. If you live in smaller towns your charity shops will be full of original Sixties gear which yo blend in with your Adidas or your crimplene. Larger tow usually have a plethora of second-hand clothes shops w you can buy freshly laundered threads. Or if you reckon your National Lottery ticket is going to hit pay dirt you ca your Mod mohair made to measure.

Fashion obsessions can always get out of hand. There a more things to life than trouser widths, but Mod isn't just hardcore purist. Jump The Gun's clientele range from thirtysomethings who are still lusting after sta-prest as w teenagers who crave the clean lines of classic English clo Mod is everywhere, from the fashion pages of Just 17 to Northern Soul all-nighters in Wigan dance halls.

"It's traditional English stuff," says Adam of his mercha "Slim-fit Ben Shermans, original Fred Perrys, Alpha Flig jackets which is more of a scooterist thing, some original shirts. We do a lot of Lonsdale as well. We're selling Ben Sherman button-down shirts for cheaper than you'd pay designer shirt. It's cut better, looks better and it is better. I education in itself wearing one of those."

Me, I'm sticking with my feather boas and false eyelash there's something about a man in a suit…

MOD FILMS/TV

"Get Carter"
"Blow Up"
"Quadrophenia" (despite Sting)
"Alfie"
"Smashing Time"
"Here We Go Round The Mulberry Bush"
"The Italian Job" (for the suits)
"A Clockwork Orange"
"If"
"Performance" (because Chas is a sharp mod)
"Pierrot Le Fou"
"The Prisoner"
"O Lucky Man"
"The Man From U.N.C.L.E."
"Randall And Hopkirk (Deceased)"
"Up The Junction"

Secret Affair

Parka Life!

If you've got this far through our Mod issue with a smirk on your face, stop. Mods may be wankers, but they're better dressed wankers than you are. But 'twas not always so. See, there's been a Mod revival before. SIMON PRICE knows. He was there. He bought the papier mâché trilby

"LOOKING good's the answer/And living by night." That's what Secret Affair proclaimed, on their Mod anthem "Time For Action". Easier said than done when you're 11, you've got f*** all money, your mum buys all your clothes and you have to be in bed by 10.

In 1979, like any other pre-teen, I was a casual fan of the big pop groups of the day: Abba, Blondie, Tubeway Army, Boney M, John Travolta, ELO, The Boomtown Rats and Sister Sledge. One night, watching "Top Of The Pops", my pop kid innocence was to end. Seven men in uncomfortably tight suits and dark glasses were doing a funny jerky elbow dance to something called "The Prince". For reasons which elude me to this day, I decided they were the best band in the world.

My descent into sickness was swift. I actually walked into a shop and bought "One Step Beyond", my first LP (as opposed to singles: this, I was sure, meant I was an adult). Several indescribably naff purchases followed: The Lambrettas, Bad Manners, The Merton Parkas. Others (The Purple Hearts, The Chords, Squire) I never actually heard, but wrote their names on my pencil case anyway. Apparently there was something called "Quadrophenia" too, but I wasn't allowed in cos it was a 15.

Skinny tie (actually an inch-wide length of ribbon with "The Beat" written on it, but you scraped that off with a biro lid – you weren't *that* naff). Yale college cardigan. Bleached stretch jeans. Braces (worn hanging round the arse). White towelling socks. Four-hole Docs. And – to cap it all – a trilby, just like the "Walt Jabsco" character on the Two Tone sleeves (by now, you owned every record on Two Tone), which was actually a seaside Kiss Me Quick hat with the slogan ripped off. Not that anyone *would* "kiss you quick" – you always hoped you'd meet a sharp-dressed Modette, but all you ever got was Shazzas in ra-ra skirts.

Worst of all was the compulsory Harrington: a black, tartan-lined bomber jacket which you armour-plated with badges: The Specials, The Jam, Mods Rule, Rude Boys. (In our school, you were allowed to be both at once, although a friend of mine was beaten up in an amusement arcade for being unable to answer the question: are you a Mod or a skin, or wot?).

Bank Holiday violence down the beach became part of local folklore. One year, a row of gleaming Lambrettas was being kicked over like dominos and set alight. In

By now, I'd also decided whose side I was on. Two Tone r weren't hits any more, but The Jam had split on a high and Weller's new Style Council were sounding good. Time for wardrobe. Shiny flying jacket covered in Northern Soul p Diamond-checked Pringles. Burgundy button-down shirts. Dogtooth sta-prests (you got your grandmother to take the – *twice* if she'd left an inch of flare). Tassled two-tone brog (never did work out how to keep the black bits black and t white bits white). I had style. I was a Mod.

This, remember, was before Sherry's, Duffer, Acupunctur Paul Smith existed. If you wanted to join a youth tribe in the Eighties, you had to make do with flimsy, plasticky mail or gear from the Melody Maker classifieds. King of the catalo was Melanddis of Carnaby Street (venue of many a pilgri on school trips to London), who made their money by look what Paul Weller was wearing on his latest record sleeve, describing it over the phone to their Taiwanese sweat shop learnt my lesson when I sent £30 for a white mac (as featu "Money Go Round"), and received, 28 days later, a lab co

Still, I made the best of it, discovered Motown, and becam incredibly sniffy and elitist about any music which didn't h "soul". I even joined the local scooter club (in fact, only one person, the hardest kid in the school, owned a scooter, and his girlfriend on day trips to Morecambe – everyone else g train), went to the discos and learnt that Wigan Casino slidey side-to-side dance. Then, on my 17th birthday, I saw The Smiths and, um, got a life. Sort of.

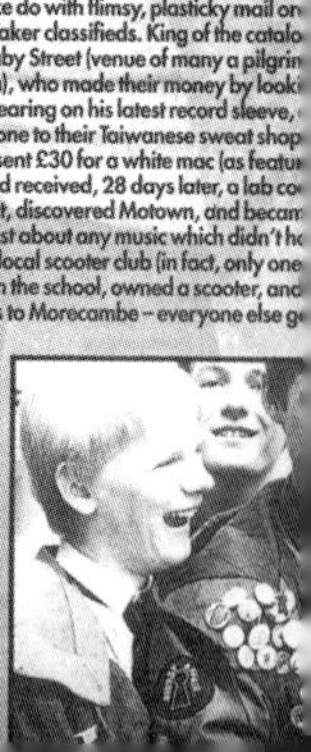

I was listening back to that Secret Affair single while writing this piece. It's a live recording, and ends with a euphoric crowd chanting "We are the Mods! We are the Mods!" But, with my

NEW SQUAD OF NEW MOD ➊

THURMAN

...man know all about indignity and hardship of musical endeavour. Guitarist Nick, his ...g brother, Simon, and drummer Diz get up ...f dawn to stack shelves in their local Boots ...s.

...he paid off, Thurman's debut single, "English

imminent and welcome demise of The Royal Family, Thurman are at pains to point out that the only English culture they truly believe in is the legacy of a golden age of British music.

"I haven't set out to sound like a south Londoner," Nick insists. "It's because I grew up listening to David Bowie, Ray Davies and The Small Faces. The biggest...

THE NEW SQUAD OF NEW MOD ➋

SAVILE ROW W1
CITY OF WESTMINSTER

MENSWEAR

...E NEW SQUAD OF NEW MOD ➌

MANTARAY

...at are Mantaray doing posing on scooters and ...g along the hallowed Mod pebbles of Brighton ...when they're a NWONW band? Sitting in a pub, ...ray smile knowingly. "We couldn't write a Mod ...we tried," demurs singer Chris. "But all the bands ...ming out of NWONW had a lot more of a Mod ...an a punk influence. Mod is about being yourself. If ...ing about Mod, it's in being yourself. To have the ...' and 'revival' in the same sentence is wrong ...s shouldn't be reviving anything, it should be ...happening now.

...ay's music has also come under the Mod ...Like that other Mod trio, The Jam, they specialise ...powered power chords and caustic lyrics.

...concedes: "Image-wise it's easy to pinpoint us ...ad but really our biggest influence is more The ...mall Faces and The Kinks. Mods have turned ...ay and they're purist Mods and they're a bit ...ed because they say we're not proper Mods ...e a bit scruffy. It's not a conscious decision to ...usic."

...re on the verge of releasing "Some Pop", their ...On the surface it's a collection of hungry pop ...lve a little deeper and something nasty's seething ...eas a lot of American bands use the recording ...alternative to getting an analyst, English pop music ...cterised by a 'pull yourself together attitude' that ...ssion fester and the music bite. Mantaray have the

sound of a band that would rip out your jugular with their incisors if you got too close. Not surprisingly for a bunch of Essex boys, their songs are obsessed with thoughts of arrogance and sex.

"If You Were A Girl" contains the chilling yet sickly seductive line, 'I started this mess/I bought you a dress', while "Closet Hetero" is not going to win them any friends. Are Mantaray fascinated by English sexual morals or are they just courting controversy?

"Those songs are about sexual fashions," says Chris. "I don't like people using sex as a fashion. That famous Brett comment inspired me to write 'Closet Hetero'. Homophobia is a very English thing but I don't think the answer is to pretend to be gay and use it as a platform. If you are gay, all well and good, then use it as a platform. But you don't have to be gay to see it from their point of view and that's what 'Closet Hetero' does."

If further proof were needed that Mantaray aren't bandwagon-jumping, then look no further than the influence of David's father on his offspring.

"When I was five my dad was ramming Elvis down my throat and saying he was the only rocker that ever lived and they'll never be a time like '56 ever again."

Chris, who blanches at this mention of The King, can't resist wrapping up the interview with a succinct sound bite.

"For the original Mods there'll never be a time like 1964 and for us there should never be a time like 1994. It's much better to create something for your era."

SARRA MANNING

LEICESTER
LAZY SUNDAYS – George's Cellar Bar, Sundays. Mod psychedelia.

LONDON
BLOW UP! – The Laurel Tree, Camden, Saturdays. Sixties to Nineties classic pop, etc.
NIGHT TRAIN – The Russell Arms, NW1, from 26 November. Two rooms playing Mod classics and rare cuts in R 'N' B, soul, ska and beat. Also live guests.
SUPER ELASTIC BUBBLE PLASTIC – The Monarch, Camden. Saturdays fortnightly. Sixties and garage disco with live bands.
SMASHING – Regent Street, Fridays. Trashy pop and live bands.
NIGHT TRAIN – Two rooms. Platform one – Mod classics

JBLE – The ... Steal House .. Maximum ...zz, soul with

...REAMS – Volks ...lays monthly. ...arage, dance. ...ACTORY – The ...ridays. Acid

...Basement, ...es Mod. ...– Gigs every ...noon. ...ND – Northern ...n – ...Northern Soul.

Monorail. Admission £4. Russell Arms, Lidlington Place, Camden NW1 First night will be Saturday 26 November.

SOUTHEND
PERIPHERY – Sacks, Fridays monthly. Sounds courtesy of Paul Tunkin (Blow Up!)

SHOPS
BRIGHTON
THE IMMEDIATE CLOTHING COMPANY, Trafalgar Street – Second-hand Mod gear
JUMP THE GUN, Gardner Street – Mod stylists. Stocks Ben Sherman, sta-prest, Lonsdale etc.
UNCLE SAMS, Sydney Street – second hand

LONDON

* Mod seems to be a southern-based kinda thang, north of Birmingham, check local listings.

FANZINES
SOMETHING HAS HIT ME
C/O Mark Raison
44 Lawrence Drive
Ickenham
Middlesex
UB10 8RW
Features on old and new bands (The Action, Brian Auger, The Stairs, etc) plus original Mod ads from the Sixties. Write for price.

EVIL EYE
Larry Grogan
3 Tulip Court, Jackson
New Jersey 08527 USA
$1. Mod newsletter

SMASHED BLOCKED

Simon Clowes & Al Richmond

Britpop proved that you could come to Mod from a different angle.

Dean Rudland

Paul Hallam: Bands like the *Stone Roses* and all that wave, certainly weren't Mods, but they were the forerunners of that Mod-*Britpop* type of look which was coming in.

Already by the mid-'90s, the media had seriously got hold of the vibe...

Stephen Twigg: *Indie* bands were listed by the *Untouchables*, at the **Night Train** in '94/'95, so they were obviously aware that what was going on was important to the scene. I used to go to the **Lava Lounge** (*Forum* - Kentish Town, Fri. night) which played a mix of '60s music - sometimes obscure, & *Indie*.

The press in '94: 'smelling' the return of Mod in the front rows of fashion...

Dave Edwards: Menswear is quite an interesting story; I remember going to **Blow Up** when it first started, in '94, at the *Laurel Tree* in Camden. There were four poor little kids, who sort of hung around together, and this was *Menswear*. They weren't actually a band. There was a guy, *Dougie*, who was a Mod, and drifted in and out of the scene over the years; he sort of started this thing that was growing up again, he got this band together, *Menswear* - they never actually played or anything, he built up this publicity surrounding this band, saying they're gonna be massive, they're friends of *Blur*, etc...

Eventually he's got this band together, four kids from *Blow Up*. That's how my girlfriend *Charlotte* got into the scene; if you look four years before, she'd gone through 'grungy', indie phase or whatever, but she'd gone to the mod thing through *Menswear*. So, through all the negative aspect of that sort of thing, there's a positive aspect; everyone's got to start somewhere and as long as people get into it, and stick with it, I'm well for it.

Maybe if I had been 15 in 1995, I would probably classified *Menswear* as a mod band, as a catalyst of getting into the scene. My girlfriend *Charlotte* would say: "At the time, I thought they were the business."

I heard that the singer of *Menswear* used to follow *The Clique*, in order to take notes about the way *Trevor* (lead singer) was dressing up... until he appeared on his publicity shots with a very similar pin striped regency jacket and the same haircut...

Touched by the hand of

MOD

Pic: Steve Gullick

Mod Life Isn't Rubbish

TAYLOR PARKES assesses the role of BLUR in the New Mod scene and finds them indirectly responsible for creating a generation of art-literate teens

BLUR, of course, aren't Mods. They're New Mod icons, sure: every time Graham Coxon steps into Blow Up, he's greeted as a homecoming hero. It's them on the peeling posters sellotaped to a million Camden bedsit walls, just above the scattered soul singles and upturned desert boots. Their audiences are filled with three-piece suits and Fred Perrys, narrow-legged boys and tight-skirted girls.

But still – whisper it – *Blur aren't Mods*. Even Graham Coxon – parka wearer and Sixties obsessive – knows as much. "The original Mods," he told a fanzine recently, "were office boys who only worked so they could afford speed and some nice clothes. That doesn't really fit in with our lifestyle."

Blur, rather than modernists, are actually POST-POST-MODERNISTS: the bulk of "Parklife" is, after all, toy music, the songs self-consciously plastic replicas of various once-glorious pop styles (these are compliments, incidentally); poised, poignant comments on the Nineties' cultural drought, quietly bubbling with a sadness that becomes explicit on the LP's two key ballads ("End Of The Century" and "This Is A Low").

But most of the kids at Blow Up haven't really thought this one out. Anyone convinced that all these Mods are genuinely sharp kiddies should dig out a recent piece in one of the glossies, in which a member of an up-and-coming Mod combo declared that, "It's really important when you're a Mod to have a good-looking girl on your arm", a teenage modette tellingly claimed she'd "always liked my dad's music", and another made a matter-of-fact announcement to the effect that Mod girls would be unwise to wear skirts "because Mod boys call you a slag" (!!!).

Blur, whatever they originally intended, are Gods of the New Mod - witness the bizarre spectacle of 500 sharp-dressed, self-consciously cool lads down at Blow Up, desperately trying to stay stylish and dance to the bouncing, gurning, impossibly uncool oompah of "Parklife" simultaneously!

The confusion is, however, easy to unravel. When Blur swapped piss-weak baggy chants for sleek, tailored pastiche- pop, they adopted a strong Sixties/Seventies look to illustrate it. The heavy DMs, shabby V-necks and tattered school shirts were hardy top Mod clobber, but look a little closer: a clearly visible parka in the "For Tomorrow" video, the Jam/Who guitar stutter all over "Modern Life Is Rubbish", the clear implications of that title spray-painted on a wall in a south coast seaside town for the accompanying photo shoot, the sleeve to their "Star Crossed" tour video (a Mod sprawled in speed-comedown agony on his narrow bed a la Jimmy in "Quadrophenia"). Mod was just one more British image to play with for the signifier-juggling art-popsters – but someone, somewhere, waiting for a Mod revival (there's always someone somewhere waiting for a Mod revival) took this as a clear signal to begin. Blur had started the scene – involuntarily.

But maybe that doesn't matter a f***. Maybe, as Kevin Pearce has pointed out, revivalism carries its own rewards. Certainly, the subsequent introduction to the achievements of a whole gallery of icons from the past makes a far better base from which to grow and develop than listening to The Wonder Stuff, smoking dope and drinking lager at the Astoria bar. The New Mods started with Blur, moved back through The Jam, The Who and The Small Faces, and, according to whispers from the frontline, are currently getting into Booker T & The MGs, James Brown, Arthur Alexander and The Temptations (as well as moving further afield and discovering Syd Barrett, Scott Walker, even Buffalo Springfield). They're reading Jean-Paul Sartre, JD Salinger and Francoise Sagan, watching the films of Godard, Roeg and Truffaut.

All this can only be a good thing. Dammit, we may even have the most art-literate generation since the mid-Sixties on our hands.

And, in a roundabout way, you can thank Blur for that.

It's A Mod, Mod, Mod, Mod World

Mods come in all shapes and sizes, from your Oasis fan to your Sixties wannabe. SARRA MANNING takes to the streets of Mod capital, Brighton, to meet the Mod multitudes

NAME: Oswald
AGE: 17
OCCUPATION: Student (income from family)
FAVOURITE CURRENT BANDS: Oasis
FAVOURITE MOD BANDS: The Jam, Small Faces
DRUGS: None
DRINK: Holsten Export

"I'm a module – it's between an indie casual and a Mod. Mod is a refined state of mind. The Mod way of dressing varies a lot from normal teenage kids. It's smarter, there's a lot of dignity to it. I get my clothes from Uncle Sam's and there's a couple of New Mod shops that have opened up. There's Merc up in London that I used to visit. I'd spend between £30 and £70 on a vintage secondhand suit. I don't like the typical Mod Fred Perrys, I'd rather have something you don't normally see."

NAME: Will Turner
AGE: 22
OCCUPATION: BR station announcer and part-time clothes shop assistant.
INCOME: £160 per week
FAVOURITE CURRENT BANDS: Comic Gain, Moloko Plus, Channel D (Mod bands)
FAVOURITE MOD BANDS: Small Faces ("they were the ultimate Mods"), The Jam.
DRUGS: Aspirin
DRINK: Vodka

"The reason I got into mod was because I saw a picture of Paul Weller and I liked his clothes and got into The Jam through that, then through them I got into The Small Faces and then into soul. I work at The Immediate Clothing Company and I get a lot of my clothes from there, plus charity shops. I rarely buy new stuff. I might go to Carnaby Street now and again but the quality's shit up there. The suit I'm wearing cost nothing but I spent £40 having it tailored. For jeans and hipsters I'd go up to about £40. When I first became a Mod about three years ago there was no one else really into it. It was clean and sharp and slightly effeminate looking, it wasn't macho."

NAME: Sean Thomas
AGE: 29
OCCUPATION: Lead singer of The Mystreated, DJ
FAVE CURRENT BAND: The Clique (London Mod band)
FAVE MOD BAND: The Creation
DRUGS: Acid
DRINK: Whisky

"I used to get a lot of my clothes from charity shops but you can't really get Sixties stuff any more. There's a lot of specialised shops in Brighton and London. I also have stuff tailor made when I've got the money. I look for authenticity really – original Sixties clothes. The thing about the Mod look is that it's really smart and there's a lot of attention to detail. People will make sure that everything is completely perfect. No, it's not sad, because that's not what it's all about. It's also the music, which is exciting and vibrant. A lot of the Mods in London who go to Blow Up seem to have got the wrong end of the stick and I'm a bit dubious about going. Mod is a collection of like-minded people and it's nice to go to a rally here or in Europe and meet up with people that you can immediately get on with because you have something in common with them.

NAME: Jane Elmsley
AGE: 20
OCCUPATION: Unemployed. Runs Colour Of Dreams (see Clubs)
FAVOURITE CURRENT BAND: Moloko Plus (Brighton Mod band)
FAVOURITE MOD BAND: John's Children
DRUGS: As many as possible
DRINK: Straight vodka

"You can look smart on the dole. I get my clothes wherever I see them. I used to get a lot of my stuff from charity shops but you don't really see much around now. I don't think women should be put off the Mod scene, there is room for them. Mod is all to do with looking sharp even if you're on the dole and you don't have much money, still having pride in what you look like. I just wear what I want to, I wouldn't wear something just because it's Mod or it's considered right to wear. They're reviving everything and it's just the latest thing to come along in, but hopefully a lot of good Mod bands will come out of it."

MOD BOOKS

Shena McKay – "Dust Falls On Eugene Schlumburger"
Kevin Pearce – "Something Beginning With 'O'"
Colin MacInnes – "Absolute Beginners"
Richard Barnes – "Mods"
Richard Allen – "Mod Rule"
Jean-Paul Satre – "Nausea"
Nik Cohn – "Another Saturday Night" (which was adapted for "Saturday Night Fever")
Jack Kerouac – "On The Road"
Allen Ginsberg – "Howl"
JD Salinger – "Catcher In The Rye"

Careless Vespa

SARRA MANNING, who you may by now have realised is pretty much The Queen Of Mod, looks at the role of scooters and Vespas in this Post-Mod malarkey

IF Mod was a category on "Family Fortunes", the top survey answer would undoubtedly be scooter. This modest, two-wheel mode of transport has become a symbol of Mod classicism and minimalism.

Tony Class of Classic Club International, which organises national Mod scooter rallies and functions, recalls the rise of the motorcycle's little bruv: "Originally we all went out and got scooters in the Sixties because they were the cheapest form of transport."

The Mods, though, with their love of detail and pride in style soon began to give the humble bike so beloved of housewives a characteristic Mod look.

"We decided to start customising our scooters to make them look smarter than average," explains Tony. "In the Sixties it was mainly lights, mirrors and crash bars. Since '79 the trend for scooters has been towards murals. Through the Eighties, murals on scooters became very, very big, although they also became very expensive to do. In the late Eighties and early Nineties the trend has gone more towards originality with both Vespas and Lambrettas; the more original it can be the better. There are models that aren't available any more."

As far as Mods are concerned there are only two makes of scooter that matter: Lambrettas, which don't exist any more, and the Vespa which is still made by the Italian firm, Piaggio. There are still 49 scooter dealers in England and in the last year their sales have started to climb steadily. Original Mod and salesman at R Agius, Claude has seen 30 years' worth of Mods onto their scooters.

"Vespa and Lambretta were the only true scooters for Mods," he says. "If you want a typical Vespa scooter of the Mod age it's going to cost £1,000 to £2,000.

"The Mod Vespa was a TS, the Lambretta was the TV or the GT200. The Vespa was still the most popular even then; there were other German scooters but the mods never really considered them."

And what does Claude think of today's breed of Mod who mix with the original article in the shop?

"The new Mods are a little on the quieter side and their dress isn't as sharp," he decides. "It looks like the gent's jackets are five times too big and they look very lacksadaisical: no shirts, no ties, hardly any collars sometimes! They were very good times. Blooming hell, when there was a stabbing it would be front page for days."

Two words – diamond geezer.

R AGIUS, 363 Edgware Road, London W2 1BS
Specialists in new and second-hand Vespas. Ask for Claude.

CLASSIC CLUB INTERNATIONAL, 42 Staveley Gardens,Chiswick, LondonW4 2SA
Any Mods wanting to attend rallies or function can write to this address for membership, which is £5 a year.

NB: Fairly good scooters can be picked up for around £200. However, if you want to save on repairs it's a good idea to get hold of a manual and do it up yourself.

THE ARCHETYPES OF MOD

THE WORKING CLASS ELEMENT.

There is a point in that. I knew some kids in the scene - top *Faces* in nightclubs - who were really proud of having minor jobs, a bit like *Jimmy* & his pals in "Quadrophenia"; Monday to Friday, 9.00 to 5.00, shit pay, no responsibilities. It's part of the whole thing, as they'd say.

I think it's a reaction that is a bit oblivious; if you've got the chance to have such good tastes, well you might as well use them intelligently, and why not end up as a major name in fashion, music & arts or in the media. Therefore there is no shame as being regarded as middle class, when your heart actually belongs to the proletarian values of this society. Mod anyway has always made me believe that we belonged to the upper class of this world, promulgating us from the bottom to the top (jumping over and avoiding the middle part), and I'm quite happy with that.

Not to mention were the people who came to the scene for a limited period only. You would spot them the next day dressed up as *Rockers* or something... having swapped their panoply for another one.

> ## I may be a waiter, but I'd go to work with a better suit than my boss.
> **Milton Astley**

THE COUPLE: Looks definitely '60s (uncannily) and so cute together. They usually hang around not far from the bar, not very inclined to communicate with other people because they are as self-sufficient as can be.

THE LONER: Normally full on *Speed*, you can often meet him at the bar where he refills his energy level with beer or *Coke*. Very smart (mohair shiny suit) & cool in his posing, he's the social entertainer that everybody knows, at least by sight.

THE TWO MATES: Guys (or gals) that always hang out together. At each party, each rally or even downtown after work, you won't see one without the other; they protect each other's back in case of an aggression fomented by *Skinheads* or *Casuals*.

Mousetrap Allnighter
Photos: Peter Roston

THE FACE: Must have been a Mod for years... and years to come. His style (clothes & conduct) is a Mod-el for anybody in the scene, and people are very proud to count him in their relations. He is one of the reasons why Mod is still alive today.

THE SKINHEAD: Normally shaves his head because he's getting slightly bald. Quite friendly, his tastes in music go for *Ska* (of course) or if not for *Northern Soul* exclusively. We are talking about a type of Mod, not the *BNP-voting/Bonehead* (who wouldn't come to our clubs anyway).

THE NEWCOMER: Very shy in the beginning, he looks around to catch ideas, and very soon starts meeting people & socialising with the scene. From the end of the 1990s onwards, his look has turned almost completely *Psychedelic*, and very often doesn't own a scooter.

the REGULAR CLUBS
In London and its vicinity

List made out of the *Untouchables* and *New Untouchables* newsletters

Some clubs lasted for ten years, some only for two months. They covered every day of the week, running monthly, fortnightly or weekly. And this is not mentioning the one-off parties that happened all the time.

A STRANGE & BLINDING EVENT

BIG

The Boston Suite, Boston Arms, Junction Road, Tufnell Park Tube, Buses 4, 10, 134, 135, C12, N1, N2)

Hits, Misses, Squarepacks & Trimes At

RELAX AND ENJOY A FREE NIGHT OUT!
EVERY SUNDAY

8- 'TIL MIDNIGHT   PUB PRICES AT THE BAR

Mildmay Tavern (Dalston)
Angel (Roehampton)
The Castle (Tooting Broadway)
Hoochie Coochie (*100 Club*)
St John's Tavern (Archway)
Mojo (*Slim Chance* -Barbican)
Copper (*Untouchables*)
Club What (*Dome*)
Gossips (*Gaz Mayall - Ska*)
Quintessence (*Psychedelic*)
60s Shakedown (Water Rats)
Mean Fiddler (Willesden)
Locomotion (Kentish Town)
Purple Turtle (Euston) became **Bedazzled** in July '94
Super Elastic Bubble Plastic Parties (*Monarch*-Camden)
Sunday Shakedown (*Water Rats* -Gray's Inn)
Blow Up (*Laurel Tree*-Camden, moved to the WAG)
Bubble Gum (*Ian Punter*-Romford)
& **Bubble Gum 2** (Barking '95...)
Magic Bus (Uxbridge)
So What (Euston)
More Than Vegas
(*St Moritz* -Wardour St)
Humpty Dump (Holborn)
Ska Bar (*Lucas Arms* -Gray's Inn)
Twist & Shout (*Rob Bailey*)
Traffic (Battersea, moved to Clapham Common in '95, then to West-End)
Smithers Soul Nite (West-End)
Get It On (West-End)
Sound Affects (Kentish Town)
R'n'B Wine Bar (Ilford)
Night Train (*Untouchables* -Camden)
Piccadilly (*Andy Lewis*)
Baby Love (Brixton)
Going Underground (West-End)
Spitfire (*Marquee* -Charing Cross)
Revolver (New Cross, moved to Gt Portland St in '97, then to Stockton in '98)

'91
'92
'93
'94
'95
'96

EVERY SUNDAY FREE   THE **BIG** CLUB   Authentic R & B Rhythm & Blues

THE BIG CLUB

EVERY SUNDAY

The **Mousetrap** has lasted since 1991 in the same venue, called successively: *Fabio's, Jaci's, Phoenix, New Orleans...*

Delegates of Soul present
ABSOLUTE BOOGALOO
We've got a brand new bag of groovy goodies and funky favourites every fortnight at London's original Hip Hammond Hangout!
Keith Moon meets Bo Diddley out on the floor for a fab blend of Soul Food and Bubblegum Breakouts.
Come shake your YaYa's to the authentic sound of swinging 7 inch kicks in an orgy of Jazzadelic Vinyl Hedonism.
THIS HAS TO BE THE ABSOLUTE BOOGALOO!
LAUNCH PARTY
FRIDAY 20th OCTOBER
(THEN 27th OCT./10th NOV.)
at
79 Oxford St., London W1.
Tottenham Court Rd Tube
9pm - 4.00am
£6 or £3 B4 11pm
pub prices (inc. draught beer)
Info line: 0171 729 2937

There were so many clubs, at some point, that you could go out almost every night.

Milton Astley: The **Bubblegum** club, organised by **Ian Punter** was in Romford, but they did a few cruises on the Thames. We would see people in other boats sitting and listening to their guide, when we would be dancing and drinking.

"Their boat looks like much more fun than ours..."

'99

Launderette allnighter (West-End)
Indigo Guy (Soho)
Get Carter
The Radioactive Camel Affair (Highbury Corner)
Da Doo Ron Ron (Highbury Corner)
Shangri-La (*Metro* -W.End)
De Rum'n'Bass (Farringdon)
MonoMedia (Camberwell)
Rollercoaster (West-End)
Homemade (Angel)
Pitstop (N.London)
Ruby Tuesday (West-End)
Je Suis Music (New Cross)
Come On Children (Ilford)
Art Gallery: **Lordy Lord** (*Clinic* -W.End)

'98

Performance (Islington)
Suss (Islington)
Hair (Islington)
Mods vs Rockers (*333* -Old St)
Pacific Bar (Camberwell)
Dirty Water (*Boston Arms* -Tufnell Pk)
Pop Corn (*P.Hallam/D.Edwards* -100Club)
Groove Tunnel (Gt Portland St)
Marmalade (Uxbridge)
Big (*Boston Arms* -Tufnell Pk)
Vincent Van Gogo (Angel)
Time Tunnel (Tufnell Pk, moved to *Wag* in '98)

'97

the CLUB SCENE in the 1990s
In the rest of Great-Britain
List made out of the *Untouchables* and *New Untouchables* newsletters

Royal George (Birmingham)
Mojo 2 (Slim Chance -Brighton)
Queen's Head (*Pid*-Manchester)
Bubblegum Factory (Brighton)
Divine (Glasgow)
Cloud Nine Beat Club
(Widnes, moves to Liverpool in '95)
Medway R'n'B (Maidstone)
became **Groovy Cellar Bar**
Lazy Sunday (Leicester)
Cellar Bar (Leicester)
Colour Dreams (Brighton)
Velvet (Liverpool)
Extraordinary Sensations
(Edinburgh)
Sunflower (Birmingham)
Reservoir Mods (Cardiff)
Duck & Dive (*Medway Aces*-Rochester)
Brighton Beach (Leeds)
A Natural Feeling (Colchester)
became **A Family Affair** in '96
Revival (Hull) became **Bass House** in '97
Basement (*Jarvis Humby* - Cleveland)
Kaleidoscope (Colchester)
Connection (Nottingham)
Junction (Sheffield)
High (Walsall)
Red Balloon (Birmingham)
Happening (Portsmouth)
became **Start**
Almost Grown (Southend)
Smarties (Brighton)
Modern World (Portsmouth)
Burton Arms (Manchester)
Understanding (Brighton)
El Pussycat (Glasgow)
Carnaby St (Manchester)
Shake Your Mini (Portsmouth)
Salisbury (Manchester)
Room 66 (Nottingham)

'94

 '95

 '96

'60s Psych & Mod (Nottingham)
Get In Touch With Your Soul (Hastings)
A Trip To Seaside (Hastings)
Roots Of A Revolution (Middlesbrough)
Birdland (Middlesbrough)
Divine (Glasgow)
Subsonic (Rochester)
Beatmaker (*Atrium*-Leeds)
Yardbird Suite (Stockton-on-Tees & Leeds)
Hideaway (Manchester)
Northern Soul Nites (Gloucester)
Modesty Blaize (*A.Croasdell* -Peterborough)
Dance Crashers (Cambridge)
Crawdaddy (Middlesborough)
Button Up (Glasgow)
became **Strawberry Fields** in '99
On The Soul Side (Bournemouth)
Club 66 (Leeds)
Soul Spectrum (Gloucester)
Move On Up (Leeds)
Lava Lounge (Leeds)
Underground Set (Bradford)
Blush (Canterbury)
The Trip (Norwich)
Robin Hood pub (Gloucester)
Crazee Daddeez (Luton)
I Was Lord Kitchener's Vallet (Portsmouth)
Uptight (Liverpool)
Shake (Manchester)
Contact High (Glasgow)
Oddin's night club (Scotland)
Brighton Beach (Sheffield & Leicester)
Soul, Ska & Scooters (Manchester)
Doug's Club Nite (Gloucester)
Total Sound (Cardiff)
Popscene (Lincoln)
Uptight (Glasgow)
Gardner's Arms (Manchester)
Modern Life (Middlesbrough)

'99

'98

'97

The 'Night Out' program from 1994 to 1995.

The clubs I used to go to were mainly the **Untouchables**' nights. From *Mousetrap* to *Night Train*...

The **100 Club** allnighter was as well, a monthly event that I wouldn't miss at the time; but you would need a lot of *Speed* in order to keep up with the party (1.00am-8.00am).

Blow Up at the *Laurel Tree* in Camden, before it moved to the *WAG*, played the best music, but was not always attended by the best crowd (Camden...).

Paul Hallam & Dave Edwards were keeping up with **The Vault Of Vibes** (which became **Popcorn** later on), at

the legendary *100 Club* on a Friday night, but it was merely a middle-aged reunion... the thing was, by the mid-'90s, the scene was seriously dying, because of a too rare new input. A new generation came around, from various backgrounds, but it never was the same, in number and in nature, as the original 'Revival' generation that came to the scene ten years before. There was a new scene coming, but that wasn't enough to take over the streets. And the attitude had changed, as well; the new Mod of the mid-'90s would never get involved into a fight, ever...

Big Beat

Sat. 7th Sept
playing
Funky Jazz
RnB
Boogaloo
Acid Soul
& other dancefloor monsters

DEEJAYS
TIM - (Absolute Boogaloo)
LYNN - (Blow Up)
ROB - (Untouchables)
+ GUEST

AT TUXEDO JUNCTION (FORMERLY SIAM CITY)
10pm - 3.30am. Admission a fiver.
NOW MONTHLY - NEXT DATES OCT 12th, NOV 2nd
A Gearhead Express Presentation

BIG BEAT

Fri June 14th
pm - 3.30am

BIG BEAT

Next dates
April 1st
April 29th

60's R & B
Soul, Beat,
Northern
etc

MARY DUNLEAVY'S
(ROYAL GEORGE, DIGBETH)
DJ'S PID & GUESTS
8pm start • £2 adm.

Caspar de la Mare: The 'Big Beat' club was in London Bridge, held by *Danny de Courtelle*, *'That Girl' Lynn*, *Tim 'Boogaloo'*.

GET LOADED 4

Starring
DJ's IAN HURFORD &
PAUL (SMILER) ANDERSON
PLUS GUEST SOUL DJ

FRIDAY OCTOBER 24th 1997
OPEN 8.30PM till 2AM

THE FINEST IN 60'S CL...
...THEN...

GET LOADED 3

Starring
DJ's IAN HURFORD &
PAUL (SMILER) ANDERSON

FRIDAY AUGUST 29th 1997
OPEN 8.30PM till 2AM

THE FINEST IN 60'S CLUB JAZZ, SOUL, R&B, FUNKY SOUNDTRACKS, AUTHENTIC MOD & ACID JAZZ,
AND HEAVY HAMMOND GROOVES. ADMISSION £3 / MAGNUMS, BASING VIEW, BASINGSTOKE.
CONTACT: LEE 01256 415751 / IAN 01256 470498

On the scene

Get Carter
Alternate Thursdays,
After Dark Club.

A VERY good friend of mine has made it his quest to collect, memorise and circulate an infinite amount of obscure music to an ever expanding circle of fellow obsessives. Dubbing himself 'The Minister of Superheavy Shake', he scours the land for unknown gems by the likes of Reuben Wilson and The Art Ensemble of Chicago; basically, anything that leaves you shakin' all over.

All this is a convoluted way to introduce the After Dark's newest night, but you'll understand when I say that 'The Minister' would be extremely at home getting down at Get Carter.

Publicity for the night promises "a wild mix of 90's britpop, 60's mod, acid jazz, northern soul, 2-tone, ska and funky soundtracks", and fails to mention the great screen onto which images from cult films flicker, included tonight are The Knack, A Clockwork Orange and, of course, Get Carter, also some cracking adverts for Vespa scooters ... God knows where they got them from but they look dead cool.

But don't be misled. If the above leads you to believe that this is a grand, blokes only knees-up, then you're way off mark. No, the ethos of Get Carter, may seem to encapsulate the essence of three generations of 'Lad', but the atmosphere is decidedly friendly with Paul and Chris really mixing things up, rather than running with one particular style.

The nicest thing about Get Carter is the fact that, despite the so-called 'mod revival', it doesn't lazily restrict itself to a six month shelf life by only playing The Who, (one song tonight) but prefers to broaden the spectrum to encompass plenty of soul, funk and wah-wah/hammond workouts. Groovy.

MICHAEL SMOUGHTON

'ISLE OF WIGHT 94'
FRIDAY 26 AUGUST
THE ACRYLIC TONES
8-2am £5:00

SATURDAY 27 AUGUST
THE JAYBIRDS
8-2am £5:00
LUNCHTIME 12-5pm ALL NEW DEE-JAYS

SUNDAY 28 AUGUST
THE AARDVARKS
7:30-1:30am £5:00
LUNCHTIME 12-3pm ALL NEW DEE-JAYS
SCOOTER COMPETITION & CRUISE 3:30pm

D.J.'s INCLUDE ROB BAILEY, CATFORD CHRIS, MICK
MARK ELLIS, PUTNEY SEAN, PID A LEE, SPEED

ALL EVENTS AT RYDE THEATRE, RYDE

Isle Of Wight - 1997 -
Photo: courtesy of Milton Astley

NO ONE STARTS AS A FULLY FLEDGED 'FACE'.
Milton Astley

Photo: **PETER ROSTON**

1991: First appearance of colour on leaflets

Various clubs in the 1990s
From top to bottom:

Suffer No Fools: **Keb Darge** & **Eon**
The monthly *Northern Soul* All-Nighter at the 100 Club: **Ady Croasdell**
The Big Club: **Alan Milliner**
Compared To What and Almost Grown: **Rob Messer**
Vault Of Vibes: **Paul Hallam** & **Dave Edwards** + Memorabilia from the first **Untouchables** rallies

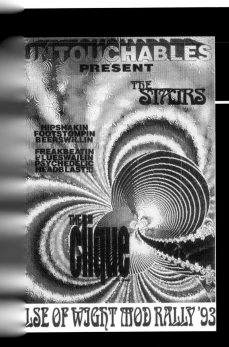

UNTOUCHABLES PRESENT
THE STAIRS

HIPSHAKIN
FOOTSTOMPIN
BEERSWILLIN
FREAKBEATIN
BLUESWAILIN
PSYCHEDELIC
HEADBLAST!!!

THE Clique

ISLE OF WIGHT MOD RALLY '93

First E.P. of The Clique - Guild records 1991
Sleeve by JON-PAUL HARPER

INTRODUCING... **THE CLIQUE**
STEREO
Guild Records

★ WHERE DID I GO WRONG? ★ THE WHOLE NIGHT THROUGH ★
★ LOOKING BACK ★ ★ TAKE HER ANYTIME ★

The Clique Mk-2
Gilles Baillarguet   Phil Otto
Chris Jordan &   Jon-Paul Harper

"Reggie" E.P. sleeve   Detour records - 1994 -
Photo FRANK NOON

The Clique were certainly the best known mod band of the 1990s, as well as the most interesting on stage.

It would be unfair to say that they were THE best mod band, because loads of other bands like **The Aardvarks** or **Skooby** were around, and well followed. But *The Clique* will definitely stay as the most popular of them all.

The Clique Mk-3:

Trevor French, Phil Otto, Matthew Braim, Jon-Paul Harper & Dom Strickland

YOU INSTANTLY FEEL KNIGHTED WHEN YOU'RE DRIVING A MACHINE OF THAT KIND...

Photos by
Steve Brown
Peter Roston
& the author.

Illustration by the author - **1994** -

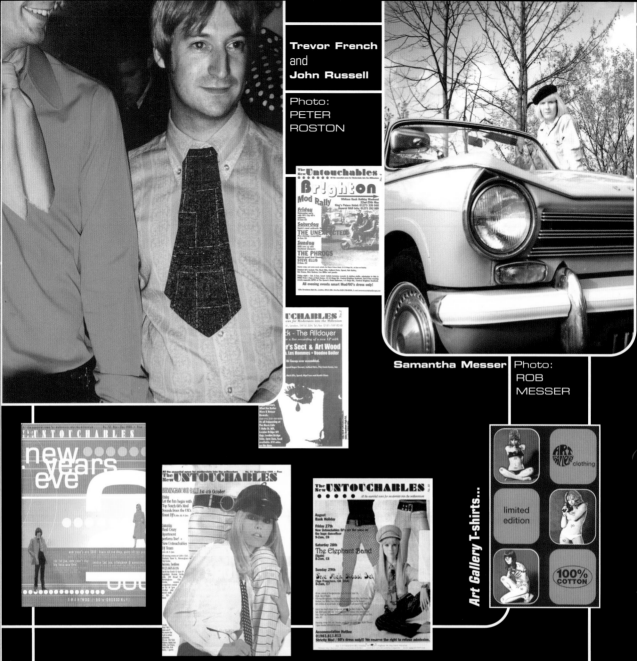

Trevor French
and
John Russell

Photo:
PETER
ROSTON

Samantha Messer | Photo: ROB MESSER

Art Gallery T-shirts...

ART GALLERY clothing

limited edition

100% COTTON

The **Mousetrap** allnighter, in Finsbury Park, was the place to go to, and to be seen at. It was entirely Mod - down to the checked floor! Everybody would dress up for that night, when you wouldn't bother too much for other nights like *Blow Up*, *Happiness Stan* or the *100 Club*. Living 'round the corner was handy, I used to be there every month. It developed onto two floors: *Psychedelia* & *British Beat* downstairs, *R'n'B* & *Jazz* upstairs. It was, in my opinion, the best night in London during all the 1990s; not for the music especially - they were playing the same tunes all the time, but for the atmosphere. It had the vibe of an authentic 1960s club.

Vincent Van Go Go

Vincent Van Gogo was a club run by **Mike 'Van Gogo',** held upstairs at the **Garage.**

Mousetrap allnighter with **Jack White** dancing in the middle and **Steph'** on the left.

Photo: PETER ROSTON

MOUSETRAP MOD ALLNIGHTER

The New Untouchables newsletter multiplied and developed over an amazing number of contacts, in England and Europe first, to the scene around the whole world. In a matter of three years, they've been printing from 2000 to 5000 copies each month (when they reached issue 13)! This newsletter, in the middle of others, has been the best designed hand-out by a long way.

Getting ready for the party - the person on the right is actually a man
Westbourne · 2000 · Photo by the author

the **Brighton Weekender** 7-8 July 2000

HIPSTERS HITS THE COAS
"For the Beatfeast Alldaye
BRIGHTON

The scene in Brighton was quite active; you had **'Scottish' Dave & Mary 'Boogaloo'** who ran a club called 'Backstreet Boogaloo', **Graeme 'Very'** who ran 'Lordy Lord' at the *Clinic* in London, **Jump The Gun** the cloth shop...

Francois **grooving at the Mousetrap**
Photo: PETER ROSTON

BACKSTREET BOOGALOO
stereo

John had promised to take her to Modesty, this weeks down payment on the scooter would just have to wait.

Milton Astley in Brighton **- 1997 -**
Photo: MARY 'BOOGALOO'

smarties
100% TUNEFUL
TAILORED BY
BACKSTREET BOOGALOO!

A GROOVY FUNK THANG!!
SATURDAY 25th SEPTEMBER 1999 THE JOINT, BRIGHTON

n my eyes, and for a lot of people that I know, Brighton has always been a 'second' London... It has also been the 'Mecca' for the mod scene since the 1960s.

Mary 'Boogaloo' - Brighton 1999 -
Photo by the author

B-right On

Paul Sawtell: I do remember walking into a pub in the West-End on the way to a club, with about ten *Faces*. We were all suited in immaculate tailored gear and razor sharp barnets. We were all carrying brollies (it had been drizzling!) We all bowled in and ordered drinks. The pub just stopped dead in admiration of us. The *Faces* that night were: *Luke Bourne* and his wife, *Milton Astley*, *'Coxy' (Steve Coxx)*, *'Irish' Pat...*

BACKSTREET BOOGALOO!

NORTHERN SOUL

100 mph STOMPERS
FUNKY GROOVERS
MELLOW FLOATERS

THURSDAY 11th MAY 1995
9 til 2am £2.00
PLUS SPECIAL GUEST DJ JOK 'NIGHT OWL' EVANS

THE VOLKS
Spirits £1.00

A TOUCH OF VENUS

A fine blend of R'nB, Tamla, Sixties Garage, Ska, Northern Soul, Soundtracks & Power Pop.

LIVE SET FROM
THE ODD NUMBERS
California's finest mod band

The Bubblegum factory

funk
jazz
Filmtrax
psychedelic
trash

Flip your wig...
At
Action A Go Go!

Every Saturday
10 -2am
Volks Tavern
madeira Drive, Brighton
£2.50/£350 non members

SMASHED BLOCKED

TOP 20
THE ACTION
CREATION
THE SPECIALS
SUPERGRASS
HAPPY MONDAYS
GOMILLA-BASS
LAMBRETTAS
'THE LAS'
JTO
BLUR
SMALL FACES
THE WHO
BOOKER T
OASIS
SECRET AFFAIR
CHARLATANS
ST ETIENNE
THE JAM
ELASTICA
'PURPLE HEARTS

NORTHERN SOUL
MOTOWN
STUDIO 1
TROJAN
BLUEBEAT
ACID JAZZ
MOWAX
60's PUNKERS
N.W.O.N.W.
X-TONE
PSYCHEDELIC
MOD REVIVAL
POWER POP
BRIGHTON POP
SKA
MERSEYBEAT
ATLANTIC
SOUNDTRAX
60's / 70's TRASH

2 X BANDS
1st BAND
ON 10:00
INFO TO
FOLLOW
LIGHTING
SHOW

DJs - *Andy Painting, The Immediate Twins, Jim Colour Dreams* & *DOBBIE*
SAT 22nd April - 9.30pm - 2am
THE RICHMOND, RICHMOND PARADE,
BRIGHTON   £3 / £2 con.
For more info, call in at The IMMEDIATE 34 Sydney Street, Brighton

A MOD IS FOR
LIFE, NOT JUST
FOR XMAS

The pub just stopped dead in admiration of us.
Paul Sawtell

The scene in *Brighton* appears on the front pages of the *Melody Maker (Nov. '94)* featuring earlier, on *page 94*. The **Backstreet Boogaloo** lot (events & fanzine) were constituted of *'Scottish' Dave* & *Mary 'Boogaloo'*, *Loz, Colin, Doug, Miles, 'Big' Jon* & *Simon Clowes*.

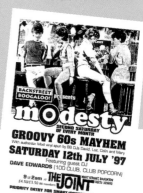

BACKSTREET BOOGALOO! presents
modesty
SECOND SATURDAY OF EVERY MONTH
GROOVY 60s MAYHEM
With authentic Mod vinyl spun by BB DJs David, Loz, Colin and Mary
SATURDAY 12th JULY '97
Featuring guest DJ
DAVE EDWARDS (100 CLUB, CLUB POPCORN)
9 til 2am at
THE JOINT
PRIORITY ENTRY FOR SMART/GROOVY 60s DRESSERS

Simon Clowes
- known as 'Mad' Simon
... top Mod from Chichester -
Photo: Rachel Harmond

It's been said that back in the 1960s, Mod originated in the West-End, but quickly spread in the East & South of London. The process seems to have repeated itself in *Revival* times, as witnessed in the previous book. Both grounds were also the home territories for two major gangs in the '60s: *Krays* & *Richardsons*. Mods were never gangsters, but you can't help to see a certain parallel between the two looks; neatly dressed, short haircut... **slick!** The best example is illustrated in the film "Performance" with *James Fox* (as well as his brother *Edward* in "Day Of The Jackal"): smart and smiling, but dangerous...

Simon Clowes: Once I was in the tube at night, going somewhere, suited & booted, seating and minding my own business, and the guy next to me said: "You look really smart; you remind me of an East-End gangster in the '60s..." he said. So I answered to him: "Pity, I ain't got my gun on me tonight"... and he freaked out! At the next station he jumped out. When you're dressed up like that, and you walk down the street going to a club or something, people usually get out of the way, because they can't work out what you are. You might get abuse from a car that is passing by in a side street, doesn't matter; you know that you like something... you might as well enjoy it.

119

Mark Raison
& Clive Roberts
promoters of the 'Orange Sunshine' club (at the Orange bar in Shoreditch) - '99/'00 - which evolved into 'Shake'...
Photo: Mark Raison

left page:

Caspar De La Mare and the author
100 Club - 1996 -
Photo:
Yann & Kim Vatiste

Mark Ralson: Most clubs to my mind are utter shite, but one that comes with a big "Something has hit me" seal of approval is Brighton's 'Bubblegum Factory'. Every Friday they play a terrific selection of '60s Psych', tons of steamy organ Jazz, a bit of Soul and Disco, as well as some new releases by the likes of *Weller* and *The Stairs*. The groovers that run the club obviously put a lot of effort to it, there are excellent lights and projections all over the place, there are films like 'Barbarella' shown on a big screen, and at Christmas there were go-go dancers, sitar players, free ice-cream, the lot!
One thing that makes the club stand out is the extremely friendly atmosphere. Although half the punters look so 1967 cool, there's none of this "Look at me, I'm so brilliant and you're so crap" attitude you nearly always get in London. Everyone just wants to have a good time and enjoy themselves dancing or just having a chat and a drink.

from 'Something Has Hit Me' fanzine -1994- (Ed. Mark Raison)

'Big Jon' Godden
Brighton - 1999 -
Photo by the author

Hastings - 1995 -
Photo by the author

I just followed *The Untouchables* around 'cos I knew their do's were always going to be good.

Paul Sawtell

The mod scene only works when everyone works together, and when it does, it's the best scene ever...
Phil Otto

There were two places I used to get my clothes from: **Caspar De La Mare** in Portobello market, who had original '60s gear (going *psychedelic* eventually), and **Mick Ferrante**, who had original stuff (pure Mod) and never worn.

When it came to tailor-made stuff, *Paul Sawtell & Leonie* introduced me to *George* (I never knew his second name), a middle-aged *Jamaican* guy living in Walthamstow, who would sew you a pair of trousers for twenty quid (!). Even in 1994/95 that was less than trousers off the peg. Of course we had to get the material first; *Bargain Centre* in Angel was the cheapest option.

I remember buying a coat from *Caspar*, one year; double breasted, B'n'W chevrons, three-quarter cut (**Hepworths** was the make)... pure 'Small Faces' gear; *Steve Marriott* would have worn that in '66. The funny thing about it, is that *Paul Weller* had come to his stall one week before, and he had spotted the coat... but it was too small for him! We obviously share the same taste for quality and stylish clothes, but thank God he's so tall (I'm still wearing that coat today).

Shopping in Birmingham with Katherine Day - **1999** -
Photo by the author

The Cavern, in the 1990s, had nothing to do with the cloth shop of the same name in Carnaby ten years before; this one was situated in Commercial Rd, specialising in late '60s/early '70s gear, quite 'dear' but always good quality, probably never worn. I must say I got quite a few things from there; original '60s *Sta-Prests*, ties...

If the white socks were the apparatus of the 1980s, by the early 1990s everybody in the scene would be spotted wearing a large white belt
The author

Milton Astley: For tailoring and made-to-measure clothes, I used to go to **Charlie**'s, who used to be still good until 1994/95. Then, as he got older, his eyes started to fail, and the trousers or suits he would make started to be a bit tight or a bit baggy. He had a guy from Hong-Kong working for him, who used to do the cutting. The first suit I had made there - blue mohair, nice hardwaring cloth - lasted me for ten or fifteen years, as far as you don't wear it too often (dry cleaning can damage it). I used to spend a lot of money, most of my wages basically.

   Katy Stephens was a tailor who used to live in a little flat near *Baker Street*. She always used to smell of whisky as far as I can remember. She was Hungarian, came to London just after the war to escape the Nazis, and she and her husband used to make shirts in the 1960s for *Georgie Fame* or *The Beatles*. She knew exactly what you wanted, she had all the patterns. She would charge £35, not including the material, but still it was fairly cheap for having a unique item.

Jump The Gun; THE Mod shop in Brighton
Photo by the author

Milton Astley and Emma Silk
who became a well-known tailor on the mod scene

Photo: Milton Astley

Real Mods don't try to be fashionable.

Mark Raison

Dean Rudland: The **PPQ** people were **Graeme Very**, **Jude**, **Dave Rabbs** who was "Hairy Diamond" - record sampling *Gladys Knight*'s "Give It Up" - and **Dave Ellis**. **Danny Hannan** (aka *Danny de Courtelle*) became a member, right at the

Peter Jackson (*Ian*'s brother) - Photo: Peter Roston

end, in 1997. Apart from *Graham*, the rest were all from the Isle Of Wight, and they all moved to London in the early 1990s. They used to run things on the Isle Of Wight; I went there DJing with *Rob Messer*, *Mace* and *Danny Hart* in 1987, called 'Cure For The Blues', which was their attempt to do a mod weekend on the island (ie. not during August bank holiday).

They started up a club called 'Hey Jude' in late '93, in a wine bar on Great Portland St, then they moved to *Eve's* on Regent St, where 'Smashing' used to be. 'Smashing' was **Martin Green**'s *Indie/Easy Listening* '60s club where all the *indie* kids used to go to, one of the birthplaces of *Britpop*. Both those clubs attracted a very similar crowd, and *Martin* & *the Karminskys* used to DJ over there, with *Jude*. Then 'Hey Jude' stopped because *Jude* went to live in Sweden, with his girlfriend.

They started a new club called 'Where's Jude?', at the end of '95. They were the best nights. Everyone who ran the club was a Mod; our first point of influence was '60s music, but we'd play anything that'd fit. It was the time when *Stereolab* had their *booggie* record out, there were loads of *French* records played, like *Jean-Jacques Perry*... so it was mixing it all up with various influences. You had new records that sounded like old, we'd play *funky* old records and '60s *Soul* & *R'n'B* records, and a bit of *Jazz* as well. The three DJs who were 'on top of the game', were myself, **Graham**, and a girl called **Emma Steele**, who was one of the best DJs I've ever played with. **'Irish' Paul** was DJing there as well; he played *E.V.A* too much, we

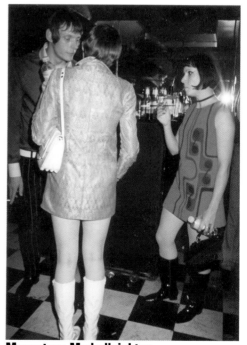

Mousetrap Mod allnighter
Photo: Peter Roston

had to ban him for that. It lasted from November '95 to the end of '96. **Percy** closed it down, and re-opened it as 'Happiness Stan'.

The crowd we used to have was very much between Mods and a trendy & *indie* art crowd. The first *PPQ* event I went to was at their HQ in Regent St (I think *Percy*'s still got the lease on it), where they had an art exhibition; they had people who became quite famous, one of them went on to win the Turner Prize...

So we were all Mods, running a very mod club, for a crowd who were a crossover between Mods and non-Mods, all in their mid-to-late twenties, probably around 120 people, full every week. It was running at the same time as 'Blow-Up', but if you were 'cooler' than 'Blow-Up' and you wouldn't go to a pure mod night like the *Untouchables* nights, then this is where you'd go.

Louise & Alex arguing again
Photo: Peter Roston

Mick Ferrante: We were talking about underpants... I don't know why, we were a few people around a table at a club, talking about that. Some prefer boxer shorts, some prefer... when suddenly, *Jude*, who was at the table with us, said: "Well, I don't wear any. Look!" And he put his trousers down, in front of us, in the middle of a pub full of people! No, he didn't wear any. We could see that. Actually, the scene almost appeared surreal to me; I couldn't believe what I was seeing. I knew that *Jude* was quite eccentric... but nothing had prepared me to see that!

Jude and **Mary 'Boogaloo'**
Photo: Nickie Divine

Caspar de la Mare: 'Do Me A Favour' was a night at the *Office Bar*, in Rathbone Place, organised by **Tim Boogaloo**, **Danny de Courtelle** & **'That Girl' Lynn**; and that was before *Easy Listening* - music for the Jet Set - became really big with the 'Blow Up' parties.

The funny thing was with *Tim Boogaloo*: he would always cross himself before dancing on a big *Northern Soul* number.

Kevin **on his Lambretta - I.O.W 1999 -**
Photo by the author

This is a man's world

The girls were the most competitive, in that scene during the early-'90s; they would stare at a newcomer if she wasn't dressed to the perfection, haircut and all... the term 'bitching' became quite appropriate in the mod world at the time.

Jayne Pountain: We did dress very manly in the late '80s. Awful! It was very strict - almost dowdy and very 'old'. Then it swung to extremes with really bright stripes and flowers - very *Pop* - then it went quite 'swinging' and 'swirly' which is where we are now really...

Milton Astley: We used to socialise together. We weren't only Mods who met in clubs, we were Mod full time. If we'd go to a barbecue, there'd all be Mods; it was a social thing as well as a fashion.

Mousetrap allnighter - Photo: Peter Roston

Guy Sissons in Carnaby Street in 2000. Sadly Guy died in October 2009
Photo by the author

Mousetrap allnighter
Photos: Peter Roston

If you look at it historically, Mod was a male invention; girls followed afterwards (trying to look like blokes). And that would explain the 'camp' thing; males wanting to compete with females, trying to charm, embellish themselves...

Women, by the late 1950s, were absolutely gorgeous; they had achieved, in terms of fashion, several centuries of evolution in order to attract the opposite sex (wonder-bra, tight waist...), so men had to find a way to become attractive as such. Effeminisation was a process that had already started at the time of *Oscar Wilde*, despite the fact that it had become associated with homosexuality. Mods didn't want that, so the best way was to create a genre, sophisticated as fuck (so to speak) but still fairly masculine.

- Al Richmond's scooter -

Photo by the author

In the next 2 pages: a story by Al Richmond

Jo from Leeds - **Brighton 1999** - Photo by the author

Al Richmond: In Canterbury, where I lived, I was one of the few Mods at school. There was a fight to be going on between all the people in my year and some rich kids, in the park. I was at the bus station, where all the Mods used to go - but I was there by myself - when all my 'supposed' friends came to pick me up for that fight. So I went over there, in this massive park called *Dane John*, and there was about 40 or 50 kids waiting for me. And they all jumped on me, even my friends - who weren't Mods - And they beat the living shit out of me. It was the one time in my life I took a serious beating. I couldn't hardly walk, so I crawled back to the bus station, and by the time I arrived there, the place was full of Mods, older than me - 25/26 years old - who recognised me and went: "Are you alright, mate? What happened? Have you been beaten up? Who's done this? Was it because you are a Mod?" And I went: "Yeah... they're all over the park". They gave me a drink of water, and we all went there like a move, like a wall. The adrenalin kicked in and we ran all over the park, beating the shit out of them. There is a wall that goes around the city, really high, and the kids were all jumping this 25ft wall to get from all these guys that I was with. It was exactly like Brighton in *Quadrophenia*, I couldn't believe it; it was the best time in my life, I was so glad that happened. The next day at school, everyone was: "All right, there?..."

From Top to Bottom:
*Andy McAvoy
*Steve Brown
- part of the Southend Mods -
Photos by the author

Steve Brown & Steve Gregory (singer of *The Impact*) **- Hastings 1999**
Photo by the author

Al Richmond: My father was a Mod, so I grew up with it around the house. A house that was never quiet; *Motown, Stax*... it was always there. I didn't know anything about it, all I know is that I loved this music, and I always used to get dressed smartly by my parents. And obviously it became a big target later on.

By the age of 12 (I was living in Kent at the time) I was pissed off 'cause all the other Mods, big brothers of my mates at school, had scooters. So I decided to borrow one of my dad's; he had an *SX 200* (same mirrors and lights I've got on my scooter now) and a *TV 175* in mint condition. Went down straight into the back of a lorry... broke my arm, collar bone, smashed my face, had a compound fracture of my little finger - which was the worst thing, it looked sickening - I was in the hospital for a long time, and when I came out, my dad said: "Are you alright son? Are you better?" I was: "Yes, I'm fine". And he beat the shit out of me, for damaging his scooter.

For a long time after that, I would freak out each time I would see a scooter, I couldn't really get into it.

London Run - 1999 - Photo by the author

To the question: "What is the most important for you, between your scooter, your clothes and your music?"
Al answered:
"It's a difficult one, but I have to say, it's the music; Mod wouldn't exist without the music behind. I need to listen to it all the time..."

Rob Messer: Talking about DJing, there are certain DJs who are only able to do a blinding set of a specific style, and I respect them a lot for that. But I never forced myself to stick to only one style; I like to play a bit of everything, *Northern Soul, R'n'B, Latin, Jazz*... because I do like a lot of different styles of music.

THE MOD TOP 100

IN NO PARTICULAR ORD

When the scene of the *Revival* years looked back to the '60s for musical influences, there were often lists of the records played in the clubs back in those halcyon days. With insight we could pick out the best of these, then delve deeper to find often more obscure but equally as good tracks by the same artists or others on the same labels and forgotten B-sides.

Many of these lists had a fair number of 'turkeys' on which may have sounded great in '64, when they were fresh, but in '84 sounded dated and boring. Also the *Northern Soul* scene, which had grown from the '60s mod scene to its commercial peak by the late '70s, had thrown up many more exciting *Soul* and *R'n'B* sides not released in the UK, which the mod scene then borrowed back.

Constant digging unearths more gems all the time, but this list is as definitive as you're likely to get from the plethora of records played in the clubs from the early '80s through to the mid-90s. This was a time when *R'n'B* & *Soul* reigned supreme with a portion of *Latin* & *Jazz* on the side, and a smattering of *British Beat*. Later in the '90s the scene would diverge further away from the original sound to encompass far more *Poppy*, *Psychedelic* and harder '60s sounds, but that's for someone else to list!

Every track here is essential for the Mod about town, and read this in twenty years' time; you still won't find a duff tune.

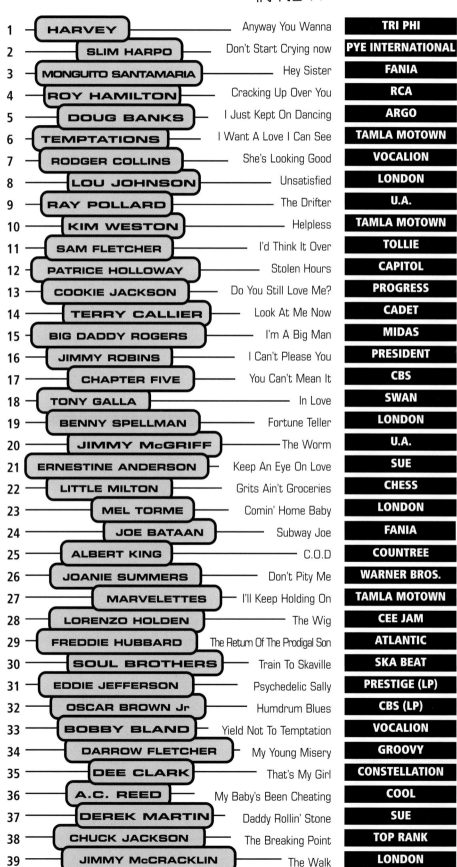

#	Artist	Title	Label
1	HARVEY	Anyway You Wanna	TRI PHI
2	SLIM HARPO	Don't Start Crying now	PYE INTERNATIONAL
3	MONGUITO SANTAMARIA	Hey Sister	FANIA
4	ROY HAMILTON	Cracking Up Over You	RCA
5	DOUG BANKS	I Just Kept On Dancing	ARGO
6	TEMPTATIONS	I Want A Love I Can See	TAMLA MOTOWN
7	RODGER COLLINS	She's Looking Good	VOCALION
8	LOU JOHNSON	Unsatisfied	LONDON
9	RAY POLLARD	The Drifter	U.A.
10	KIM WESTON	Helpless	TAMLA MOTOWN
11	SAM FLETCHER	I'd Think It Over	TOLLIE
12	PATRICE HOLLOWAY	Stolen Hours	CAPITOL
13	COOKIE JACKSON	Do You Still Love Me?	PROGRESS
14	TERRY CALLIER	Look At Me Now	CADET
15	BIG DADDY ROGERS	I'm A Big Man	MIDAS
16	JIMMY ROBINS	I Can't Please You	PRESIDENT
17	CHAPTER FIVE	You Can't Mean It	CBS
18	TONY GALLA	In Love	SWAN
19	BENNY SPELLMAN	Fortune Teller	LONDON
20	JIMMY McGRIFF	The Worm	U.A.
21	ERNESTINE ANDERSON	Keep An Eye On Love	SUE
22	LITTLE MILTON	Grits Ain't Groceries	CHESS
23	MEL TORME	Comin' Home Baby	LONDON
24	JOE BATAAN	Subway Joe	FANIA
25	ALBERT KING	C.O.D	COUNTREE
26	JOANIE SUMMERS	Don't Pity Me	WARNER BROS.
27	MARVELETTES	I'll Keep Holding On	TAMLA MOTOWN
28	LORENZO HOLDEN	The Wig	CEE JAM
29	FREDDIE HUBBARD	The Return Of The Prodigal Son	ATLANTIC
30	SOUL BROTHERS	Train To Skaville	SKA BEAT
31	EDDIE JEFFERSON	Psychedelic Sally	PRESTIGE (LP)
32	OSCAR BROWN Jr	Humdrum Blues	CBS (LP)
33	BOBBY BLAND	Yield Not To Temptation	VOCALION
34	DARROW FLETCHER	My Young Misery	GROOVY
35	DEE CLARK	That's My Girl	CONSTELLATION
36	A.C. REED	My Baby's Been Cheating	COOL
37	DEREK MARTIN	Daddy Rollin' Stone	SUE
38	CHUCK JACKSON	The Breaking Point	TOP RANK
39	JIMMY McCRACKLIN	The Walk	LONDON

Artist	Title	Label
BUD HARPER	Wherever You Were	PEACOCK
MONGO SANTAMARIA	Cloud 9	CBS
BOBBY FREEMAN	C'mon And Swim	PYE INTERNATIONAL
THE QUIK	Bert's Apple Crumble	DERAM
IRMA THOMAS	Don't Mess With My Man	SUE
BROTHER JACK McDUFF	Duffin' Around	ATLANTIC (LP)
SOUL CITY	Everybody Dance Now	CAMEO PARKWAY
ETTA JAMES & SUGAR PIE	Do I Make Myself Clear	CHESS
BRIAN AUGER	Black Cat	ATCO
DAVE BRUBECK QUARTET	Unsquare Dance	CBS
SOUL BROTHERS SIX	I'll Be Loving You	ATLANTIC
CHUCK JACKSON	Hand It Over	PYE INTERNATIONAL
BOBBY SHEEN	Dr Love	CAPITOL
BO STREET RUNNERS	Baby Never Say Goodbye	COLUMBIA
TONY CLARKE	Ain't Love Good, Ain't Love Proud	PYE INTERNATIONAL
FABULOUS PEPS	With These Eyes	WHEELSVILLE
JOHN LEE HOOKER	Think Twice Before You Go	BLUESWAY
BOOTS BROWN	Trollin'	RCA
DEAN PARRISH	Skate	STATESIDE
BO DIDDLEY	You Can't Judge A Book By The Cover	U.A.
HECTOR RIVERA	Do It To Me	BARRY
COASTERS	Love Potion No 9	PARLOPHONE
MOHAWKS	The Champ	PAMA
QUINCY JONES	Soul Bossa Nova	MERCURY
DYNAMICS	Misery	LONDON
V.I.P's	Straight Down To The Bottom	ISLAND
RAY CHARLES	I Don't Need No Doctor	HMV
JOHN MAYALL	Crawling Up A Hill	DECCA
TOM & JERRIO	Boomerang	HMV
JUNIOR WELLS	I Got A Stomach Ache	VANGUARD

	Artist	Title	Label
70	DEREK MARTIN	If You Go	SUE
71	SYLVIA ROBBINS	Don't Let Your Eyes Get Bigger Than Your Heart	SUE
72	IKE & TINA TURNER	I Can't Believe What You Say	SUE
73	GOOGIE RENE COMBO	Smokey Joe's La La	ATLANTIC
74	MAYTALS	Dog War	BLUE BEAT
75	DETROIT CITY LIMITS	98 Cents Plus Tax	OKEH
76	BROTHER JACK McDUFF	Hot Barbecue	PRESTIGE
77	Mr DYNAMITE	Sh'mon	SUE
78	JACKIE ROSS	Jerk And Twine	CHESS
79	ROGER & THE GYPSIES	Pass The Hatchet	SEVEN B
80	PRINCE & PRINCESS	Ready Steady Go	ALLADIN
81	THE CONTOURS	Can You Jerk Like Me	STATESIDE
82	NINA SIMONE	Save Me	RCA
83	MAXIMILIAN	The Snake	LONDON
84	SLIM HARPO	Baby Scratch My Back	STATESIDE
85	BILLY STEWART	Secret Love	CHESS
86	LITTLE RICHARD	Get Down With It	COLUMBIA
87	YOUNG HOLT TRIO	Ain't There Something Money Can't Buy	BRUNSWICK
88	RUFUS THOMAS	Memphis Train	STAX
89	RAY BARETTO	Soul Drummers	FANIA
90	JIMMY SMITH	The Cat	VERVE
91	JUNIOR WALKER	Hip City	TAMLA MOTOWN
92	RUSSELL BYRD	Hitch Hike	SUE
93	JOHNNY NASH	Love Ain't Nothing	PYE INTERNATIONAL
94	GUITAR RED	Just You And I	PYE INTERNATIONAL
95	HERBIE GOINS	Cruisin'	PARLOPHONE
96	DARROW FLETCHER	Pain Gets A Little Deeper	LONDON
97	SOLOMON BURKE	Stupidity	LONDON
98	LOU DONALDSON	Everything I Do Gonna Be Funky	BLUE NOTE
99	SKA KINGS	Jamaican Ska	ATLANTIC

the regency craze is back...

- from top left to bottom left:
top dancers Steph',
'Scottish Joe'
and Claire

- centre:
Gavin Evans (DJ)

- bottom centre:
Paul Owers

- right:
*Rufus
*Louise Howlett

Photos: Peter Roston

At the end of 1997, **Rob Bailey** decided to split up with the rest of **The Untouchables**, and started his own 'society': **The New Untouchables**. And suddenly, all the venues - like the Isle of Wight and other rallies around the country - got booked by the *New Untouchables*, as the old lot announced their retirement. They were at the peak of their career by then, organising most of the mod rallies in Europe as well as England. But they wrote in their newsletter: "Rob is a very very naughty boy".

Claire Strickland: *Rob's* position in the *Untouchables* had become untenable. The reasons were varied and insurmountable, but the decision to ask him to stand down was not taken lightly since we didn't want to end up with a split in the already dwindling scene. *Rob's* DJing position was not affected, it was just the administrative side.

Around this time we heard that *Rob* had set up on his own as *New Labour*, I mean **New Untouchables**.

I know for a fact that all of them were on the edge of retiring, after more than ten years of promoting, DJing and travelling all over the country; *Maz Weller* was getting engaged, as well as *Phil Otto*, *Claire* got married to *Dom Strickland*, and they most probably had enough of the busy life that is running clubs and rallies everywhere in the country and abroad, while they were still sticking to their day jobs.

THE UNTOUCHABLES PRESENT ' THEIR LAST EVER' 1999 NEW YEAR MINI RALLY

All events will take place at Churchill's Nightclub, 19-22 The Paragon, Ramsgate

Phil Otto: It was great at the beginning and as everyone felt a part of it.

Then as usual it all started to get too serious and some used the society for their own gain; and the dirty tricks and back stabbing started, this was again divisive. Although the members at the time, to their credit tried to hold it together, it eventually split again. This time I feared the scene would not be strong enough to repair itself.

Dave Edwards: *Rob Bailey*, as a promoter, learnt everything he could from **Tony Class**. He was his main DJ for years, and *Tony* taught him all the ropes of: how to run a club, and get it successful. *Rob* made loads of contacts, basically built up enough cash to put on do's. I have a lot of respect for someone who eventually involved his whole life into his passion, and works really hard at doing what he does.

LIVE ON STAGE
SMALL WORLD
Saturday Night at Brighton '98
UNTOUCHABLE

"I've got some good news and some bad news; the good news is that I'm retiring, and the bad news is Rob Bailey isn't."

SMILER

The following year, on August Bank Holiday '98, I went to Brighton. *Rob Bailey* and his *New Untouchables* were doing the Isle of Wight, but the original *Untouchables* had put up a pirate rally in Brighton on the same weekend. And by spirit of complacency, I had decided to attend, with a few friends, this rally instead of the usual I-o-W. The venue and organisation were poor, but we were there to support them anyway.

By midnight on the Saturday, the police turned up and switched the lights off; they had apparently received an anonymous letter, mentioning the presence of cocaine dealers at our party. On top of that, I'm not sure if the pub -situated far east on the seafront- had a licence to be open after 11pm...

Anyway, we all waited for the *Filth* to go away, put the music back on and danced all night. The difference was that the only drink that was available from then on was that terrible Bacardi/Coke, coming out of a dodgy bucket.

It didn't spoil the party, but everyone has always wondered who had had the idea of writing to the police...

From top to bottom:
*Rob Bailey **(I.O.W - 1999)**
*Guy Joseph **(I.O.W - 1999)**
*Colin Fribbens **(I.O.W - 2000)**

Photos by the author

Coast To Coast, club run by **DJ Cello** since the late 1990s.

Claire Strickland: Over the years, loads of Mods had been running the *Untouchables*, and people contributed what they could when they could. PUTNEY SEAN, SMILER, PHIL OTTO, HAYLEY, ROB BAILEY, MAZ WELLER (BERINI), DOM STRICKLAND, ANDY SMART, JOHN KIDD, ALAN McKEOG, JAYNE TAYLOR, CLAIRE STRICKLAND, SIMON PERSAUD, TREVOR FRENCH, PETER DEW, MAURO BERINI, MARTIN MELLORS and for a short time, FLAZ. DAVE EDWARDS also had a fair bit of input over the years.

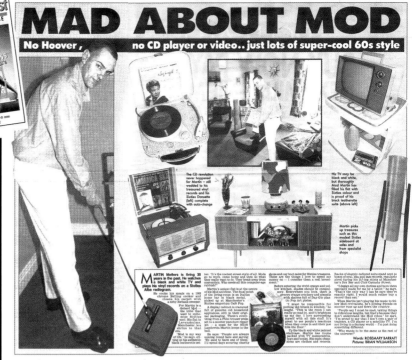

MAD ABOUT MOD
No Hoover, no CD player or video.. just lots of super-cool 60s style

MARTIN Mellors is living 30 years in the past. He watches a black and white TV and plays his vinyl records on a Sixties Alba radiogram.

He cooks his meals on a 1969 chrome Belling cooker and cleans his carpet with a nutty Ewbank sweeper.

For Martin is a diehard Mod – the tribe that used to symbolise Sixties cool. His flat in Leytonstone, Manchester, is a shrine to that era.

"Mod is my way of life," he says, sitting on his authentic black leatherette sofa. "It's the coolest street style of all. Mods go to work, come home and then do what they really want to do. They break away from convention. Who needs all this computer-age rubbish?"

Martin's unique flat is at the centre of his Mod universe. The focal point of the living-room is an Italian home bar in black metal, covered with Sixties ephemera Cash Pop.

A display cabinet is crammed full of genuine old household appliances, still in their original packaging. There's everything from a Pifco trouser press set to a scooter puncture repair kit – a must for the MX16 Lambretta Martin keeps in the hall.

He says: "People are always coming round here and saying: 'We used to have one of these. I'll spend days scouring charity shops and car boot sales for Sixties treasures. Those are the things I love to spend my money on – I consider them a real investment."

Before entering the weird orange and yellow kitchen, shades should be complusory. Everywhere you look, there is groovy orange crockery and utensils with shelves full of flop-flip plastic Sixties gear.

"I must be responsible for putting the kitsch in kitchen," he laughs. "This is the room I can really go mad in, and it brightens up my day. I love surrounding myself with all this stuff. It's great to see people's reactions when they come in and their jaw hits the floor."

Up the black and white painted staircase, Martin has rooms packed with TV memorabilia, toys and books. His main obsessions are clothes and records.

Racks of sharply-tailored suits stand next to boxes of soul, ska and jazz records, regularly aired during his DJ-ing stints at Manchester's Dry Bar and Club Carnaby Street.

"I design all my own clothes and have them specially made for me by a tailor," he says. "That's the only way I can be sure they're exactly right. I would much rather buy a record than eat."

When he's not playing his music to fellow Mod revivalists, he's joining friends on scooter runs up and down the country.

"People say I must be mad, taking things to ridiculous lengths, but that's because they don't understand the Mod ethos," he says. "I'm proud to say that I don't own a pair of trainers, a CD player or satellite TV. I'm not living in a fantasy world – I'm just doing something different.

"Who wants to be the same as the rest of the universe?"

Words: ROSEMARY BARRATT
Pictures: BRIAN WILLIAMSON

The CD revolution never happened for Martin – still wedded to his treasured vinyl records and his Sixties Dansette (left) complete with auto-change

His TV may be black and white but thoroughly Mad Martin has filled his flat with Sixties colour and a proud of his black leatherette suite (above left)

Martin picks up treasures such as this modest Sixties sideboard at sales and from specialist shops

---

Claire Strickland: There was also STEVIE J and TONY NEWMAN who had been invaluable on the ever unpopular door! There were a lot of other people who mucked in over the years to keep it all going and also the main regular DJs: DAVE EDWARDS, PID, CATFORD CHRIS, LEE, MICK.

I can definitely say that it was a real privilege to have been part of this. The people we met and the friends made, the satisfaction of the hard work paying off with a successful rally or club. It was great.

Phil Otto: To be honest, we have made **Rob Bailey**. In the beginning he was hanging around with *Gamba* (*Guy Joseph*) & *Dom Bassett*, asking for DJ slots. He was very young and persevered. **Dom Bassett** was the main DJ at the *CCI*, and when he had a tussle with **Tony Class** (they argued and split) *Rob Bailey* was there and turned back to *Tony* at the last second, who gave him the best spot. *Dom Bassett* hit him later with a brick in front of the *St John's Tavern*. It all went a bit nasty for a while; a lot of people said that they were going to split away from *'Classie'*, when they actually turned back at the last minute, and *Rob* was one of them. When we started the *Untouchables*, he just jumped ship, once again at the last minute, to be part of it. He became a runner for us. And like with *Mark Johnson*, it's the runner who eventually took the whole thing over.

Still, a lot of us carried on going to the rallies; even if *Guy Joseph* was into *Acid Jazz* in the early '90s, he would however always attend the *I-O-W* with the last scooter he'd restored.

Top: Martin Mellors (Mirror article - 1999)
Right: Catford Chris (Barcelona - 1995)
Photo: Dom Strickland

Dave Edwards: I tried to do more specialist events, like once a month rather than once a week, 'cause I find it too much hard work, really. We've done **Popcorn** at the *100 Club* with *Paul Hallam*. Doing a place like the *100 Club* every week is really hard work. People don't understand how much work goes into it. You're there for seven, eight hours, and then you have to find money. If you're forking out £1200 a week to hire a venue, it's a lot of pressure as well. So you don't really get to enjoy it.

Whereas, if you do something once a month, it's a bit more special, I think the punters enjoy it more as well. Otherwise it's easy to get stuck in a routine; you're gonna play the same tunes week in, week out. Also the rallies; you go to the rallies, four or five times a year, at the most. Some people do the seven or whatever the number it is... but if you only go to three or four of them, you're gonna have more fun, because it's more of an event.

Paul Hallam: I can't dress like a Mod, I'm too old and too fat, but you still got an air about you, you still wear a *Smedley* top, you still wear tailor-made trousers, you still wear smart boots or whatever, you still crave for a scooter. And you still get that feeling when you see maybe ten scooters down on the road, you still get that feeling in your heart.

The principle of being a Mod is to stay young.
Des Mannay

Phil Otto: So like *The Clique*, *The Untouchables* was an ideal that people saw as if it was their own. It worked until single minded people tried to control the beast, or use it to their own ends. A scene, especially the mod scene, only works when everyone works together, and when it does, it's the best scene ever…

When I first met **John Finch** - not a long time ago, he told me that he couldn't be a Mod anymore because for him, Mod was about youth. You couldn't stay a Mod as soon as you grew older, it was for him directly connected to a youth cult and nothing else. Which I disagreed with, straight away; from *Paul Hallam* to *Paul Weller*, you can decide to be a Mod all your life, and there is no shame or embarrassment about that, it's a natural thing.

Top left: **Caspar de la Mare**'s very stylish double-breasted jacket.
Top right & left: Mousetrap allnighter.
Right: **Jo** in Brighton.
Photos:
Peter Roston

Mick Ferrante: I was talking to this old Mod once, who bought me a drink in a pub, a Welsh guy. He used to come up every weekend and spend Friday night to Monday morning, when he'd be driving back to Wales for his job, pilled up. I said to him: "How did it work out? How did the mod thing go from the early '60s through to the mid-'60s and then into the *hippie* thing, how did it work? What did you do?" He said: "Look, we were of the first generation, we came into it in about '62 when it really was just starting to pick up and '63, '64, you got from 16 to 18... in '66 you were about 20 and you're going with the fashion thing because it's *Modernism*, you're just following what's happening. Of course, the mod thing died, but fashion keeps going, and if you're a Mod you go with it, so just like *The Small Faces* went from Mod to *Psychedelia* to *Hippiedom*, so did the fans, the fans followed through. Everyone was living on that same conveyor-belt." They didn't stand still, that's my whole point.

THE TWO TYPES OF **MOD**

HARD MOD: Purist, cropped hair and 3 to 5-button suit, or more casually *Ben Sherman* shirt (with chequered pattern) & tailor-made trousers. Very much like the smart 1960s *Skinhead* look, he is the closest link to the original Mod in his attitude; always 'crisp' and well-mannered, but hard as well in his conduct. Music period: 1964/66 only, always *Soul* related. Definitely working class. Called 'Soulies' by the other camp.

Isle of Wight 1999 - Photo by the author

SWIRLIES: *Swinging London* explosion; reviving the late 1960s, they left the suit for a *Regency* jacket and a pair of stripey flares. Definitely effeminate - almost camp - and coming from a more recent background with a completely different attitude; they are the reason why *Skinheads* were invented, as a reaction to it. Music period: 1967 onwards... to *1974*? *Freakbeat* & *Psychedelia*, *Hippie* & *Prog Rock* (!). Middle-class background. And so what?...

THE LOOK CHANGED DRASTICALLY BY THE END OF THE 1990s; SUITS WERE SWAPPED FOR CORDUROY FLARES & BEADS, AND THE HAIR GREW TO A 'BRIAN JONES' SHAPE.

Illustration by the author - **1999**
Based on a *Skinhead* illustration (cartoon that appeared in a French fanzine during the
1990s: two *Skinheads*, one smart and the other 'rough', watching each other
suspiciously, thinking at the same time: "Fuckin' Punk!... Fuckin' Mod!").

To assume that *Rob Bailey* is responsible for the split of the scene at the end of the 1990s, is certainly unfair. Half of the scene turned *Hippie* (*psychedelic* music & *Freakbeat*), when the other half became even more hardcore (strictly *Northern Soul* and nothing else); it was bound to happen. The scene cannot stay still; every day we're looking for new records, for new clothes... and the styles evolve from that.

The Mods of the last decade took exactly the same route as the Mods in the 1960s; we all were sharp and smart in the early '90s, and then the *Swinging London* vibe took us over, one by one around '97...

The first time I realised people were dressing more Psychedelic was at the 'Lordy Lord'.
Caspar de la Mare

Top left: **Angie** - on the left - bassist of The Surrounds
Bottom left: Mousetrap Allnighter

Right page: **Jo + The WAG**
Photos: Peter Roston

Very important were the **Blow Up** compilations that were released in the late 1990s, as a reference to proper *Lounge* music, and the work of the **Karminsky Experience** as DJs.

Commercialisation
of Mod

There was nothing more annoying than those middle-class kids, who were attending our clubs (ie. 'Blow Up' or any mod club around Camden or the West-End). They had nothing better to do than take the piss out of our clothes...

Dean Rudland: I don't think nowadays it's about a club that is Mod or non-Mod. It's about the size of the club itself, really; if you're running a club of about 100 people, the people who are going to go there are pretty much there for the music. If you're going bigger than that, then you can't get the same quality of people. As 'Blow Up' was growing bigger, 'Where's Jude?' was getting a more 'hip' crowd of people. Whereas 'Blow Up' was getting all the *Britpop* scene who were discovering this kind of *Easy Listening*, 'Where's Jude?' was attracting a more 'arty' type of crowd who knew about this music. To my mind it was a true mod club. Mixing old and new music, but always with the right attitude.

Mixing old and new music, but always with the right attitude.
Dean Rudland

Brighton New Untouchables Rally - 2000 - Photo by the author

THE KIDS ARE ALRIGHT

THERE was a time when their visits to the coast would have attracted all the wrong kind of attention.

But today's mods are more likely to attract admiring glances from people along the seafront of Weston-super-Mare.

And the stares will be more than welcomed by most mods who, like the originals, spend a fortune on their scooters and clothes to ensure they always look their sixties Sunday best.

Local club Bristol Mods is keen to keep the spirit of the sixties alive, even if, in many cases, members missed the genuine article by a good decade.

And Weston provides the perfect backdrop for their retro days out.

The original mods would flock to the seaside town on bank holidays and many of the greasy spoons and arcades have hardly changed since mod culture had its last big revival in the late 1970s.

Reinforced by the cult film *Quadrophenia* in 1979, mods have been inseparably linked with the rockers – and with violence.

But in reality, most mods would probably be too precious about their

Pictures: ANDY BUSH and GRAHAM EASTLAKE

mohair suits and Italian leather shoes to take part in punch-ups, according to Jon Drake.

Jon, one of the founders of Bristol Mods, explains: "Mods were sharp dressers. They'd spend a fortune on their suits and shoes. The look wasn't really compatible with fighting.

"The whole mods and rockers thing was just something the media latched on to, blew out of proportion and then you'd get people tagging along looking for trouble. But that wasn't what it was about."

Jon rides a £4,000 Lambretta and also owns a GS 160 Mark 1 Lambretta, an original 1960s model and "one of the top mod scooters".

Jon grew up with the lifestyle and the music.

"It all began in the late 1950s and early 1960s in the Jewish and Italian communities and the espresso bars," he revealed.

"The look is all about being individual. The scooters were all painted differently with added lights and mirrors."

● To find out more about Bristol Mods go to www.bristolmod.co.uk or contact one of the founder members Mike Pick on 0117 9574753. The society has 70 members and, between them, the largest collection of vintage scooters in the country.

epnews@bepp.co.uk

In the spotlight: Mod Nick Tolley

Standard Friday 17 August 2001 | eswheels | 5

Mods v Rockers (but this time it's friendly)

In the Sixties they fought pitched battles on Brighton seafront. Now they're all mates and still heading for the seaside at bank holiday weekend, says **Daniel Lee**

nk holiday, 1964. You're on rough Speed Twin bike ng through the ryside, an Elvis song ng in your head. The open ches ahead as you aim for with 30 like-minded friends. 've been in work a few saved every penny to be fford a leather jacket and the that will deliver incendiate

assic image that created the Rocker and gave birth of imitators who will be a similar route on classic bank holiday. "The e full of passion, from the aking bikers, later this rd racing was one of its

patrons' memorable activities.

Bikers dropped a coin into the jukebox and raced to a given point and back before the music ended. The snack bar's fame ensured that, even after closure, its site on the North Circular's junction with the Harrow Road remained the place to meet.

"There are youth clubs and there are youth cults, but you know when Rockers have arrived," says Wilmoore, who owns five classic British bikes: a Triton T66 or, Norton Commando 850cc, two 700cc Triumph Bonnevilles and a Triumph Thunderbird 650cc.

Period machines are the Rockers' favoured hardware, but many resort to more-reliable modern equivalents.

even if the bikes are not English. The Harley Davison Electra-Glide is a favourite.

Their enthusiasm may be hard to match, but Rockers will not be alone on their rides over the bank holiday. Just as they fought in the Sixties, so too will the revived retro rebels — the Mods.

Rob Bailey, 39, runs Mod revival organisation The New Untouchables and owns two scooters, a 1965 Vespa GS and a 1968 Lambretta SX. He has been a Mod since he was 15. "Bikes are OK if you like getting your hands dirty and you want to wear all that extra protection," he says. "But on a scooter you can dress up and feel good."

Mod style has a cleaner image than

the Rocker look, because earlier bikers were from a generation who could only just afford their motorcycles, let alone state-of-the-art clothes, Pete Meaden, who discovered The Who, encapsulated the idea, calling it "clean living in difficult circumstances".

Mods are also on the rise, helped by the recent popularity of scooters, such as the Vespa T5. "There are now Mods all through the country, but focused on London," says Bailey. "Being a Mod is a frame of mind. You always look for new music and try to keep ahead of the game."

Both cults have gone through numerous revivals, most notably at the end of the Seventies in the wake of The Who film *Quadrophenia*, but

their relationship has not always been easy.

In the Fifties, teenage bikers were an intimidating presence. There were stories of bike-back sexual antics and rampaging young motorcyclists. Images fuelled by films such as James Dean's Rebel Without A Cause and Marlon Brando's The Wild One, banned in mainstream British cinemas for 19 years after its mid-Fifties release.

When Mods came along in the early Sixties there was bound to be trouble. They were sharper clothes, listened to soul or rhythm and blues music. They shouted a desire to be up-to-date and upwardly mobile. No only Britishes for them.

Brighton seafront became the infamous battle ground for the two groups one mid-Sixties bank holiday. James Cooper, 92, was one of the early Rockers in the Fifties. "Many of us remembered the war and when you got on your Triumph or BSA, you felt like nothing could stop you," he says. "Everyone took notice until the Mods came along."

Each group saw themselves as the true face of the British rebel, even though, paradoxically, Rockers drew heavily on American youth images and Mods used Italian clothes and scooters. They seafront battles came about more by and distorting footage about rampaging

Consersid animosity with Rockers even helped down. "I different and Thi also made and once clashe helped. ● kit mik revolved spit the most anyone to relive the word I under interesto

rs: mods Paul and Amanda Carr of Medway Aces Scooter Club, left, and rockers Phil Woodhams and Mick Mair flank mod Steve Howard — aka Jurassic Mod

Rocker kit

g kit

, baggy parka, with a fleece lining. Mods ock.

E: They had and for own lavom, such f lipurt and own "member" tie when on biker d their cshout.

S: Plain wh ne, the modern Vespa wo Rocker has ock more affordable than the reveal of parcels you any year ocket.

Mock kit

JACKET: Mock leather, decorated in later years but if possible always from Lewis Leathers in London. A chain would be worn across the chest from the shoulder.

TROUSERS: Baggy workwear in the early years and later dungaree jeans.

BOOTS: Baf war surplus or Mark if cops.

LANGUAGE: moreorlessshut. HELMET: Pudding basin.

BIKES: 500cc Triumph Bonneville or Speed Twin or 500cc Tiger 900, Norton 650 TI, BSA 650cc, (two) Triton (a Triumph engine in Norton frame).

The Seaside Scandals Of '64

eswheels
Friday, 17 August 2001
www.eswheels.co.uk

ACE CAFE LONDON

Brighton rocks to rivals' return

By John Bedford

THEY were sworn enemies and the scourge of seaside resorts; parka-wearing, scooter-riding mods and leather-clad, motorbike-revving rockers — but this week, those who once used Brighton beach's deckchairs to hit each other are returning to sit on them, and reminisce.

The event is the biggest gathering of mods and rockers in their favourite coastal haunt since the Sixties — and not one of the 15,000 who rolled into town from London was looking for trouble.

Among them was retired security officer Steve Howard, better known as Jurassic Mod. The 53-year-old proudly declared himself a mod since 1962, through 40 years and two marriages.

He said: "I remember buying my first scooter for £1 and I was hooked from the beginning. I just wanted to be different. I loved the way the mods dressed.

"The whole thing kicked off on Whitsun Bank Holiday, 1964. A huge group of us went to Margate and the locals, mainly rockers, didn't take kindly. A bloke from the press offered us a fiver to cause trouble. Little did we know the rockers had been offered more. They started waving tenners at us and it sparked a massive punch-up." The violence was nothing to laugh about, however: Mr Howard recalled bike chains, bottles and knives being used.

But today the two groups, mellowed with age and family responsibility, are happy to exchange stories about their youth and discuss their bikes.

Cabinet maker and rocker Mick Mair, 55, who lives in Brighton, said: "It's strange seeing a lot of the faces from back then again. I suppose we will just grew out of it, although it never entirely goes away. Other things become more important. There's no trouble now, just a lot of respect."

Anyway conflict this week is unlikely: Brighton's obscure one-way system has ensured both groups are using up all their energy trying to find each other.

Jayne Pountain: I was at nearly every rally from '88 to present day... I did more than 10 *I-O-W* rallies! A bit sad though to see the turnout of Mods went from *700+* to maybe *200-300*...

ds vs Rockers See page 5

The Underground
mod society
since 1999

Dave Edwards: I think, *The Underground* have got a lot to learn. In terms of: they sort of jumped out of a frying pan into a fire. They've said: "Well, I don't like what *Rob*'s doing, I can do this better". What they've neglected to do is to try putting on a club. They've gone straight in and put on a rally and, obviously, their first one was a good do. But after that, it became a little bit complacent. They rested on their laurels and not really progressed.

Claire Strickland: The Manchester mod scene was really strong and we invited *Martin Mellors*, who had DJed at Cattolica, to do more with us. We had a new club, **Flamingo's**, where we concentrated in early *Soul* and *R'n'B* sounds and tried to get away from the *Psychedelic* sound that had become more prevalent. We carried on with the rallies in England, and also went back to Cattolica on the back of the previous year's success. But

behind the scenes we were on the receiving end of so much personal aggravation and too many sabotaged club & rally nights to make it worthwhile carrying on. The *Untouchables* was a bunch of Mods who had got involved because they had something to offer and wanted to do something for the scene. By this stage, the hardcore of us decided that we didn't have anything left to offer and we put our last do on New Year's Eve 98/99 at Ramsgate.

> **I heard some records the other night that I hadn't heard before;**

London Run -1999 -
Photo: Peter Roston

At the same time, a reaction to 'hippy' Mods was on its way, 'engineered' by the *Northern Soul* scene.

Suddenly, crowds of Mods left *Rob Bailey's* clubs to find the music they loved in the *Northern Soul* circles (from the *100 Club* allnighters to clubs in the north of England: Manchester, Stoke-on-Trent...).

The scene really broke down at this point, and the two camps nearly started to hate each other.

We were into Mod to discover new tunes, rare good records; old or new, as far as it's good, you would go and dance. But if you hear the same thing every time... I remember at an *Untouchables* rally, waiting all night for a new original & interesting track that would drag me up to the dancefloor!

you still get that old tingle up your spine.

Paul Hallam

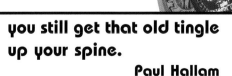

London Run -1999 -
Photo: Peter Roston

The **Art Gallery** and the **Lordy Lord** club, at the *Clinic* in Gerrard St, were run by **Graeme Very**, & **Cess** (amongst others). It became the time of the 'Rod Stewart haircut'.

Graeme 'Very' & Amy Photo by the author

The **H e a v y Load** club run by **R o b Whitmore**, is where M o d t u r n e d i n t o Hippie.

Photo: Peter Roston

V.I.P. ENTRANCE INTO CIRCLES

SMILER: I hadn't been to a Mod rally since 1995 -*Rhythm'n'Soul Set* rally organised by *Mace & Rob Messer*. Around '96, a lot of the *Acid Jazz* wave was dying out; *Jazz Hip-Hop* was getting far more into hardcore *Rap*. All the bands like *Galliano*... had gone; there wasn't a scene anymore. Around the same time, I was putting together a *Vespa GS -Mark 2- 160cc*, and decided to turn up at the Isle Of Wight on August Bank Holiday '97, with my 'pride & joy'. I can remember entering the club, I was wearing a white crew neck *Stone Island* top, black *Paul Smith* trousers - Italian mod cut - & *Patrick Cox* loafers, so I still looked very smart, modern day Mod. And I was really choked, because I'd never seen the '*Austin Powers*' type -the *swirly* type- ever, in a rally; I couldn't relate to it. I was so shocked... I knew nothing of it; I just turned up, on my *GS*, thinking I'd be getting some stick, because I was wearing modern day but still decent, designed mod clothes. I thought I looked really smart, and I couldn't believe what I saw; everyone looked so effeminate. To me, it was such a long way from when we were at '*Sneakers*', where there would still be that sort of Hard Mod image; the short crew-cut hair, the suits, the classic sort of '64 look, to being quite an effeminate *psychedelic* look. And to be honest, most of the people at this rally wouldn't have been allowed into *Sneakers*. There were, in the 1980s, some *psychedelic* people who would be seen at the *Phoenix*, like '*Psychedelic*' *Sean*; but everyone accepted him because he looked really '60s and different. You had the *Circles* club as well, run by *Alan Milliner*, in the late '80s. But it was still seen as a separate scene. We tolerated each other, basically. And that *psychedelic* lot would have hated to do anything under the mod banner; they weren't Mods.

That's the difference nowadays; a lot of things go under the mod banner, which are not specifically Mod.

> ## That's the difference nowadays; a lot of things go under the Mod banner, which are not specifically Mod.
>
> **SMILER**

HAIR: Little club in Islington, hosted by a young Mod called *Roman*.

Dylan (Brighton - 1999)
Photo by the author

The look of the mod girls changed drastically after '95. The very stylish girls used to wear suits by the late '80s; they were more masculine, and, I have to say, they were a bit more clued up than their younger counterparts. With the new arrivals during the *Britpop* wave, the skirts became shorter & shorter, with patterns that were massively influenced by the paintings of *Mondrian*...

***Mike 'Van Go-Go'**
promoter of a monthly night at the Garage (Islington)
*'**Speed**', DJ for the New Untouchables
(Carnaby St -1999)

Photos: Peter Roston

Milton Astley: Since the split of the *Untouchables*, in 1997, all the apples have been put in one basket; you haven't got the choice you had seven or eight years ago - like it or lump it. I still have a good time when I go out, it's just not so much now because of the old age, I suppose.

From top to bottom:
*Giles & Emily (I.O.W - 1999)
*Katherine Day (Birmingham - 1999)
*Graham & Sharon Simmons (I.O.W - 2000)
Photos by the author

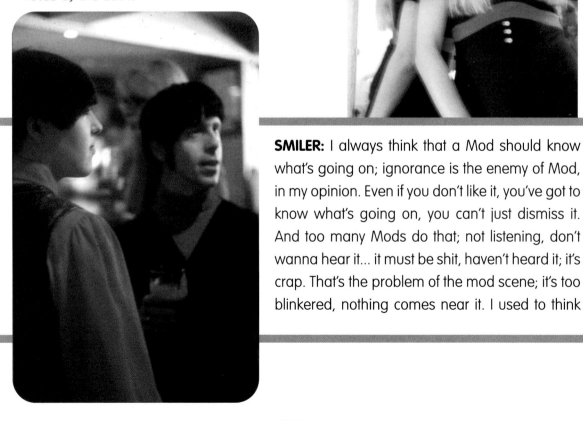

SMILER: I always think that a Mod should know what's going on; ignorance is the enemy of Mod, in my opinion. Even if you don't like it, you've got to know what's going on, you can't just dismiss it. And too many Mods do that; not listening, don't wanna hear it... it must be shit, haven't heard it; it's crap. That's the problem of the mod scene; it's too blinkered, nothing comes near it. I used to think

It was a lot better during the *Britpop* time, 'cause you had a lot more people.

Paul Hallam

60s r'n'b & garage, pop, beat and soul from Blow Up DJs and guests

£5 with this flyer!

FRIDAY 1ST OCTOBER
at **GOSSIPS**
69 DEAN STREET, SOHO W1
10pm to 3.30am

LIVE **SMASHING TIME**
GUEST DJ LEWIS (LORDY LORD)

baby **blow up**

Milton Astley: Eventually, there weren't enough people to go around; if you'd attend an *Untouchables* do once, next time you'd try a *New Untouchables* do. At the end the *Untouchables* put a Christmas party on, where hardly any-body turned up.

Milton Astley: I don't know whether the scene is dying or dead already, but it's certainly changed; I'm sure all the people that go out do it religiously, probably get-ting as much fun out of it now, as I did eight or nine years ago, maybe because they don't know any better, or because they like the way things are now. The music's certainly changed, you don't hear all the old *Motown* and classic *R'n'B* songs that people like *Rob Messer* used to play. He always used to do a brilliant set, a set for getting people up and dancing, whereas now everyone seems to be going for obscurity rather than quality and it does show.

'Welsh' Clare - Photo: Peter Roston

that way, but I left the mod scene when I started being involved in other music; I felt at the time that rather than diluting the scene, I'd walk away from it and do my own things. To me, a Modernist (in the true sense of the word) is a magpie who will steal and use the best and most sussed elements of the past and the present, and use them in a positive way to move forward.

MODS: FASHION or MOVEMENT?

Mousetrap allnighter
Photo: Peter Roston

A fashion is unanimously followed by people who don't know each other.

A movement is made of people who want to get to know each other...

Even if the 1990s looked similar to, and seemed to be a continuity of the 1980s, in fact the last decade of the millennium will appear (and stay in the future) much more revolutionary than any other decade of the twentieth century. In a matter of ten years, computers popped up absolutely everywhere, mobile phones passed over the technology of *Star Trek*... and music had come to a dead-end street.

But in terms of fashion, it is funny to come to the realization that we actually went backwards...

There are phases, though not as many and fast-changing as there were in the 1960s.

Mark Raison

I remember looking at the windows of remote boutiques around Oxford Street and Mayfair, in 1995 and seeing that the fashion was becoming the same as in the early '60s. Suddenly three-button jackets were back in every shop... big brands of the 1960s were coming back as well (*Clarks, Ben Sherman...*).

And everybody had been laughing at me - when I was in Art school five years earlier - as I was saying that it would happen!

The Mod thing has become so credible and fashionable that, personally, I find it quite laughable knowing that I went through twelve years of shit and piss taking, to now see everybody trying to dress like I do.

Dave Edwards

PSYCHEDELIC TENDENCIES

Dave Edwards: I think a lot of people feel that downstairs at the *Mousetrap*, rather than being '60s, it's more like early '70s, because of the girls; a lot of skirts and dresses that they are wearing are not '60s. A lot of it is '70s. If you watch things like "Man About The House" and it's '72, '73, you see their source of inspiration. But once again that's evolution. What is their evolution is not my evolution. Me, I'm quite happy to stay how I am.

We were badly offended when "Austin Powers" got released. We had recreated the style, and someone was taking the piss openly. *Swirlies* didn't get inspired by the 'Man of Mystery', it's rather *Mike Myers* who got inspired by the 1990s London mod scene.

Jack White - Dawn Carrington - I.O.W 1999 - Photos by the author

Skinheads in the mod scene

Suedehead at the Isle Of Wight
- 1999 -
Photos by the author

> There was a real respect towards the real Skinheads in the scene.

Seen sometimes as the real survivors of the Mod movement straight from the 1960s, the *Skinheads* and their relatives (*Suedeheads... Rude Boys*) have nevertheless suffered from a bad reputation, unlike the 'Hard Mods' who used to attend the mod clubs.

Milton Astley: The *Skinheads* have been labelled as having solidarity with the far right and the *National Front*, especially since the late '70s and the early '80s, when there was a *skinhead* revival, after the mod revival. That's when they became tainted with it - I'm sure a lot of them aren't and some of them are (that's the difference between *Skins* & *Skinheads*) - but that's the same thing with any types, whether it's football fans or music fans. In any kind of scene you will always get some people who are and some who aren't. Just because someone is a Skinhead doesn't mean that he's a fascist, but the way the media perceive it, is you get tainted with a brush even if you're not one. The use of the *Union Jack* as well, although I think it's taken the flag almost as *Pop-Art*, it's like an everyday usable object and you use it as a decoration, not a political statement.

Faces & Braces
all meet at
THE
SKA
BAR
at the
Lucas arms
grays Inn road kings cross
6t's ska reggae
and rocksteady
from your boss
d.j.s. chris & dave
plus guests
8-11pm free
September 11th / 25th

6T's REGGAE, SKA SOCIETY

Faces & Braces
all Meet at
The
SKA
Bar

LUCAS ARMS GRAYS INN RD KINGS X
CHRIS AND DAVE
Return with special
guests bringing you the
HOTTEST
SKA, ROCKSTEADY AND REGGAE
MUSIC FROM 1960'S JAMAICA
SUNDAYS 8-11
FEB 12th and 24th - -

SUNDAY AUGUST 14th
BOSS 6T's
REGGAE
SKA AND
ROCKSTEADY
AT THE
LUCAS ARMS
Grays Inn Road
Kings Cross
7.30 - 11.00pm
D.J.'s
CHRIS & DAVE + Guests

THE
3RD
SESSION
SKA+REGGAE
AT THE
PENNY BLACK
FARRINGDON RD
DJs
SPIDER JOHN
ROB MURPHY.
SEAN.
ALAN+IAN.
FRIDAY
1ST
JULY
ADMISSION 2 QUID.
STARTS
7-30 TILL 11-30

Dalston Danny
(Brighton - 2000)
Photo by the author

Skinhead Jon
Photo: Steve Hall

> The *Skinheads* are very much dedicated to their scene; you'll see them attend any Do they're invited to, and will quite often be the first ones on the dancefloor. From a mod point of view, they are the most true to their kind; their entire life is dedicated to their scene, from music to fashion...

Everybody knows **Skinhead Jon**... even *Madness* and *The Specials* know him!

I shared my flat with him for six months... quite an epic journey! He told me that joke he played on a guy one night, who was asleep at a party; he covered his hair with depilatory cream... the bloke had turned into another *Skinhead* overnight!

Dave Edwards: I used to work with an original *Skinhead* and he said that the main reason was they wanted to be like their older brothers - his older brother was a Mod, but because the nature of the mod thing being always evolving, they were evolving by having their hair shorter which was also a reaction to the *hippie* scene. So they see people growing their hair and they get theirs shorter. And it's just as the whole scene moved on. They still listened to Black dance music, *Reggae* became more important than *Tamla Motown*. So it was sort of reversing it 'round a little bit but keeping the same ideals. In that respect I would say that it was the natural continuation of it. As opposed to the *hippie* thing. It's a reaction and a continuation, if you like.

It's the business!

The ultimate guide to business in Gwent – every Tuesday in your Argus

Return of the super Scooter

Mods back in gear for sixties revival

STYLISH: Steve Power, from Newport, on a Custom-built 1961 Vespa GS

ON PARADE: Club founder member Brian Humphreys, of The Italian Job scooter shop

PROUD OWNER: Peter Hustler, from Newport, at the launch of the All Wales Mod Scooter Club, on his 1972 LI 150 Special which he rebuilt and customised himself

Pictures: **ADRIAN WHITE**

By Jane Heinich and Gareth Phillips

IT was like a scene from cult mod film Quadrophenia is scores of Vespas, Lambrettas and their sharply suited owners descended on Newport.

It was a day of classic modernist revivalism, with a ride down to Penarth pier for an afternoon of music and then it was all back to the Kings Hotel in Newport for a night of Northern soul and authentic rhythm and blues music.

Saturday marked the launch of the official All Wales Mod Scooter Club, dedicated to all things 60s.

Stow Hill in Newport looked like Brighton Pier in the 1960s as scores of revival mods met outside the Italian Job scooter shop next to St Woolos Hospital just after midday, turning the heads of shoppers.

Just before they left for Penarth, one of the founder members, Nick Tolley, said: "It's cracking. A few more have turned up than we thought."

Brian Humphreys, owner of the Italian Job and another founder member of the club, said the scooter owners were mostly from Wales but some had come from as far away as Hereford and Bristol.

"There was a need for a new mod scooter club covering the whole of Wales."

It is intended that similar events will be held regularly, and Mr Humphreys explained the appeal of the scooters – "it's just style".

One of those taking part in the rally was Peter Hustler, who was astride his 1972 Alloy 150 Special Lambretta, which he restored himself.

He said he had been into the scooters since he was a teenager. "I was just bitten by the bug," said the 46-year-old father-of-two, who lives at the Coldra, in Newport.

His youngest son, 19-year-old Ian, is now following in his father's tyre tracks.

Mr Tolley explained the 'triangle theory' behind the mod scene.

He said: "The three points represent music, clothes and scooters. If you are into any one of them, or preferably more, then get involved. Our club is open to all Welsh modernists that are still hibernating since the 60s!"

If the *Triumph Herald* was the mod car of the '80s, and the *Austin Mini* the appendage of the *Casuals*, surprisingly enough, the *Mini* became the mod car of the 1990s.

Next page, from top to bottom, clockwise:

Photos by Toski, Milton Astley, the author (how to get into the car - Hastings '92) Janine Snow and Darren Russell.

Mods & Cars

Milton Astley: I had an **Innocenti Mini-Cooper**, from 1974. *Innocenti* -the company that made the *Lambrettas*- had a licence in the '60s to make *Minis*. Fantastic looking car, went like a rocket... but when it came to repairs, you could never get any parts for it; none of the standard *Cooper* parts could fit, because they were all a few millimetres smaller.

    Luke Bourne had a red *Mini-Cooper* & *Pat Lee* had a yellow *Triumph Spitfire*; we organised a race at night, from Finsbury Park to Dalston. We started all the alarms on the cars as we passed by, because of the noise, it was hilarious.

This page:

*Lumumba
(Cartoon by **Gordon Wallace**)

*Dansette
(Modzine ed. by **Helen Barrell**)

Next page:

*Painting by **Justina Dewhurst-Richens**

Representation of a mod fruit, or personification of the mod girl? (the author)

Sharp (*Emma & Rob*)
Tailor Made (Chippenham)
Boys About Town (Scotland)
New Modernist Express (Cambs.)
Fire'n'Skill
Sawdust Caesars (Dave Edwards -London)
All Our Yesterdays (Middlesbrough)
Summer In The City (Nottingham)
Psychedelic Mushrooms (Scotland)
Promo 4 (*Paul Lobb*/Bournemouth)
Action Time (Chesterfield)
Almost Grown (London)
Groovin' (Worcester)
Jam Start! (W. Midlands)
Changing Faces (Edinburgh)
Funky Ass records (Newbury)
Kynd newsletter (Bucks.)
Call It Something Nice (Hillsborough)
Sussed (Southampton)
Brian Cant's Pants (Norfolk)
Lumumba (Birmingham-cartoon/*G. Wallace*)
Dansette (Birmingham/*Helen Barrell*)
The Modernist Review (W. Yorks.)
Do The Dog (Berks.)
Die Screaming (Leeds)
Hey Sha-Lo-Ney (Gordon Wallace/Birmingham)
Sixties Direction (Cheshire)
Circa 60 (Cambs.)
Bewitched (S. Yorks.)
On Target (W. Yorks.)
Pulped (Scotland)
Steve Ellis' Love Affair (Herts.)
Shindig (ex-**Gravedigger**/Salisbury)
Beatin' Rhythm (E. Sussex)
South East Scooter Scene (Kent)

'92

'93

'94

'95

'96

'97

'98

Modzines
in the 1990s.

Don't Wanna None -o- That Groove Thang & The Raver - Ed: SMILER
Something Has Hit Me - Ed: Mark Raison

TEN HERE

Out now!!

ginger 60

Issue 3

To receive a copy of this glorious publication send an A5 SAE to: Nikki Hirst, 9 St Michaels Road, Aldershot, Hants, GU12 4JF or email: Nikhla.Hirst@virgin.net to find out more.

Start!

THE SMART WEEKLY NEWSPAPER

No2   SATURDAY 24 SEPTEMBER 94

Published by SMART.26 Barclay Rd.Leytonstone.E.11./556 7837

SO YOU'RE SICK OF BEING CALLED A MOD

Ask any one what"Mod"means and you'll invariably get a number of different answers,from coastal fighting yobs to the coolest humans to walk on earth. The word"Mod"is an abbreviation of the word modern meaning up to date : i now. So what's so b-i   when
                                    ng.
                                  the
                                    to
                                  book
                                    or see
                                  ake.

OVER UNDER SIDEWAYS DOWN

NO 2

Backstreet Boogaloo was most certainly the best designed fanzine at the time. Editor: *M a r y 'Boogaloo'*, printed by her husband *Dave* in *Brighton*.

A.D. 2000 #1 - free

the zine for Mods, Swingers and the fancy free!

R&B LIV

LONDON'S RHYTHM AND BLUES

FREE!

INSIDE THIS ISSUE:
'G
TINGS IN AND AROUND LONDON
★
REVIEWS

WEAVER

THE TWO TONE STORY

By Ge

sussed

Issue No 1 January 199

OUT NOW

THE ULTIMATE GLOSSY ZINE AVAILABLE FROM: P. O. BOX 491 SOUTHAMPTON SO14 2XJ £2.00 + A4 SAE MAKE CHEQUES PAYABLE TO: G. WYRILL

contains: live reviews, Paul Weller, Oasis, Skooby, R'n'B, jazz, soul, singles, albums, clubs, scooters, features and loads more...

Moke Magazine (Birmingham)
New Breed ex-Modernist **Review**/ex-'60s **Direction** (W. Yorks)
The Spirit (Cheltenham)
Modern Times (Australia)
Lament For A Trapped Spy-novella (*Helen Barrell*/Birmingham)
Cat O'Nine Tails (W. Yorks.)
Fire & Skill (P. *Sawtell*/Cambridge)
Jamdown (Berks.)
Scooterist Scene (Kent)
Parade newsletter (Middx.)
Sixbeat (Lancs.)

'99

THERE ARE BUT FOUR **SMALL FACES** AND ONLY ONE BOOK

small faces the young mods forgotten story

by **PAOLO HEWITT** foreword by **KENNEY JONES**

AND ITS OUT JUNE 1995 ON **ACID JAZZ** BOOKS

£14.99

MOD! A VERY BRITISH PHENOMENON

The 1990s saw as well the arrival of books about the subjects: '60s music history, *2-Tone* & Mod culture, like never before... photographer **Rebecca Lewis** published her own book, while **Terry Rawlings** and **Paolo Hewitt** furthered their career as writers on the genre.

SEXDRUGSANDNORTHERNSOUL

Slap bang between the handbag joints and done-out boozers Britain's most enduring musical cult, Northern Soul, is alive and well. Buzz met its patrons, The Mods, Skins and Soulies, at Cardiff night Fabulous and Riverbank for a taste of the alternative on the trail of Northern Soul.

Text **Mathew Blythe** Photography **Gareth Hiscock, Roy Clark & Rob Watkins**

Hard faced men with pin-stripes or Fred Perry's populated the fringes of the dance floor at Fabulous. A handful of 60s originals moved through the 30-something throng, their finer tailor work marking them out while a lone female Skinhead weaved through the crowd. Mods and Scooterists rubbed shoulders and shared dances with skinheads; braces, crew-cuts and all. The floor was sprinkled in talcum powder to allow for slicker spins and in one corner a DJ with an immaculate pin-stripe suit kept the clientele moving with 4x4 arse kicking northern soul.
"There're loads of types here," said Lawrence Cullen, a Mod revivalist since the early 80s. "But everyone loves northern soul. It's different because there's no youth cult or underground cults any more, just us. I don't want to sound old but the youth of today just don't do it. They all look the same but here we're still dressing as individuals."
Northern Soul came to be in the late 60s when music archaeologists started digging up ghetto and obscure soul from the archives of reord companies. These rare grooves were shipped to the UK where, to break away from the Funk heavy clubs of the Soul, allnight clubs started playing it on account of its fast and regular four-four beat. Nights and faces have come and gone but essentially both Fabulous and its sister club Riverbank are just the latest generation in a family of northern soul clubs harking back 35 years. Fashions and the music have been kept alive by life-long Mods, Skinheads, Scooterists and Soulies giving Fabulous, a time-warped feel similar to the latest run of Brit flick, cockney capers.
The faces behind Fabulous include Gerry McGonagle and DJ Steve Morris, Mods from the 80s revival scene and still regulars at scooter rallies and northern soul nights around Britain. They started Fabulous two and a half years ago with the idea of bringing their scene closer to home.
"We were always going off to dances at the weekend in Manchester, Scarborough and that, but there was nothing close to home and Steve was dying to play his records somewhere louder," explained Gerry.
"Fabulous still doesn't have a regular slot because we have to put it on around the Scootering weekenders we go on."
"The scene was pretty dead before we started up in 1998," said Steve. "We used to have scooter parties with the Cougars in the 1990s (Cardiff scooter club) but they were very infrequent. We play 60% northern soul but we also play other Mod sounds like Ska and Paul Weller. I got into northern soul at the scootering weekenders we went to as kids. The best Northern Soul dos are all-nighters and we'd like to do an all-dayer around here if we can find a venue."
Fabulous' sister soul night is a bi-monthly club held in the Riverbank Hotel, Riverside, Cardiff run by the M4 Soul Club. Together they share an uneasy alliance entertaining South Wales' northern soul fans but they are by no means the same. Riverbank is a purist's night playing northern soul or nothing, its DJs, such as long-time Northern Soul man Mike Wilks, play 'newies' as opposed to the predominantly 'oldies' sets to be heard at Fabulous and its 'only the latest dug up tunes' policy has represented Cardiff as more cutting edge.
"As soon as Mike and me started Riverbank there was a buzz about getting something going at this end of the M4 again," explained Mark. "We're now searching for a venue to out on an all-nighter."
It was after a lifetime dancing at northern soul clubs and all-nighters like Wigan Casino, The 100 Club in London, The Twisted Wheel in Manchester and T in Doncaster, that Mark started his night. His introduction to northern s ical of the trip had by many music f have entered the scene's heady, tw world. The scene had more in com the outdoor raves of the late 80s an 90s than a pub disco.
"It was the most bizarre night I've e confessed the ageing groover whim met hundreds of northern soul fans service stations thanks to this bloke earlier in the evening. When we got last one it was absolutely heaving w

"I wouldn't say anyo would get hit or don over but the scene's always had very sp ways of enforcing its own rules."

with 'bags' on, playing tapes and se records. By the time we got to the c (Stars and Stripes in Yate near Brist 2am. There was a big car park and could hear the music echoing acros watch the silhouettes of these peop ning and dancing and shuffling from side. I got in and sat down and it ble head away."
At the time (1978) Mark was a punk ditched his spiky red hair and leathe for a pair of 'bags', leather shoes ar He started travelling around the cou going to as many all-nighters as he afford, learning about the scene tha

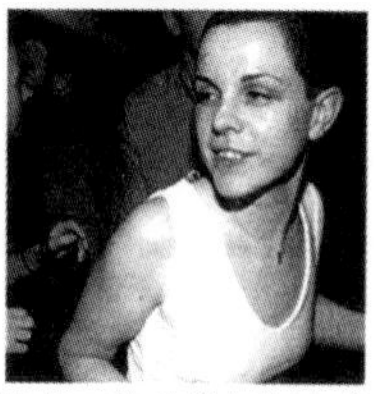

BUZZ

Free Welsh Magazine

Top Row : Fabulous, Torch Club Patch, Cardiff to Barry Charity Scooter Push 1981, the Fabulous crew.
Bottom Row : Stateside 7", Fabulous, The Legendary Cardiff Cougars 1983.

already been going for 10 years.
"The northern soul scene has got very strict, unwritten rules and one of them is the style of dancing," explained Mark. "It tends to be a shuffle from side to side with lots of foot work (feet shuffling) and fast spins. People used to be a lot harder and crueller in the old days. I wouldn't say anyone would get hit or done over but the scene's always had very special ways of enforcing its own rules. Wigan Casino had a tradition that the best dancers always occupied stage right at the front. Woe betide you if you went in there because you'd find your feet would get trodden on, just 'accidentally.' One of the best ways the scene has enforced its rules is people just stop and look. You've got to be able to take sarcasm as well; if you've bought the wrong record, if you bought it on the wrong label, if you bought a bootleg pressing thinking it was the real thing or if you bought bad gear. It's quite an elitist scene but I've always wanted people to embrace it because to me it's always been worth it."
The roots of the northern soul scene are in the Mod scene. Mods were dancing to soul and what was to become northern soul way back in the early 60s and again during the revival of the late 70s and early 80s.
Although Cardiff had little or no look-in in the 60s, fast forward to the 70s and Blackwood, Ebbw Vale, Merthyr Tydfil and Pontypridd had become the biggest centre for Northern Soul outside Northwest England. Riverbank DJ Mike Wilks found his niche when in 1974 the Skinhead discovered northern soul and left reggae and commercial soul behind:
"That year I went on holiday with my girlfriend to Torquay where we visited the Compass Club. They had four levels of dance floors with ordinary disco, funk cum commercial Soul and on the middle floor there was this other sound that fascinated my wife and I. We couldn't recognise it apart from the fours beats: very Tamla Motownesque music. And my wife was fascinated with the fashion that went with it like Oxford Bags, flat leather shoes for the boys, Hawaiian style bowling shirts and 60s dresses for the girls."
Back in South Wales Mike found Northern Soul alive and well at Tiffanies, an all-dayer, and Belinda's, which evolved into the Bierkeller just off Blackwood High Street.
"We were hit by the music straight away. I can't explain it," enthused Mike. "It was completely original. We fell in with the northern Soul community and soon we were travelling to Wigan Casino where there were thousands of people dancing all night.
"Every week there used to be a 72 seater bus travel from the Butcher's Arms in Blackwood to the Blackpool Mecca and Wigan Casino, including an individual who later became Steve Strange. He was 15 and called Steve Harrington at the time."
Mike took this newfound love home with him and started Newport's first Northern Soul night in early 1975 in The Kensington Club, Maindy, Newport. There were no northern soul clubs in Cardiff but there was the West Indian soul and reggae scene including the Casablanca and Big Windsor clubs.
"The cultures did occasionally cross," recalled Mike. "You had groups like the Q - Tips (lead singer Paul Young) and DJs like me occasionally play Casablanca and another club called the Monk's in St Albans, Newport. There were very few coloured lads into the northern soul scene. It was classed as a white scene even though it was black music. There was no problem on a racist basis."
When the Kensington Club burnt down Mike started a night in the Pink Flamingo, Newport Centre, which fell into a watery grave when a gang of punks rearranged the plumbing in the basement flooding the place. It had run tandem with a now thriving northern soul scene in a Porthcawl club night in the Stone Leigh Club but the dance floor's acrobatics forced a move to the Manor Suite, a massive venue run by the late Mark Paine and his side kicks Eddie and Nigel.
"They used to attract a massive crowd from South Wales... and I'm talking 700, 800 to 1,500 people," said Mike, whose club closed after workers from a fairground next door clashed with scooter clubs on the dance floor. "It was all coming from the Mod revival and The Scooter scene was taking northern soul as their main musically influence. The Manor Suite drove the South Wales scene up until a few years ago; they were legendary nights."
Northern Soul did not reach Cardiff until the very late 70s when the Ocean Club opened on Rover Way and was patronised by scooter clubs like The Cougars, Street Life (Pontypridd and District) and Barry Echoes. From the age of 17 Cardiff main man Richard McCarthy ran a string of Mod and Northern Soul nights in the 80s and 90s starting in 1986 in the Central Hotel, St Mary Street.
"I got into it aged 12 hanging around Central Station about 1981." There had been Mods hanging around Cardiff Central since 1979 hence their name The Station Mods. They were the Faces. "There were 150/200 Mods there every Saturday morning. It wouldn't happen today, the only thing close is football and rave cultures. By the time we were 15, 16 there were youth discos like the Embassy on Cathays Terrace (now Cathays Community Centre). On a Friday night it used to be quite a gathering place and on Saturday morning, if you went down to Garth Street we were at the old Transport Club, which is just being knocked down now. It started out as a youth club disco but by the end of it there were 200/300 Mods down there dancing to northern soul and ska.
"They were pretty close to Fabulous and Riverbank but the only hang up I have with those nights is that they are done more as a nostalgia society rather than something that's current."
Richard went onto run Mod and northern soul nights in the New Ocean Club, Rover Way (now demolished) - 200 or more scooters could be seen outside and came down from Pontypridd plus punters from Norwich, Metros, Reservoir Mods at the Riverbank Hotel, Etahplus (Sulphate) and finally Total Sound, first in Metros, then The Loop, The Emporium, The Grand Hotel and The Touca site in Westgate Street.
Here and now Mike is set to open a new Soul and Northern Soul night in Sam's Bar St Mary Street on a Thursday night.
"It won't be about nostalgia but introducin new people to the sounds of northern sou

The roots of the northern soul scene are in the Mod scene. Mods were dancing to soul and northern soul way back in the early sixties.

*** Fabulous, Dempseys, Cardiff. Saturday 10th February (9pm - midnig Tickets: £3. Info: (029) 2033 7398 www.fabulousonline.co.uk**

*** M4 Soul Club, Riverbank Hotel, Dispenser Street, Riverside Cardiff. Saturday 10th February (9pm to mid night). Tickets: £3. Info: (07771) 541**

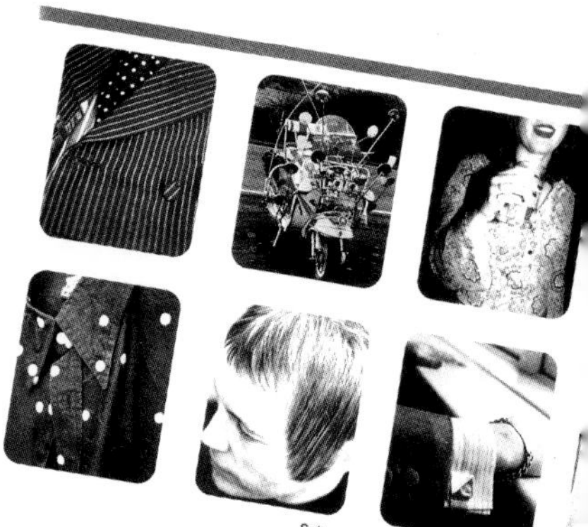

Suits (Michael's, Gloucester Road, Bristol), **Dre**
Shoes (Nick Franholis, The Arcade, Penarth) **Sh**
Haricut (Steve's Hair Studio, 3 Howell St, Cilfynydd, Po
Cuff Links (merc, London) **T**

We Are The Mods.

All you need to be a mod.... a bird, a scooter, a suit, loafers and a Paul Weller hair cut..
Photography **Jon Rizing Damp**

Speaking from an entirely personal point of view, I attended mainly gigs in the 1980s.

In the 1990s I got hard core into the London Untouchables Club scene and did the rallies.

Paul Sawtell

TREVOR FRENCH, singer of The Clique - Photo: Tina Vaughan

ROYAL ALBERT HALL
GENERAL MANAGER D CAMERON McNICOL
THE FACE OF THIS DOCUMENT HAS A COLOURED BACKGROUND
TUESDAY 4TH DECEMBER 1984
AT 1930. DOORS OPEN AT 1845.
M C R
PRESENTS:-
THE STYLE COUNCIL
PLUS SUPPORTING ATTRACTIONS
ADMIT TO:-
BALCONY 'S'
ENTER BY DOOR 5
PRICE (INC. VAT)   ROW   SEAT
574 0977 N   £6.50   6   83
THE BACK OF THIS DOCUMENT CONTAINS AN ARTIFICIAL WATERMARK
TO BE RETAINED   See Reverse

DOMINION THEATRE. Tottenham Court Rd.
M.C.P. presents—
The Style Council
plus Special Guests THE QUESTIONS
WEDNESDAY   14   Evening 7.30
MARCH   Doors open 6.45
STALLS
£5.00
L   40
Retain this portion   Licensed Bars
No Ticket Exchanged nor Money Refunded

ODEON
Hammersmith   Telephone 081-748-4081/2
Rank Theatres Limited VAT no. 425 2843 E
Please retain this portion
201040
ASGARD PRESENTS   SEATING AREA
J O H N   L E E   H O O K E R
02 X 58   7.7.90   SATURDAY   REAR-CIRCLE
BLOCK ROW SEAT   DATE   DAY   8.00   12.50
                                 TIME   PRICE

03105 DOWN   1   29   11.00
EVENT CODE SECTION/BLOCK ROW SEAT PRICE
£ 11.00   DOWNSTAIRS
SE 2.00
PRICE
DOWN   SJM PRESENTS
SECTION/BLOCK   GALLIANO
CH 1   29   NO UNDER 18 S
1   29   THE FORUM
A-TYPE   KENTISH TOWN. LONDON NW5
58546   TUE 31-MAY-94 7.00PM

Sol Entertainment presents The Radio 1 American Music Festival
MIDSUMMER BLUES
BUDDY GUY - ALBERT COLLINS + The Icebreakers
John Campbell - Pops Staples - The Mose Allison Trio
The Jimmy Smith Band with Jimmy McGriff - Terry Garland
hosted by JOHN HAMMOND
The Crystal Palace Bowl
SATURDAY 4th JULY 1992   Gates Open 12 noon
£20   PROGRAMME STARTS NOT LATER THAN 1PM   No 14832

KILBURN
NATIONAL
KILBURN HIGH RD. LONDON NW6
HARVEY GOLDSMITH ENTS by arrangement
with PRIMARY TALENT present
KRISTMAS IN KILBURN
PAUL WELLER
MOVEMENT
plus guests
OCEAN COLOUR SCENE
£10.00   TICKET NO
IN ADVANCE   02205
PRICE
WEDNESDAY 18th DECEMBER 1991
8.00 p.m.
RIGHT OF ADMISSION RESERVED
TO BE RETAINED

Terry Rawlings was right when he said that the mod scene collapsed when it stopped supporting its bands; the new mod bands, from **The Clique** to **Corduroy**, didn't get half the attention or the following from fans, unlike the **Purple Hearts** or **Secret Affair** who had benefitted from the support of thousands of people in their time. Therefore the gigs in the 1990s didn't catch the eye of the media, and this made the bands 'age' quite quickly. Anyway the charts would have retouched their image and their sound, to make them look 'acceptable' by the masses...

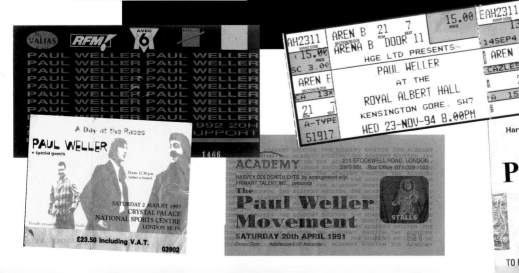

ALIAS RFM AVEC 6 BARCLAY
PAUL WELLER PAUL WELLER
PAUL WELLER PAUL WELLER
PAUL WELLER PAUL WELLER
PAUL WELLER PAUL WELLER
PAUL WELLER PAUL WELLER
PAUL WELLER PAUL WELLER
PAUL WELLER PAUL WELLER
PAUL WELLER PAUL WELLER
PAUL WELLER PAUL WELLER
992 20H
SUPPORT
1466

A Day at the Races
PAUL WELLER
+ special guests
Doors 12.30 pm
(subject to licence)
SATURDAY 2 AUGUST 1997
CRYSTAL PALACE
NATIONAL SPORTS CENTRE
LONDON SE 19
Proudly presented
£23.50 including V.A.T.
03902

15.00   EAH2311
PRICE   EVENT CODE
AH2311   AREN B   21   7   SEAT   13X
EVENT CODE SECTION/BLOCK ROW SEAT
£ 15.00   ARENA B   DOOR 11   14SEP4
SC 3.00   HGE LTD PRESENTS   SECTION
PRICE   PAUL WELLER   CAZLE590
AREN E   AT THE   AREN B
CA 13X   ROYAL ALBERT HALL   21
21   KENSINGTON GORE. SW7   15.00
ROW SEAT WED 23-NOV-94 8.00PM   7
A-TYPE   51917

071-326 4444
CREDIT CARD BOOKING
24 HOURS SEVEN DAYS

ACADEMY
HARVEY GOLDSMITH ENTS. by arrangement with
PRIMARY TALENT INT. presents
The
Paul Weller
Movement
STALLS
SATURDAY 20th APRIL 1991
Doors 7pm   Admission £10 Advance
211 STOCKWELL ROAD, LONDON
SW9.9SL   Box Office: 071-326 1022

Harvey Goldsmiths Ents and The N
A LAZY SUNDAY A
With
PAUL WE
+ FULL SUPPORT
FINSBURY P
LONDON N
SUNDAY 9TH J
GATES OPEN 11
£22.50 IN ADVANCE (SUBJE
SUBJECT TO LI
TO BE RETAINED

Dave Edwards: (continued from Vol.1) There have been three bands called **The Direction** to my knowledge; the first from Shepherd's Bush, *Tony Burke* and his brother. They became **Big Sound Authority**; had a couple of minor hits in '83, went about at the same time as *The Truth*.

There was another band - they played at the Elephant & Castle, around '86 - called *The Direction*.

The last band - *The Direction* from about '94 - was two brothers, *Carl & Paul*, I think *Paul* lives in Coventry. They've been in the mod scene since '79, and never really done something. *Paul* told me that he'd worked with *P.J. Proby*, on a cabaret circuit. They were with this guy, *Russell*, and formed this mod band: *The Direction*. *Russell* didn't last long. *Paul* went to join **In My Life Story**; He's the bassist in that band. *Carl* went to *Italy* with his wife, and has been there for about seven years.

> ## The way music was brought into the market has changed a hell of a lot since the Revival time.
> Dave Edwards

SMILER: Apart from the *Acid Jazz* bands, you had **5.30**, **The Revs**, early *Manic Street Preachers*...

The La's were pretty much an *R'n'B* band, but not looking like an *R'n'B* band. Their album is completely british *R'n'B*, and that was in 1990. Unfortunately they imploded themselves, because *Lee Mavers* (their singer/songwriter) wanted everything to be recorded on '60s equipment. Basically, big bands like *Oasis, Blur...* would have never made it if it hadn't happened for *The La's*; they broke so much ground at the time.

The reputation of the mod bands after the **Revival** period ('78/'82) was the following one: **too confined**! And the media therefore closed their eyes on anything that had the smallest connection with the '60s culture. You would never become famous if you were a mod band! You'd have to change direction...

Dave Edwards: That was another strange point; in '94, once again a few bands copped out: there was a band called **The Revs**, from Twickenham -they were linked with a sort of *grungy* band called **The Senseless Things**, who were quite good (for what they were). *The Revs* didn't look like anything 'moddy', but they had a guitar with *The Who*'s target sticker on it. They were a three-piece band like *The Jam*; they sounded like *The Jam* mixed with *The Who*. One of'em was about six foot five, skinny as fuck and curly hair. The other one, *Jake*, was a bit smarter, and they had the *Revs* logo written in a arrow -there was like black'n'white symmetry. The sound was a '79 type - really fast energetic sound. The music press would take notice as well, because they sounded like *The Buzzcocks* meet *The Jam*.

There was this little ball-rolling when *The Direction* came along; there was a little bit of rivalry there, 'cause *The Direction* were a bit suicidal, though they got on really well with *The Revs*.

Playpen
i-D's music section

Joe Smooth, Boys Wonder, Renegade Soundwave, The Cranes, Flowered Up, Deep Joy and more healthy sounds than Cynthia Payne's bedroom!

Edited by John Godfrey and Matthew Collin
Contributions from Mike Noon, Robert Yates and Ronnie Randall

Fuck Art Let's Dance
BOYS WONDER

The problem with Boys Wonder, some people say, is that they're too rock'n'roll [they're too hard to be different]. And you mean just like it when they look their shorts off on stage. Get real! Well, the news is that Boys Wonder have taken a cool check on their career trajectory to date, and decided that it's time to change tack. After half a dozen band members, three singles and 400 gigs, they have taken stock, realised that something is amiss and made their best record to date. The six track EP 'Radio Wonder', released on the 'very independent label' Flat Records, is a record bursting with ideas and influences more associated with Chaka Khan than four lads who have played 50s and '70s rock/pop more thoroughly than Tone Loc. That's right, Boys Wonder have made a dance record. "We realised that what we were doing, we were doing for our own benefit - it was something we were enjoying but nobody else was," says guitarist Scott Addison. "We looked around and saw that everybody was dancing, so we decided to start dancing too." Cold and calculated? Bloodyand commercial chameleons? Ask singer Ben Addison and he'll blurt - "You can see i-D loves Boys Wonder has sold out if you like." Actually, i-D says that the Quincy Jones and Aretha Franklin records their parents used to play down house finally triumphed over the pastiche pop. Almost. There's enough of the Gary Glitter Experience and Anthony Newley humour to appease old fans, but the riffs are pure funk. You will be surprised. "I hope people will be surprised," adds Ben. There's a lot of people out there with imaginative vibes to us. They still think we're Sham 69." Still smarting from their experience with Sires Records ("one of our biggest mistakes") Boys Wonder are wary of major label deals but still welcome sensible offers. "After all, we want as many people to hear us as possible," says Scott. "We've been too far out on a limb." Boys Wonder might have twisted their boots for dancing shoes, but don't expect to see them on the dancefloor. "Oh no, our idea of a good night out is still doing a gig," says Ben. JG

The EP 'Radio Wonder' is released on January 22 on Flat Records. They will be doing a nationwide college tour in February.

Dressed to thrill? Boys Wonder photographed by Wayne Gambino. Hair and Make-up by Michelle Rahner from Opera. Styling by George Goodman.

BEN & SCOTT ADDISON

Corduroy and **Mother Earth** used to tour together and swap headlines.

Corduroy did five studio albums, and one live recording in *Japan*. And many pirates were done after that...

Mother Earth, who were more *psychedelic*, have played with many great musicians on top of their line-up; **James Taylor**, **Graham Day** (*Prisoners*), **Gregory Isaacs**, **Kenney Jones** (*Small Faces*)... even **Paul Weller** played harmonica with them.

SMILER: The Stairs were an *R'n'B* band. **The Prime Movers** came out at the time, with **Graham Day** (*Prisoners*) & **Fay Hallam** (*Makin' Time*). **The Revs** around '92/'93 had a very big mod influence; target or arrows on their guitars, they were using a lot of the mod iconography and they definitely were linked to *The Chords, The Jam*...

SMILER: Around 1994, another band that I thought were bording on being quite Mod, were **These Animal Men**. They were getting a hell of a lot of airtime, and you could really see the Mod link in them. But unfortunately they had a big 1970s influence as well, and they ended up being quite camp. I think it came from what they were told to look like, but in their early days they had a big following; they were mentioned in 'Scootering'... they even covered "I Can't Explain".

M.C.P. PRESENTS
THESE ANIMAL MEN
Plus Special Guests
THURSDAY 20th OCTOBER 1994
L.A. 2 (LONDON ASTORIA 2)
165 Charing Cross Road, London WC2H 0EN
TICKETS £6.00 Advance
Doors Open: 7pm
R.O.A.R.   NO RE-ADMISSION
00363

JAZZ ★ FUNK ★ SOU
NITE
MONDAY 27TH DEC 93
£1.00
RING AN
ON DET AI
TO TENS
EN
8 TILL 12:0

POONTAN PRESENTS!!!!!
THE SOLID SOUND FOUNDATION
AT THE CROFTLEY ROOMS LIGHTWATER WOKING
ON MONDAY 27TH DECEMBER

THE SOLID SOUND FOUNDATION!!
LIVE AT BLADES BAR, BASINGSTOKE ICE RINK
SAT 6TH AUGUST ● TILL LATE
STOMPING DJ's ► PAUL ANDERSON KEITH PARSONS
+ SPECIAL GUESTS
SPINNING MIND NUMBING PUNK, JAZZ & RAP
£3.50 before 10.00pm
after that NO CHANCE!!!
ADMISSION FREE   8-12pm

Richard Searle: I was in the scouts when I was a kid, and my patrol leader was **Clive Jackson**, who happened to become the wacky doctor of **Doctor & The Medics**. In 1982, when the new *psychedelic* revival started, sparked by *Paul Weller* as an evolution of Mod, we did our first recording on *Wham records*. The manager of *Mood 6* decided to produce us, only for one record after which we were supposed to split up. But we kept going; we used to play at the *Clinic* (new *psychedelic* club) *Batcave* (*goth* club), and various *psychobilly* gigs... nothing else really happened. Then we helped start a club called *Alice In Wonderland*, at *Gossips*. **Alex Biankov** who was the lead singer of **The Marble Staircase** (also my scout leader) used to hang out there and later became our tour manager. The club was very popular. We got a proper manager, **Andrew King** (who used to manage *Pink Floyd*), and played there most months.

It's at that time, after the music had gone through many style trends, that it came back to *Psychedelia*. We got signed to **IRS** records. Because we had been playing to large crowds - we'd been touring with *The Damned* and *The Fuzztones* - we had a real big following composed of *Punks*, *Goths*, *Psychobillies*, *Psychedelics* and Mods. So we went into the charts, straight away. We had a No1 hit with "Spirit In The Sky" (1986). Toured the world, went to *Stringfellow's*... but we got dropped, from *IRS*, by the end of the '80s; bear in mind that at the time, our original fans went off us because we sold out. As soon as you're not in the charts anymore, the 15-year-old schoolgirls stop buying your records, and that's what mattered. Dropped!

Richard Searle: At the end of the '80s, my favourite band was **Boys Wonder**, which was managed by **Alex Biankov** (him again!). They looked cool, and their bass player - *Chris Tate*, who was very good- got sacked just before a gig where they were supporting *The Hoodoo Gurus* at the *Forum*, so I filled in. Had to learn their set for a week, did a gig at *The Marquee*. Then *Tony Barber*, from *The Buzzcocks*, took over. They sacked him, the drummer and guitarist *Graham Jones* (ex-*Haircut 100*). As *Doctor & The Medics* was near the end, I got offered to join *Boys Wonder* again. But, what they didn't tell me was that they just had been dropped by their record label *Sire* which was run by *Seymour Stein*, big name in the music industry, in 1989. Me & *Steve* (guitarist from *The Medics*), joined up in 1990, when they were at the bottom! The new drummer - **Rory Lyons** - who used to be in *King Kurt* before, got massively into *House* and *Dance* music. So after a show where we were supporting *Living In Texas* in *Paris*, the twins - **Ben** & **Scott** - decided that we were gonna rip off *Dance* music, instead of *Rock* music. *Rory* had loads of contacts, like *Cathy McGowan's* daughter. So the twins got an interview on *ITV*. Because of that publicity, *Ronnie Fowler*, big old-time manager, who saw a video of us, offered to manage the band. He liked the look of the whole group. But the twins wanted to be a duo with the rest of us as a back-up band. They turned *Ronnie* down, and that was the end of *Boys Wonder*.

But around this time, *Alex Biankov* had a night once a week called "Okey Cokey Karaoke" in a comedy club in Greenwich. He wanted a *jazz* band for New Year's Eve. That band became **Corduroy**. Now **Simon Nelson-Smith**, who I knew since I was fifteen, had a band; very nice instrumental *Jazz*. He became the guitarist. That's how we got the *Corduroy* sound together; the twins (drums & keyboards), me (bass), and *Simon's* guitar & repertoire. After a couple of gigs we worked on more material and tried to get a deal. We went to *EMI*, and **Acid Jazz**; the latter put us in a studio one week later... within a few months we had an album out; the rest is history.

CORDUROY
plus *skooby*
Friday 16th May
Followed by Dabbledoyah (11pm-4am) £3.00
£8.00 entry
£7.00 members
Alleycat Live

Loads of bands reformed - bands from the 1960s - during the 1990s; despite the flop of **The Animals** and **The Pretty Things** in the 1980s, **The Action**, **Creation**, **Yardbirds**, **Downliners Sect**, **Rupert's People**, **John's Children**... made a comeback that was well appreciated by the new Mods. Though I remember saying to *Colin Fribbens* at a rally

in Brighton, that they couldn't fit in their original trousers anymore! Still we both agreed that it was fantastic to see these guys on stage, after 30 years.

It became almost fashionable, as bands followed straight away: *Secret Affair* (as **The Affair**) came back on stage, surprisingly, as well as *Madness, Sex Pistols, Damned, Buzzcocks, Stiff Little Fingers*...

SMILER: Martin Blunt, Bass player of *The Charlatans*, was in a band - between *Makin' Time* and this band - called **The Gift Horses**, with **Graham Day**, and they used to do a cover version of "Hush" (previously covered by **The Prisoners**). **The Prime Movers** (*Graham Day & Fay Hallam*) recorded a very good version of that song. I think *Martin Blunt* just took the impetus from it, and did it with *The Charlatans* on "The Only One I Know".

The Chords reformed for an exceptional gig at the *100 Club*, organised by *Paul Hallam*, just after the I.O.W in '96. That was amazing: the queue was the longest one I'd ever seen in front of that club.

The Chords are performing now as **Pope** - **Chris Pope** with the same crazy 'T-shirt man' at the drums (**Buddy**) and the former guitarist of *The Way Out* **Matthew Wiles**, on bass - and they haven't lost their energy...

The only time I got really pissed off, is when we went to see **Brian Auger** at a *New Untouchables* club, in 2000; he didn't even bother dressing up or playing his '60s stuff. It was all new *lounge jazzy* incredibly boring middle-class shit that he was playing during the whole gig! When I think of all the people coming from all over the country to see him...

Everything turned *Flower Power*, *Swinging London*, and it started as soon as the early to mid-'90s (for *faces* like *Trevor French* or bands like *The Aardvarks*) soon followed by the rest of the scene during the later part of the decade.

The Prisoners reunion in 1996 - second concert after they split up in '85 - is for me the best gig I've ever seen in my life! *Graham Day* was playing his solos with a bottle of beer...

Dean Rudland: The Prisoners' reunion in 1994 was sparked by a listing in the *NME* as one of the great 'lost bands'.

Graham Day, after **The Prisoners** had split up, went on to forming **The Prime Movers** with *Fay Hallam* (ex-*Makin' Time* keyboard player and singer), then did an album with his new band **Planet** in 1995, and eventually formed **The Solar Flares** by the late 1990s with former *Prisoners'* bass player **Allan Crockford**.

The Aardvarks (from Ealing) were, after *The Clique*, the main band on the mod scene, at least during the first half of the 1990s.

The Aardvarks - Photo: DARREN RUSSELL

BRITPOP EXPLOSION: WHEN MOD MET CASUAL

We, as purists, never took **Oasis**, nor **Blur**, for the new wave of Mod bands when they appeared in the early '90s. We were quite impressed by the return of **Paul Weller**, even if he didn't sound the same and got the blame for becoming too 'folky'; he was at least bringing in his shade the genius of bands like **Ocean Colour Scene**, **The Bluetones**... who were closer to the sounds that we wanted to hear from new mainstream 'Mod-influenced' bands.

OASIS/BLUR: NEVER ACCEPTED BY REAL MODS

Blur and Oasis appeared at a time when the media were ready to accept only one kind of trend: **the casual image mixed with the mod image**. It was the only way to get Mod back into fashion, even if we got seriously ashamed to be associated with these two bands (though I've got some respect for Blur...). Still, it brought a lot of people to the scene, new blood that was absolutely needed, because the scene was getting older and older... the difference being that some of the new comers were not that young anymore.

Stephen Twigg: I think Britpop had a very positive impact to the Mod scene as it got a lot of people interested in music again, with some of the bands under that banner being heavily influenced by mod bands and sounds from the past. Indie clubs would play more mainstream '60s sounds, which only helped the scene get noticed.

SMILER: "The Only One I Know" -The Charlatans- was getting a lot of plays, but some of us, at the time, were pretty much into our '60s music, so we took it as an insult, a betrayal to the Mod scene. At the King's Tavern, I took the record and smashed it, and I think to this day John-Paul Harper's still got it.

SMILER: One of the best gigs I ever saw was, back in 1991, two bands that appeared on 'Band Explosion', at The Marquee in Charing Cross; Manic Street Preachers, who sounded quite punky at the time - a bit like The Jam - and **5.30** - they were from Oxford - who had been previously a mod band. I had seen them in a rally in Clacton in 1984; absolutely appalling, they sounded like a Jam tribute band. But 5.30, as a band who had mod influences, who progressed through bits of Funk, bits of Manchester sound, became a fantastic band. They used to support Slow Dive, who were part of the shoe gazing trend - which was getting quite big at the time. But we would go to see 5.30, who had this little introduction to their gig; they would always come on stage with Alastair Crowley's front door. They got extremely good reviews, were compared to The Who, and suddenly their drummer decided to go back to college... and they seemed to fade.

Dave Edwards: If you look back to, say 77: a lot of people nowadays say that *Eddie & The Hot Rods*, "Do Anything You Wanna Do" is a really early mod record. I go along with that; I think *The Revs* were that sort of equivalent: a little bit before their time. You look two years later, *Blur & Oasis* made it really big; they're using the mod thing, because being a mod band is being cool again.

THE REVS

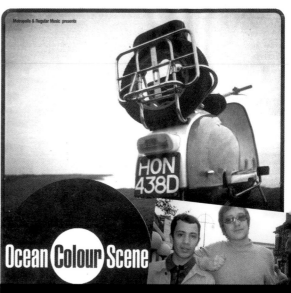

Ocean Colour Scene

Milton Astley: With *Britpop*, Mod became mainstream again, as before it used to be an underground movement; *Weller* came back and the media took advantage of it. Bands like *Ocean Colour Scene*... to bands like **Kula Shaker**, who were more into *Psychedelic*. '60s was back in fashion again.

Milton Astley, here with Simon Fowler from OCS
Photo: MILTON ASTLEY

SMILER: I didn't like the first **Ocean Colour Scene** material; it was a bit too wishy-washy. They started as **The Boys**, played in a mod rally in Bournemouth, in 1988. I've got to say, they were absolutely dire; they were a cheap *Jam* cover band. But when they did evolve, they did it well. I never underestimated *Steve Cradock's* guitar talent, but wrong place wrong time before that, absolutely terrible at the time.

SMILER: So many bands... and so much potential. But none of them got anywhere, really. It is sad to think about it now, because we'll never see them again...

the Clique

BIG BOSS BRITISH BEAT

brighton beach

The CLIQUE
brighton beach
Friday 22 September

SMILER: Going back to the late 1980s, there was quite a split between a few of us (including the members of *The Clique* -

Dave Edwards: The original line-up of **The Clique** was **Phil Otto** at the bass, **Paul Newman** on guitar/vocals & harmonica, and **Gilles Ballarguet** on drums. They were just a three-piece band. Then came **Jon-Paul Harper** after a while, at the guitar. *Paul Newman* decided to leave and they went through a series of singers, **Chris Jordan** was the replacement, followed by **Trevor French** who lasted quite a long time. Then it was **Speed** and a girl called **Alex Petty**. *Peters & Lee* they were called; *Peters & Lee* of Mod.

Paul Newman, Jon-Paul Harper -

In 1992 *Gilles* left and was replaced by **Matthew Braim** on drums. **Dom Strickland** on keyboards had joined in 1991, at the same time than **Trevor French** (lead singer). *Jon-Paul* left the band in 1994, to form **Knave** with *Trevor French* & **James Braim** (little brother of *Matthew*, on drums). *Jon-Paul* was replaced by legendary *Milkshakes/Headcoats* crazy drummer **Bruce Brand**, who happened to be an excellent guitarist. *Trevor* left the band in '96, to concentrate on *Knave*.

'our' band) being really into *R'n'B* and *British Beat,* and the *Northern Soul* crowd; more friendly than bad rivalry.

Let's Talk About:
THE CLIQUE

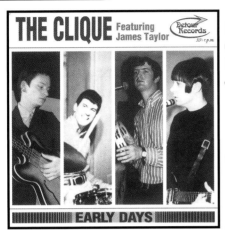

THE CLIQUE Featuring James Taylor
Detour Records 33⅓ r.p.m.

|||||||||||||| **EARLY DAYS** ||||||||||||||

Second release (1989/93) Featuring **James Taylor**

— THE RHYTHM & SOUL SET —

presents

'THE ONE YOU'VE BEEN WAITING FOR'

HAYLING ISLAND

SEE THE NEW YEAR IN
at
THE SOLENT CLUB
SEAFRONT
on
FRIDAY, 30th DECEMBER — 7.30pm - 2.00am
SATURDAY, 31st DECEMBER — 7.30pm - 2.00am
SUNDAY, 31st JANUARY — 7.30pm - 2.00am

RHYTHM & SOUL SPINNERS

B, MACE, DOM, STEVE, JON,
D, IAN JACKSON, RALSTON

Y, 31st DECEMBER — 12 noon

LIVE — LONDON'S FINEST
THE CLIQUE
Admission £1.00 on door (all proceeds to Band)

RESS ONLY   Admission £3.00 per evening
Weekend Ticket £7.00
Send SAE to:
Rob Messer, 16 Chilham Close,
Pitsea, Essex or
Andrew Mason, 88 Abbotts Dr
Sneyd Green, Stoke-on-Trent

Paul Newman & Phil Otto

Photo: DARREN RUSSELL

Phil Otto: *The Clique* was a band that had an ideal which evolved out of and similar to the reason 'The Jukes' were formed. That ideal was to form a band of mod musicians from the clubs and play the music that we listened to down the

THE CLIQUE
Detour Records

BAREBACK DONKEY RIDING

Fourth release (1995) with **Bruce Brand**

THE CLIQUE
REGGIE SHE DOESN'T NEED YOU ANYMORE
Detour Records

Third release (1994)

All are **Detour records**

Chris Jordan, Jon-Paul Harper, Phil Otto & Gilles Baillarguet

clubs. Simple in principle not so in practice. So over the years the line-up and the style of music evolved as the scene did. Starting with more *R&B* dance tunes and leading through to *Garage* mixed in with our own stuff. I think by the end we had covered most styles covered by the mod umbrella in one way or another.

BAND
MATTHEW BRAIM
WOODSTOCK SAARBRUCKEN '94

SHOUT & SCREAM
Detour Records
THE APEMEN • THE CLIQUE • THEE CHERYLINAS

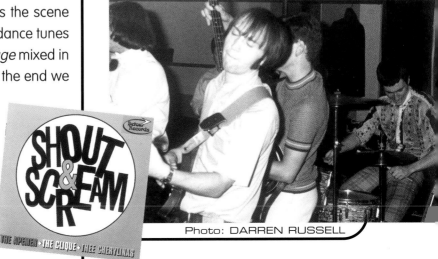

Photo: DARREN RUSSELL

Phil Otto: This was our third trip to Blankenberge, a small seaside town on the Belgian coast. We had decided this time to hire a coach to take our equipment, we didn't have our own van at the time, and if we could find some loyal fans to come with us it normally paid for itself. So we filled it with DJs, *Noj* and *'Catford' Chris*, band members, girlfriends, guitars, drums, amps, beer, you get the picture, and off we set for the night crossing.

After a very drunken crossing (or was it just rough?), we all arrived tired and hungry. Remembering we are not ardent travellers and most of this motley crew hadn't seen life outside of a *London* night club, looking for some breakfast was quite a comedy of errors. Nothing was open, there was an old man in dressing gown and slippers walking his dog along the seafront, even our hotel was closed. After a while we found a friendly hotel willing to try and feed 45 or so 'Mods'. Of course, all we wanted was a fry up, after a lot of negotiation we ended up with scrambled egg and salad!

Later we returned to our hotel and spent the rest of the day sorting out that night's entertainment. The rest of the gang found out that they could drink at the hotel bar without paying just receiving a small piece of paper with numbers on it! Others realized that if they misled the barman about their room number someone else had to pay. The only problem was we were the only people in the hotel! *Noj* got landed with a bill for £80.

The day drifted into the evening, and those who could, got ready and made their way to the end of the pier. This was a great venue with the entrance into a seated area with the bar across the back wall. To the side of the bar was a corridor leading to a similarly sized room with a small stage in the far corner.

The whole place had a *'50s* seaside feel to it and always felt busy as most people were either at the bar chatting and drinking, or while the band played, in the back room dancing. As usual, we were greeted by an enthusiastic crowd and were playing well, but at the same time there was a different feel to the night. There had been an edge to the atmosphere all night; the venue had filled with Mods and Skinheads from France Belgium and Britain.

It was getting late, about three in the morning; many of the *London* crowd had gone back to the hotel. I was sitting right at the entrance to the venue at a table, talking to *Dom* and *Larry*, discussing the gig, We then noticed a kerfuffle in the corner, we turned and noticed *'Black' Guy* being held up against the wall by his neck! Three or four other large *skinhead* types were now heading towards him. I think they started on him as he was black. I launched myself at one of these *Skinheads* by instinct. Clinging around his neck I suddenly realised that my feet couldn't touch the ground. I was hit sharply on the back of the head by a knobbly glass ashtray. If that was not enough someone else hit me with a bottle. I fell to the floor, not a good place to be as anyone down is fair game for a 'kicking'. At this point *Dom* and *Larry* intervened by picking up the table and using it as a battering ram against the fresh onslaught. However, as I tried to get up, the table then landed on me. I was not happy and a little stunned as I crawled under a nearby table. Somehow I came to be outside. Of course you then go back in! As I staggered to the door *Cousin Chris* came out covered in blood, followed closely by *Nick* in the same state. At this time I didn't realise I was hurt; I tried to pass *Nick's* girlfriend who was trying to gather the wounded for a hospital trip, 'You're not going anywhere' she said and led us away down towards the pier. The owner by now had rung the police and we were greeted by them, *Nick's* girlfriend was so determined to take the wounded to hospital she demanded that they use their car to take us. It was a short trip to the hospital and once there we were shocked to see a steady influx of casualties. Once we were stitched we were taken down to the police station, we believed we were in serious trouble. In small groups

BLANKENBERGE
a story by Phil Otto

Jon-Paul Harper, **Guitarist Composer of**
The Clique and Knave
Photo: DARREN RUSSELL

we were taken into rooms to be questioned. As it turned out they helped us to write our statements and sent us on our merry way back to the hotel.

Back for breakfast at the hotel we swapped yarns as the others woke to find out what they had missed. What follows is hearsay... we heard stories of guns, windows being shot out, records being hurled into the sea, knives, stabbings, arms being broken, girls being kicked and punched, *'Catford' Chris* starring as Mr Hong Kong Phooey, disguised as a mild mannered DJ!

Returning to the club, in the cold light of day we saw the devastation, the club was boarded and the owner was sweeping up the debris as we scuttled in to retrieve our equipment.

Finally on the ferry, as we stood at the bar drinking to soothe our wounds someone noticed that everyone that had stitches in their head had been clouted from behind. That's when we decided they were not fighting to Queensberry Rules!! All in all it was quite a good weekend and I'm sure we didn't play that badly!

THE CLIQUE HASTINGS '92

Where did I go Wrong
Crying Days
Security
Take Her Anytime
Lookin' Back
Crawlin' up a Hill
Wrackin my Mind
Baby never say Goodbye
125
Why do I cry
Make you Mine
Jons little Diti
The Quest

Sookie Sookie
Memphis Train

Leavin' Here

I was their 'enlisted' DJ, and I would always get up and introduce them on the mike at rallies & gigs.
SMILER

SMILER: Another time I was DJing on one of the *CCI* rallies, and I put on "Get Out" by *Harold Melvin & The Blue Notes*, which's got a slow start; a big crowd came on the dancefloor - the *Soul* lot - it was one of *Tony Schokman*'s 'spins', one of the big tunes... everybody looked at me, thinking: "How come you're playing this *Soul* record?" And just as it was about to start, I thought: "Fuck that!" took it, smashed it, and put on **The Clique** (the original '60s combo) "We Didn't Kiss, Didn't Love, But Now We Do Do". All the *R'n'B* lot got on the dancefloor, with all the *Soul* lot stranded in the middle. It was all friendly banter though.

Trevor French - **Brighton 1999 -**
Photo by the author

the clique
Detour Records

BACK IN ACTION FEATURING THE ACRYLIC TONES & SUPPORT

Self Preservation Society

FRIDAY NIGHT AT THE GARAGE
NEAREST TUBE HIGHBURY & ISLINGTON
ON THE 10th OF MARCH '95
ADMISSION £2 (with this flyer) 8 TILL LATE

Matthew Braim: I joined **The Clique** in 1992 - prior to that I played in several bands since the age of *13*, stopped for 4 years... I wanted to play in *The Clique* since I first saw them in 1987. I knew that around 1990/91 they were having trouble with their drummer, and I pretended I could do better. In March '92, two weeks before the Hastings *Rally* - first one of the year - they gave me an audition and I got the job (I knew I was on the cards anyway). First gig we played I was terrified; most terrible moment of my life.

MATTHEW BRAIM
Last Drummer of **The Clique**

And we carried on. After that, things seemed to happen; we got some offers, used to be interviewed in a lot of fanzines... we did a promo-tape, that everybody seemed to want. That was recorded in **Toe Rag** studio (in *Shoreditch* at the time) by *Liam Watson*, who had just got hold of the *Abbey Road* equipment (the same that *The Beatles* used for their recordings) for a very cheap price because it was out of date. He was fascinated by our music, as we were by his equipment. We did a version of "... The Quest" which was seven minutes long, with rain effects, all kind of effects we tried on that song.

The Clique were famous anyway, almost legendary. For me to come out of nowhere, and straight away gain a kind of status, was great and really changed my life. We knocked out a few singles; they just sold in masses.

We went on a tour in *Italy*, starting with the *Rimini* rally and then everywhere, small towns big towns... we had the ambulance at the time to carry our equipment, but it was incredibly badly organised. Though we had such fun. First gig we did, there were crash barriers in front of the stage; when we got on stage, about 200 people ran from the back of this massive hall into the barriers... the security didn't know what to do. When we played in Rimini, the hall was packed with about 1200 people; not only it was packed - on a Sunday afternoon - but they knew all the words in the songs! That was incredible; they'd never seen us, but they had our records and they knew all the words...

I have to say: there was never any ego in the band. But *Jon-Paul* was a 'Rock star' and things started to crack as soon as '94/95.

I was in another band with him, *Paul Newman* and *Kate White*, called **The Fixed**.. We played in '93 in Bruxelles; people came from all over *Europe* to see us, but very soon they started to mix the two bands.

With *The Clique* we did a tour of *Europe*, with *The Apemen* (Germany) and *Thee Cherylinas*, which has been the reason for **Detour Records** to put out an album called "Shout & Scream". Once again that was terribly badly organised; we did 2000 miles in one weekend! We went through Austria to Italy, came back up to Austria, played in Vienna then in Munich (South-East Germany). Then we had to go to *Belgium* for a gig and a radio show; we left the gig at five o'clock in the morning to the studio, completely pissed, with a bottle of vodka... that was *The Clique*. Then we had to get back to Saarbrucken (at the border of France/Germany) for the *Modstock* festival; that was in 1994.

Jon-Paul (guitar & writing) left, and was replaced by **Bruce Brand** who started pro-ducing us as well. Suddenly we did an album, but *Trevor* (singer) decided also to leave shortly afterwards. We got *Speed* - the DJ - to join in, but he was very nervous. We were playing, by then, in big venues: *Garage*, *100 Club*, we played in Barcelona...

For some reasons we got this girl called **Alex**; she had been spotted by *Phil Otto* at a rally when coming back to the hotel with some friends, she had started singing some kind of *Gospel* on her own - she has a fantastic voice. But I was totally against it; because you need a focus. You can't have this sort of 'Peters & Lee', 'laly-laly' twin thing going on; male or female, you need only one of these people - the 'front man'.

What gave me a bit more fear is that for some reason MTV had heard about us, showed up, got on stage and started filming us, interviewing us and did this thing about us and the scene. Which I found good but scary at the same time.

In Bed With
THE CLIQUE

Fifth release (1996)

Sixth release (1998), which is a kind of Best Of, featuring all the members of the band since the beginning.

Phil Otto: Myself, *Dom*, and *Bruce* believed that the album line up had had its day, and that it was hard to continue promoting that material after losing such a distinctive voice as *Trevor*'s.

I had thought that with *Alex*, we could reshape the band and do a complete new set, a bit more *Rhythm & Soul. Matthew* wanted to continue with the old set, which I thought was tired, and so we ended up with neither until it fizzled out.

The Clique first & last album (1995)

SMILER: I remember saying to *Dom Strickland* that *The Clique* could never make it at the time, with the image that they had. All they had to do was to dress down slightly; if they had worn stripy tops, white jeans & desert boots, they would have had a chance. But the public at the time could not relate to a mod image.

If they had worn stripy tops, white jeans & desert boots, they would have had a chance, but the public at the time could not relate to a mod image.
SMILER

Curse Of The Mod Bands

from left to right, anti-clockwise: Gilles Baillarguet - Paul Newman - Phil Otto

Photos: DARREN RUSSELL

Matthew Braim: *Alex* left later on anyway, and we sacked *Speed* (who lived in *Nottingham*) because he didn't show up to rehearsals for about three months. We thought he'd left. I think it's *Phil Otto* who saw him one night, and went to apologise for getting him out of the band: *Speed* didn't even know about it.

Then we got **Chris Jordan** back in the band, who was the original singer of *The Clique*. But when he drinks... he can do fantastic things, as he can do terrible ones.

That's when we got approached by *One Little Indian*. One of them had heard the album and seen us live, and thought we were the greatest thing in the world. Then the owner of *One Little Indian Records*, **Derrick Burkitt**, arranged a meeting. We met him, we met the accountants, we met the A&R people, we met all sorts of great people. We got taken out to dinner, had formal meetings and informal meetings at the pub with them; they were just chatting us up. We were really open-eyed about it, we wanted certain things, we actually wanted lots of stuff. And they seemed to be saying: "Yeah, that's cool." We were told we were being unreasonable, and we thought: "we are just great." We got a few hundred quid, and got offered our own rehearsal studios and any equipment needed, we got offered guaranteed minimum salaries even, just in case we didn't gig enough. We got offered a choice of managers, we got offered our own lawyers we could go to, they would pay for them, our music industry guys. We got offered **Brendan Lynch**, who was producing *Paul Weller*; he wanted to re-record the album. We did a session at *Olympic Studios,* in front of a room full of people. And that was the final thing. 'Cause I had been very sceptical, I just thought it couldn't happen, because it was the one thing I had always wanted. So they just asked if we could sign as one of their new acts on *One Little Indian*, which was fantastic, money wise; basically I thought I can do this full-time! Then we went to loads of receptions; we went to a *Skunk Anansie* reception, we got introduced to all these international people, which was very nice.

The day we were meant to sign the contract, they didn't want to see us. And instead of going to the offices, like we were expected to, we went to the pub next door. We just thought: "Nah, it's alright, let's go to the pub next door." We were told that Bjork, who was their number-one person, had pulled out of her tour, because somehow, and I don't know how this could happen, a fan sent her a video of him killing himself. I mean, you killed yourself and it's great you managed to put it on a video but, still, I never figured that one out. I mean: how can you commit suicide, film yourself and then send the video through the post?.. well I thought it's quite clever, but Bjork pulled out of her tour, and all the money had to be pulled out to pay all those people.

Art by DOM STRICKLAND

KNAVE

Paul Newman at the organ; another instrument he played to perfection...

Photo:

Phil-Hip Beauvais

KNAVE had this amazing act, with go-go dancers on stage! For a while it was *Trevor's* beautiful girlfriend at the time, *Jackie* (apparently, she'd been a model for *Penthouse* magazine...).

They definetely were the most professional mod band on stage.

Once again, it would be nearly impossible to list the full amount of mod & mod-related bands throughout the 1990s, only in the UK without daring to cite all the combos from all over the planet, who contributed a lot to our entertainment, at places like the Isle of Wight and other rallies; **The Jaybirds** from Austria (who had the quality and the sound of *The Yardbirds*), **The Apemen** from Germany (more of a *Revival* sound than '60s, but still very appreciated to this day for their presence on stage), **Statuto** from Italy, **Brighton '64** from Spain... the list would be endless.

LIVE AT THE LAVA LOUNGE.
H.Q's Camden lock NW1 On
SATURDAY 10th JUNE 2000.

T h e Revelation was the last attempt I saw, that *Trevor* did - as a band - before he disappeared from the mod scene, shortly after 2000.

What we were trying to do was to record in the

Another combo that *Trevor French* put together for a few rallies, was a tribute band entirely dedicated to *The Small Faces*: **Musn't Grumble**, that must have been around '96/'97...

It is absolutely needless to deny it; probably more than 90% of the *Garage* '60s influenced bands in the 1990s came, and not only from England, to record at **Liam Watson**'s studio in French Place (Shoreditch - East London).

TOE RAG studio

Knave in Germany
(Unkel festival),
Stuart Duffield on bass,
singer **Trevor French**

Photos: Alex Hussenet

**same style as
1960s bands.
Phil Otto**

Phil Otto: First of all, **Toe Rag** studio is not a valve studio, as it has always been taken for. *Liam Watson* had a lot of old equipment; some of the bits were coming from studios where *The Beatles* apparently had recorded... he would use old mikes, that had degraded over the time. He was still recording on *1-inch* to *2-inch* tape, and on the old virtual reels, which most of the studios had by then stopped doing. (He had an engineer setting up his equipment...). So, that attracted a lot of *Punky & Rock* bands, as well as '60s bands to it -I think *The Aardvarks* were the only band not using it. What we were trying to do was to record in the same style as 1960s bands: the whole back line in a first time, then over-dub maybe some backing vocals and a bit of tambourine.

Quant

Matthew Braim: We had it in our hand, I didn't want to believe it, and it never happened. Anyway, the day after we split up, I got a call from *Rob Bailey*, who had a band on the go. I said: "Look, I've been down that road... I don't wanna play in pubs anymore". Alright, it wasn't the aim anyway, but I definitely got in charge over there; I didn't write anything, but I had my say over it. I could say I don't like this, change that... three weeks after we started we went to studio, because I wanted to start recording with that band. They were called **Quant**. I was probably suffering from this massive failure with *The Clique*, but I had to be in charge. The singer couldn't sing - *Rachel* that was - so I asked who was her favourite singer and she said: "That's *Robert Palmer*". And she started singing like *Robert Palmer*, instead of being a little girl. Little things like that help, because I'd been on the road for such a long time; I knew every little step to get a band professional. I said to her to get her mike out of the stand and things like that.

The line-up was initially: **Jack White** at the guitar, **Stuart** on bass, **Rachel Croft** on singing and **Francois** who just turned up on stage, playing tambourines & stuff, and he was great. But *Stuart*, for whatever reason, was terribly unhappy with the world, and turned up one day completely pissed out of his brain (in a gig we did in Brighton) it was the night *Princess Diana* died (August '97). He started attacking me; I was getting really upset, because I was gonna clobber him. But then he went for *Rachel*, and she hit him across the face, with a glass of gin & tonic.

We then got a friend of mine **Little Phil** (a keyboard and sax player originally) very talented, who took the bass on. I used to live 'round the corner from him. We did the *Hope & Anchor*, played in Tower Bridge... we went to Spain...

The Hoodwinks were one of the best *British R'n'B* combo's of the late 1990s... and their bass player one of the best musicians I've ever met.

The Phrogs were in my opinion the most 'moddish' band of the late '90s, the right mix of proper mod sounds coming directly from the '60s.

Milton Astley: The thing is, you'd see a band every week, and to be honest with you, you wouldn't pay much attention to them; time to get the drinks in. Unfortunately, that did happen a lot; you'd be there for the records.

The Phrogs - Photo: Nickie Divine

THESE GUYS'RE DIGGIN' SO COULD YOU!!!!!
at The Garage, Highbury Corner Tuesday 7th
£5 entry/ £3 with flyer

TAKE IT TO
THE BRIDGE

Saturday 17th August
KNAVE

Saturday 21st September
THE PHROGS

Saturday 26th October
THE KYND (T.B.C.)

Other bands you would see at gigs during the 1990s, in London or at rallies: **Jarvis Humby, The Embrooks, The Mystreated** (who were a *psychedelic* band with a mod following).

Matthew Braim: So this tour in Germany hadn't ended really well, and we were going to America to play at a festival in San Diego, organised by my ex-girlfriend, **Anja**, with *The Chocolate Watchband - Phil* got busted for carrying illegal substances on our way to the States. We also did a little tour in California. In San Francisco we played in a few clubs, and that was amazing; as a member of *The Clique,* probably the coolest time of it all.

They've got a brilliant '60s scene in San Francisco, but a very bad mod scene though. It's anti-everything; one of the Mods I met there said he wanted to move from his flat because the area was full of working-class people... things like that. But the '60s scene on the contrary is very cool, and I don't mean *Hippies* & beads but more similar to the 1966 *'Swinging London'* type. And that is due to San Francisco and its atmosphere.

We ended up - with *Quant* - splitting up just after that, because my little proteges thought they could all do it by themselves. *Jack White* had his own project; he formed **The Standard Wonder Band**. I went to a band called **The Surrounds**. By this time, *Quant* had two singles out.

THE JAMES TAYLOR QUARTET

Even **James Taylor**, who after the split with **The Prisoners** had started with a pure 1960s-influenced *Boogaloo/Jazz* sound, was becoming groovier & groovier as soon as the 1990s had begun. Up to a point where it was quite difficult to follow him in his remote '*funky* valley'. But respect to the guy; he's put enough albums out to have nothing to prove anymore. He is, for a lot of people, the great genius issued from Mod, and will probably stay in our mind the ultimate mod composer.

Apparently, *James Taylor* was involved in many other bands, like **The Apostles, The New Jersey Kings**... and touched the heart of the real *Jazz* lovers.

available from all quality record outlets

The James Taylor Quartet EXTENDED PLAY

JAZID110T/JAZID110CD

ACID JAZZ

because music just isn't funky enough

Still, it is difficult to say that, because he is incomparable with **Paul Weller**, whose career has been unique and so well achieved. Nobody could say, as we reached the '90s, that he would make such a comeback after the end of **The Style Council**. Today I don't think his association with **Mick Talbot** was a failure at all; listening now to their first album - "Cafe Bleu" - I find a lot of *jazz* vibes that were really daring at the time, on the horizon of British *Pop*.

The James Taylor Quartet
Penthouse Suite

(J. Taylor/D. Taylor/J. Willmott)

JTQ came on stage at 10pm and started off their set with an excellent cover of 'Mission Impossible'. The band seemed in good spirit and went into their version of 'Mrs Robinson' and 'Wade In The Water'. 'The Cat' was soon to follow, and then 'Blow Up' which was ten times better than on vynil. The drummer began to excel himself, and before long the microphones & cymbals hit the floor. This caused much amusement to everyone including the band. After settling down, JTQ finished with a mega cover of Booker T's classic 'Soul Limbo'.

from Listen Here (fanzine-1988
Ed. Steve Piper & Darin Gosling)

Discography:
(At the end of the last century)

Mission Impossible (1986)
The Money Spyder (1987)
Wait A Minute (1988)
Get Organised (1989)
Do Your Own Thing (1990)
Absolute (1991)
Supernatural Feeling (1993)
Extended Play (1994)
In The Hands Of The Inevitable (1995)
A Few Useful Tips About Living Underground (1996)
Penthouse Suite (1999)

Mixed by James Taylor & Eddie Piller
String & horn arrangements by Mike Smith

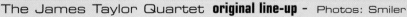

The James Taylor Quartet **original line-up -** Photos: Smiler

Les Hommes were not a mod band, but their *jazz* influence and their simplicity (two to three-piece combo, with massive *Hammond B-3* sound, light drums and sometimes xylophone) got them a big mod following.

Photo: PETER ROSTON

Skooby were absolutely amazing! They were one of the only bands I knew, who were able to get their public dancing at a gig. Once I saw them at the *100 Club*; they had a big following, who started dancing at the first note... it looked a bit like a 'Ready Steady Go' session.

Then came **Big Boss Man**, who were the best *Jazz/Funk* combo for the end of the 1990s.

At the same time, a great *jazz* band from *San Francisco* worth seeing, **The Nick Rossi Set**, were surprisingly similar to *Georgie Fame*, in sound and quality.

100 Men were a *ska* band, led by **'Stig' Mick** who used to work at *Merc*.

The 1990s mod bands wouldn't have had so many records released today without the passion of **David Holmes**, a.k.a **Dizzy Detour** who, despite being in a wheelchair, found the energy to create the **Detour Records** label, which was to record nearly the whole panorama of mod bands throughout the decade.

A PASSION FOR
MOD MUSIC

Dizzy is also the founder of the 'Bin Liner' Label, which he started in 1997, dedicated to *Punk* bands.

---

01 **The Persuaders**
Finished Forever / In The Night
Limited pressing 300 copies - 30 promo copies black vinyl
01/01/93

02 **The Tin Soldiers**
A New Beat / Girlfriend / Get Up & Go
Limited pressing 1000 copies clear vinyl
28/06/93l

03 **The Direction**
Yesterday / The Kids Wanna New Direction
Limited pressing 1000 copies black vinyl
26/05/93

04 **The Buzz**
Tell Her No / Well I think It's Already Dead
Limited pressing 1000 copies black vinyl
05/07/93

05 **X-Axis**
The Wild Bunch / Deep Dark City
Limited pressing 500 copies black vinyl
02/07/93

06 **The Clique** Early Days ep
Ground Ginger / Crying days / Leaving Here / Tee-Ni-Nee-Ni-Nu
Limited pressing 1200 copies black vinyl
20/09/93
Second pressing 130 copies green vinyl
Third pressing 130 copies white vinyl
Fourth pressing 370 copies yellow vinyl

07 **Vox Pop**
Cor Blimey / Pretty Impossible
Limited pressing 900 copies black vinyl, 100 purple vinyl
11/10/93

08 **The Bogeymen**
Let Me Give You My Love / You've Got No Scruples / Gimme Little Sign
Limited pressing 900 copies black vinyl, 100 blue vinyl
Second pressing 500 copies black vinyl
12/11/93

009 **The Revs**
Do The Right Thing / Stay In Touch / Anna
Limited pressing 900 copies black vinyl, 100 blue vinyl
Second pressing 500 copies black vinyl
15/12/93

DR010 **The Acrylic Tones**
Girl / Theme from The Acrylic Tones / The Rainbow Song
Limited pressing 900 copies black vinyl, 100 pink vinyl
Second pressing 500 copies black vinyl
20/01/94

DR011 **The Persuaders**
Waiting For The Nowhere Express / Girl / The Paperchase
Limited pressing 900 copies black vinyl, 100 red vinyl
15/03/94

DR012 **The Most**
Days, Days, Days / Take You There / Six Fifteen / Our Time
Limited pressing 900 copies black vinyl, 100 white vinyl
23/02/94

DR013 **Los Flechazos**
Try It / You Drove Me Crazy
Limited pressing 900 copies black vinyl, 100 red vinyl
Second pressing 500 copies black vinyl
10/05/94

DR014 **The Clique**
Reggie / She Doesn't Need You Anymore
Limited pressing 900 copies black vinyl, 100 red vinyl
Second pressing 500 copies black vinyl
16/07/94
Third pressing 500 copies black vinyl
Fourth pressing 500 copies black vinyl
Picture disc pressing 200 copies
11/05/95

DR015 **The Strange**
I Don't Care / Mint Sensation / Bad Scene
Limited pressing 900 copies black vinyl, 100 pink vinyl
19/07/94

DR016 **Now!**
Fatal Attraction / Prying Eyes / New Direction
Limited pressing 900 copies black vinyl, 100 green vinyl
Second pressing 500 copies black vinyl
13/06/94

DR017 **The Mourning After**
Doin' Me In / Out For The Count
Limited pressing 900 copies black vinyl, 100 blue vinyl
Second pressing 500 copies black vinyl
01/12/94
Third pressing 450 copies black vinyl
06/03/96

DR018 The Aim

Call Your Name / Out On The Streets

Limited pressing 900 copies black vinyl, 100 blue vinyl
Second pressing 500 copies black vinyl
01/10/94
01/12/94

DR019 The Day

Another Country / Gospel

Limited pressing 900 copies black vinyl, 100 lime green vinyl
Second pressing 500 copies black vinyl
01/08/94
01/11/94

DR020 Squire

The Place I Used To Live / Make Love To You / Over You

Limited pressing 900 copies black vinyl, 50 white vinyl
Second pressing 360 copies black vinyl
Third pressing 588 copies clear splattered vinyl
01/09/94
12/05/95
03/09/96

DR021 The Apemen

Love Train / Let The Good Times Surround You

Limited pressing 900 copies black vinyl, 50 purple, 50 pink
Second pressing 500 copies clear vinyl
Third pressing 500 copies black vinyl
17/10/94
12/02/95
14/06/96

DR022 The Cybermen

Word / One Spy Too Many

Limited pressing 900 copies black vinyl, 100 red vinyl
06/03/95

DR023 Groove Tunnel

Rainy Day / How Do You Feel

Limited pressing 900 copies black vinyl, 100 white vinyl
Second pressing 500 copies black vinyl
12/01/95
02/03/95

DR024 Kickstart

Sweet Sorrow / Let's Fall Down /
Topical Fashion / Plastic's Mouth

Limited pressing 900 copies black vinyl, 100 red vinyl
Second pressing 500 copies black vinyl
15/02/95
06/03/95

DR025 The Curtains

In My Street / Family Affair

Limited pressing 900 copies black vinyl, 100 blue vinyl
06/03/95

DR026 The Shreds

Brutally You / The Love I Knew / Never Too Late

Limited pressing 900 copies black vinyl, 100 white vinyl
08/06/95

DR027 The Clique

Bareback Donkey Riding / Security

Limited pressing 1900 copies black vinyl, 75 orange vinyl
03/07/95

DR028 The Chosen

New World / Doesn't Matter Anyway

Limited pressing 900 copies black vinyl, 100 purple vinyl
02/05/95

DR029 Sharp Kiddie

Time Again / So You Say You Love Me

Limited pressing 900 copies black vinyl, 100 lime green vinyl
18/07/95

DR030 The Lost Minds

Now I'm Alone / You Cr

Limited pressing 900 copies black vinyl, 100 lime green viny
Second pressing 500 copies black vinyl
22/06/9
09/02/96

DR031 The Shambles

(We've Got A) Groovy Thing
Nothing Can Be Everything / A Girl To Kill Fc

Limited pressing 900 copies black vinyl, 100 orange vinyl
Second pressing 500 copies black vinyl
29/09/95
19/06/96

DR032 The Odd Numbers

The Easy Life / Clubbir

Limited pressing 900 copies black vinyl, 100 orange vinyl
Second pressing 500 copies black vinyl
03/07/95
28/03/96

DR033 The Mourning After

You're Lying / What's Going Dowr

Limited pressing 900 copies black vinyl, 100 red vinyl
17/08/9

DR034 The Itch

Wigan To Brighton / Eyes Across The Roon

Limited pressing 900 copies black vinyl, 100 clear vinyl
Second pressing 400 copies black vinyl
20/09/9
06/02/9

DR035 Now!

Keeping Up With The Joneses
Insanity Begins At Home / The Weak Mc

Limited pressing 900 copies black vinyl, 100 clear vinyl
19/09/9

DR036 The Lazy Sundays

Dion Sire's Game / It's Not A Faded Picture

Limited pressing 900 copies black vinyl, 100 yellow vinyl
Second pressing 500 copies black vinyl
26/02/9
16/05/96

DR037 The Knave

Bachelor / Canc

Limited pressing 1400 copies black vinyl, 100 red vinyl
16/05/9

DR038 End Of The Beginning

Maniac / Into My Mir

Limited pressing 900 copies black vinyl, 100 red vinyl
19/01/9

DR039 Hipster

I Can't Help It / Love Me, Leave M

Limited pressing 900 copies black vinyl, 60 orange vinyl
19/01/9

DR040 The Acrylic Tones

A Place I Used To Know / Jol

Limited pressing 1400 copies black vinyl, 100 orange vinyl
22/05/9

DR041 Thee Cherylinas

We Were Happy / Let's Make Love
So Nice / Pictures Of Matchstick Me

Limited pressing 900 copies black vinyl, 100 blue vinyl
14/10/9

DR042 The Ravengers

Bottletop / When The Day Doesn't Com

Limited pressing 900 copies black vinyl, 100 white vinyl